The Justice

by

Janine Rennie

Copyright © 2024 Janine Rennie

ISBN: 978-1-917129-14-5

All rights reserved, including the right to reproduce this book, or portions thereof in any form. No part of this text may be reproduced, transmitted, downloaded, decompiled, reverse engineered, or stored, in any form or introduced into any information storage and retrieval system, in any form or by any means, whether electronic or mechanical without the express written permission of the author.

This is a work of fiction. Any names or characters, businesses or places, events, or incidents, are fictitious. Any resemblance to actual persons, living or dead, or actual events is purely coincidental. Certain long-standing institutions, agencies, and public offices are mentioned, but the characters involved are wholly imaginary.

www.publishnation.co.uk

Dedicated to:

Bobby my soulmate. We were destined to be together.
My children and grandchildren. I hope you are proud of me and the sacrifices were worth it.

The wolf within

I was ill and had been for a very long time. My sickness was much deeper than physical illness as it came straight from the core of my being. From a very early age I knew that the world wasn't right. In those days in the early seventies the world on the surface seemed okay. People played in the forests without worrying too much about danger and would wander far from home with parents not being too concerned if they returned before dark, often muddy and hair full of grass and twigs. I played all day and often into the night running wildly through the countryside surrounding the concrete jungle. Life passed on day by day with the usual routines the same as any other child and I made friends easily. Nature was an intense mystery that I embraced and experienced with joyful abandon at every season.

But something was wrong. With every day that passed I felt the danger and felt it was everywhere. Other people didn't see it so I did not feel inclined to mention it in case people would comment that I was going mad. From an early age I saw things in people that I felt that others didn't see. It was as if I could sense things intensely. At night I would squeeze My eyes tightly to avoid seeing the faces that were just behind my eyelids. Those images would make tears burn the backs of my eyes.

As the years passed, I managed to subdue the feelings and entered life the way that others did. Life was fine on the surface of things, and I had the usual aspirations to succeed, to fall in love and to form a perfect family.

School was a strange experience in that I never quite felt connected with anyone. I was popular with many friends, but I always felt that the relationships formed were on the surface and the interests that others had didn't connect with my own desires. It was then that I learned to wear masks for every situation in my life. Soon I found that I could be like a chameleon. Friends came from many different groups, and I found fitting into each group easy as I merely told them what they wanted to hear and became what they wanted me to be.

By night escape came from painting and writing poetry sitting up for hours and hours pouring feelings onto paper. The next day reading what was written or looking at what was painted would bring confusion and no memory of completing the work. Radio Luxembourg was always on the background, and it was the time of worry about nuclear war. Like many people at that time, I would obsess about the potential of death and destruction and the regular bulletins on the radio would further feed my fears.

It was hard to define when the illness started. There were early memories of walking to school doubled up with pain and nights filled with strange and dark thoughts of the potential of the end of the world. By day things were normal with adventures and sunshine.

As the years passed the illness intensified and after a time, I was unaware of how it felt to be well. There were constant visits to doctors with no explanations and I began to feel like I was really losing my mind. The dark shadows persisted, and I spent hours considering whether the illness was of the mind. However, the images of something out of memory seemed real, purely glimpses, or flashes of something but something that existed.

Throughout life I became convinced that there must be something more and that the images must mean something, but I could never find the answers. I would spend hours staring into the flame of a candle or laying spread after spread of the tarot but there was a barrier to understanding that would block the ability to be well.

Days and years would pass, and I would throw myself into many situations and many disasters would ensue. I knew deeply if the answers could be found the pain would pass. One day I would wake without the clawing nausea of body and spirit.

I started working in the charity sector and I always wondered how the work I did was connected to my destiny. It was the strangest world for so many reasons with complex and complicated situations and people.

The dark places

It started one morning on what had started as a regular day. I was working for a charity that supported people. One of the clients came into the charity and asked to speak to me. He sat huddled in a chair so sunken into himself that it seemed like he just wanted to disappear. His voice was rambling to begin with, jumping from one topic to another, confused and scared. Hardly able to express what was inside his mind and his body while it was racked in pain. I felt helpless as I couldn't understand what he wanted to say and what he needed from me, but I wanted to reach out to him and make the pain better.

Suddenly he looked at me intently and lucidly.

"I have to tell you something" he said "I don't think you will believe me, but I am being followed by my abusers. I feel that they will harm me"

"Have you reported it" I said "I can go with you to the police?"

"I can't" he said "I don't know who might be involved and the police may not help me"

He returned to his pattern of talking in a disjointed way jumping from one topic to another, staying for about another twenty minutes before leaving and thanking me for speaking to him.

The following week he returned. This time it was obvious that he had been attacked with dried blood all over his face, large bruises, and an obvious limp.

"We have to go to the police this time" I said "you are clearly at risk, and I have to take that forward you know I do".

"I want to go" he said "I am afraid, and I have to find help somewhere or I think they will kill me."

We sat for a while before leaving and he told me much of the background of his life. I wasn't his counsellor so had only heard what most others who encountered him heard that he was abused by so many people in the local area. Much of it felt to many of us as part reality and part imagined. Like the previous week he became calm again and he explained his past abuse.

At the age of seven he became a choirboy at the local chapel with several other boys. He was so excited at what felt like an honour and he was close to his religion which at that time he never questioned. The priest was young and inspiring to the boys giving them constant encouragement and friendship. The client had awful problems at home. His mother was very ill with multiple issues, so he had been sent to live with his older sister and her husband. The experience of being away from his mother was confusing and frightening. He always wondered when he would be allowed to go back, and he often felt he must have done something wrong.

The priest would listen. He was kind when he was quiet and withdrawn because of the beatings he had started to receive from his sister's husband. The chapel became a place of escape, and he grew to trust the priest as someone who would keep him safe. He became involved in activities organised for the choirboys. The priest would take a group of them swimming at the local pool where there would be other men who appeared to be friends of the priest. Gradually he and the other boys came to trust the other men and they enjoyed their company as they were so much fun. It felt like an escape from the troubles at home.

One day it all changed. The day started in much the same way as other outings but the boys were taken on an excursion to a local derelict building with grounds and woods. He remembered a cloth being put over his face that smelled funny and he blacked out. When he came round, he witnessed one of his friends being held down by one man while another raped him. He was aware that he was in pain, and he became terrified that the same thing had happened to him. He became aware that there were seven men there and that even if they were able to find the ability to fight, they would be overpowered. Each of the boys was abused by the men taking a turn until finally it stopped. The boys were warned that if they told anyone they would be killed, and their family members would be killed.

As time passed the boys were taken to several locations and they were always too afraid to tell anyone or to speak out. Life became an ongoing nightmare of one dark day to the next even though the seasons passed. The client became aware his stepfather had put him in touch with the original man and that he was selling him and his siblings to the ring. They were taken to a cellar that had been built in his stepfather's house. He remembered babies being brought there to be abused with photographs taken. He felt terrible that he couldn't stop what was happening and the cries of the babies haunted him every night. The abuse went on until he became a teenager and then the men seemed to lose interest. He was so confused about who he was, and he found himself becoming involved in sex work and in unhappy sexual experiences.

After telling me about his past he turned to me in fear and said "they are everywhere in this area. They will hurt me or kill me. They will suspect I know who they are"

I was very afraid for him and stressed again that we should go to the police.

We travelled to the local police station in my car. He said "they won't help me. The people who abused me are very important here. It will be covered up"

"I'm sure it won't" I said "the police are independent even from those in power"

On arrival at the station, we went to the custody desk and were ushered into a side room where we were joined by two police officers. They placed a huge file down on the desk and looked at the client in a condescended manner saying, "you have accused a lot of people in this file, who is it this time?" I was shocked as he was sitting clearly covered in injuries, but it was not being taken seriously. I asked what was going to be done about the assault and they sighed and said, "okay we will take a statement" Nothing happened from the statement and no action was ever taken.

Some weeks later he appeared really excited saying that at last his case was to be taken forward. He seemed so well and content. He enjoyed his groups so much more interacting with his friends and going to lunches and nights out with them.

Ingrid one of the other managers met him on a train coming back from Glasgow and he was so happy and talking openly about at last achieving justice. He told her that local councillors had been involved in abusing him and at last they would be held accountable. She later discovered that he was telling anyone that was willing to listen the same things. Ingrid and I were worried that he would be putting himself further at risk. He told his other worker names of the abusers, and she wrote them in his file. She supported him in further disclosures to the police. The more the implications of who may be responsible became obvious the more worried for him we were.

His other trauma worker from the NHS fed back that since the case was being taken forward his mental health was improving beyond recognition. He was lucid and clear on what had happened, and he spent weeks coming in and photocopying paperwork and statements for his case. Everyone in the team enjoyed seeing the change in him and he would sit regularly and have a cup of tea with various staff.

One day he came in to see his worker and it was obvious to everyone that something had changed. He looked confused and hurt and he was unable to make eye contact with anyone. After his session he explained that for some reason his case had suddenly been dropped. He said that he thought the other boys who came forward had been threatened to not give evidence.

Over the next few weeks, he would text others in his group to say he wanted to die, and Trudi my colleague, attended hospital with him on many occasions to ensure that he was safe and not at risk. Gradually nobody heard from him one of the other clients said he was hiding in the attic of a family member as he had been beaten so many times.

Nobody who had met him felt able to leave aside their fears about his wellbeing and we all discussed what we could do. The Board and I realised that we were dealing with a very serious situation, and we knew we would have to act. The client had spoken out on a DVD to raise awareness just before he disengaged. About a month later the office was broken into.

We had started thinking that the office may be bugged and that phones tapped so we arranged to meet in a pub in a small village to discuss what to do. While this seemed far-fetched it was not unusual for strange things to happen in our work. We decided that it would be important to access support and advice from outside the local police as we realised that would maybe be a risk with the abuse ring being local. We contacted a child abuse expert from an area in England where a major abuse ring had been exposed. She had been the person who carried out an independent report into it. I emailed her and was shocked to receive a response. I was even more shocked when I was told that a charity in that area had been shut down for exposing what was happening with abuse rings. I met the expert in a café in Glasgow, rushing away from a charity event to meet her. I explained the clients' situation and that our charity was facing attacks. She told me that she could completely relate to it as being like the other case and the destruction of the charity there. She told us to meet with the child abuse unit and to speak to an investigative journalist. She promised to send on contact information.

Strange things happened with staff being followed, a man sitting outside the office in various cars, and threatening calls. We met with the child abuse unit and told them everything about the client's case and other really frightening cases we were aware of through our work including one disclosed in the prisons. The unit seemed concerned, but they said they didn't think there was much they could do without additional evidence and corroboration. We were shocked and asked them to pursue it as we had provided names of perpetrators and clients. We spoke to a journalist, but we were too scared to take an article forward to protect the client and keep him safe. At the time of us speaking to the journalist another young man came forward to say that he wanted to be involved in raising concerns about his abuser who was an ex-janitor in the same area. He was still living next to a school. He said he would speak to the journalist. I agreed to go with him to the local education department to raise the concerns. We drove down and when we arrived, we were taken to a meeting room. On the way through the corridors the council manager asked who I was. When I explained he said "we fund you don't we or do we" smirking as if it was a threat.

In the room was a woman who was ready to take notes and she explained she was a human resource manager. The client explained his concerns and the manager said, "you raised this ten years ago and you were not believed then."

The client became very upset, and I was horrified by what he said "that is not true. The case not going forward does not mean someone is not believed it just means there is no corroboration."

The manager smirked again "well there was no case then so what do you want us to do?"

"He should never be near children. If you don't do anything I will," the client said

"That sounds like a threat"

"I just meant I would warn the parents!"

We ended the meeting as it was pointless and returned to the office. The client thanked me and left.

The next day we spoke to the journalist and the client told me the police had appeared that morning to warn him not to act by informing the parents. The journalist was interested in the story, but she said if no-one from the organisation was willing to be named, she could not do it. We were too afraid to be named due to the threats we had received, and I felt we were stuck with no way forward to achieve justice.

Over the years I became overwhelmed at the number of similar cases and the danger we faced.

One of the strangest characters to play a part in my life story called himself 'hyper haggis'. He seemed to feel it showed a combination of drive and enthusiasm while connecting with his Scottish roots. Unfortunately, his energy came from using large amounts of speed with alcohol to come back down from his high. After many drunken conversations I felt sure he had killed two women. They were drug users, and the deaths were recorded as drug related deaths. I felt compelled to find out the truth. I wanted justice for them. I spoke to the police repeatedly about my worries but they dismissed them.

My journey was all about justice. I supported people who had experienced serious abuse and trauma throughout life. They were the hidden and lost people all around. They were a threat to the power structures that led our lives. I was conflicted. How would it be possible to expose the perpetrators of abuse and those who protect them while keeping myself and my family safe. I had entered a dangerous and confusing world.

Jim had experienced a life of serious abuse from early childhood. He was sent to a residential care home due to severe violence from his father. His home life was a daily torture. The family lived in a Glasgow tenement with a close that smelled of urine and vomit. Each day his father would go to work then straight to the pub. Sally, his mother was kind and timid. There were four children in the family, none of them the result of sex that she had consented to. Bill, her husband would come home from his nights in the pub, roll on top of her with no permission sought and most times not use a condom. If as in the early days, she tried to protest he would beat her until she was bruised all over. He avoided her face to ensure the neighbours wouldn't know. On Jim's 10th birthday his father beat him so badly he was hospitalised when he tried to defend his mother. From that day he blamed her, rather than his father and that was to set the scene in his future relationships.

On a winter morning Jim was released from hospital and driven to a care home in the countryside. It was a beautiful place with massive grounds. It was so different from Glasgow, and he felt overwhelmed and excited. The excitement was not to last. The abuse that he experienced there was replicated in many care establishments across Scotland. Jim became like many of the children and adults I went on to support throughout my working life. The difference was they did not go on to kill.

"The man in the shiny suit"

I was sitting at home waiting for a joiner to attend to give me a quote for my kitchen when my husband Chris called me.

"Have you seen the paper? Guess who is the new chair of a very important review?"

"I haven't seen the papers today"

"It is a tiny article, but it is the possible "man in the shiny suit!"

I was silent and Chris asked if I was still there.

"That is completely unbelievable. Are they mad? That man has associations that make him the worst possible person for that role."

After I had some time to think I called our lawyer. He advised me to call the police, so I called a police contact.

"I know nothing about this" he said. "I will check if anyone further up has any awareness of it."

I called the lawyer back and he suggested writing to the review team to raise concerns followed by press contact if there was no response. He wrote a very strong letter mentioning his associations with the paedophile ring and his close relationship with the head of the paedophile ring. It had been the worst ring in the country with eight of them being connected. They filmed themselves abusing babies. He had joined the Board of an organisation at the same time as the main ringleader joined as CEO and they had worked together five years before on various studies and papers. A client who was involved with the review told me that he was a close advisor to someone from the church hierarchy who had been accused of inappropriate behaviour. The review team did not respond so I was set up with a television interview. I was very uncomfortable as I had known him for years and we operated in the same professional circles. I knew what I was about to do could affect friendships.

The interview very cleverly managed ensuring I made no accusations, as I still didn't know if there was any guilt, just concerns, but they showed his connections to the paedophile ring on camera. The television company contacted me afterwards to say the programme had been delayed as he was on holiday. In the meantime, a client had contacted the review and he was invited to a meeting with the CEO the following Monday. He invited me along with his support worker.

On the day after the contact with the media company I was shocked that the charity he had recently worked for were all over the news and newspapers in a very positive light. The organisation was on both television channels with large features. There were articles in newspapers even local publications. This level of press coverage for something insignificant was extremely unusual and the timing of being after the television filming very strange. I contacted the press officer to ask what was going on. He said it was probably just a coincidence, but I felt very tense about it.

On the Monday I travelled to the meeting with the review team, extremely nervous. I met the client and his support worker in a café in the venue. We all felt the situation was bizarre and the client commended me for standing up and going public, protecting survivors who had raised concerns about public exposure. We went to the desk, and we were taken in a lift to the top floors emerging to a very prestigious looking office suite. We entered the room and were introduced to the Chief Executive and the public relations officer. When we sat down the client gave a long speech on his concerns about the appointment. He asked how the recruitment took place, why survivors were not consulted and why his associations were not investigated. The public relations officer followed his questions with accusations that approaching the media had not been necessary as the concerns could have been answered. I was furious "you had no intention of responding to our concerns. You only gave us this meeting because the press officer contacted the media".

"I realise I have been told off by you now!" I said.

"No, it isn't about telling you off" the press officer said "I am just saying you could have given us more time. The CEO was on holiday abroad."

"Interesting" I said "so the CEO was abroad, and the subject of the news story is still abroad. Very convenient."

I explained the background I knew about the situation. The CEO seemed alarmed by the account, but he responded defiantly.

11

"What can I do about this? These are allegations but no conviction. If I terminate the employment of somebody without a conviction, I could be facing legal action."

"Well how did you appoint him?" the client said, "you have not answered any of my questions."

"He was recommended by the police and the government. We felt that was a very high-level recommendation."

I was shocked that he seemed to be connected to government. I already knew he had associations with the police but his likely association with government was interesting in view of issues we had experienced with them.

We left frustrated that there had been little progress. The CEO ended the meeting by saying he would discuss it with the new head of the review on his return from holiday.

The media decided to go forward with the taped interview despite me trying to have it stopped. I was terrified to see it, but it was very well filmed as it did not accuse him of anything, and my interview came across very well. We expected to be contacted by journalists the next day as all other TV coverage had been followed up in that way. There was complete media silence. It was so strange, and it felt almost eerie. I had a sense something was very wrong, but I had no idea what was behind it all.

That evening and for days afterwards I was contacted by several people who had similar concerns thanking me for doing the interview. No contact came from my professional colleagues. A survivor told me one of his contacts had killed himself after contact with the same person when he worked with the church. He had refused to offer any help and support to the survivor or to hold his abuser to account. There was an emerging pattern. When I spoke to him there was a significant echo on the phone. This was a pattern.

I wrote to the police to ask if they had recommended him. I was very surprised to receive a letter from a detective chief inspector at a very senior level to say that the police had nothing to do with the appointment. This was to come back to bite in a serious way.

Family matters

My family life had always been difficult and distressing. From very young I had realised that my sister was favoured by my mother. I could not understand why as Morag, my sister, was not liked by anyone either in the family or in the neighbourhood. She had a vicious and jealous nature. An early memory for me was still very upsetting to recall. I had a small hairy black caterpillar that I was fascinated by. It was beautiful and as a young child I loved it. Morag asked to hold it and as she held it in her palm, she smashed her hands together killing it. I was never able to forget the shock or the satisfaction in her face. There were many other incidents throughout our childhood. One day we were walking home from school and some friends were laughing with me and we were running around having fun. When they went off in a different direction to head home she threw a brick at me, and it bounced off my hip. I rushed home to tell my mum and show her the large bruise and she asked me what I had done to deserve it.

When we were teenagers, our mother bought us a dog. I loved the dog so much. She became my constant companion, sleeping in my bedroom and following me everywhere. Morag asked if she could come with me for one of my walks. We took the dog out to the woods near our house. There was a steep incline on the country path down to a stream at the foot of the hill. Morag had been fine walking along until suddenly she pushed the dog down the hill whipping her with a leather lead as she tried to recover and climb back up. I screamed and cried but she wouldn't stop. The dog managed to break free and run away. I felt so relieved when I returned home, and she was waiting. The explanation Morag gave was that the dog preferred me to her. Throughout our lives she would endlessly compete over our mother. It wasn't necessary as my mum had always made it clear that she bonded better with Morag. She told me often that when she was in labour, she was given a drug that made her lose her memory. She told me when she came round, she would not believe that she had given birth or that I was her baby. She would then describe how perfect it was when she gave birth to Morag and how immediate the bond was.

Growing up in a single parent family in the 70s was unusual. All my friends had a mum and a dad unless through bereavement. Divorce was barely spoken about. My dad left when I was six. All through my childhood I would pretend that he was still at home. I didn't want to feel different. My mum didn't seem to be able to be affectionate or loving. It was as if when her relationship ended something shut down in her. She was beautiful with huge dark eyes and sallow skin, but she seemed to be shut down to letting anyone else into her life. Her mother died when I was four and from then when I tried to take her hand, she would brush me away. If I tried to hug her, she would shrug, grunt and usher me away. I learned never to seek affection from her. My sister was different. As a young child I couldn't understand why my mum would cuddle and coo over my sister but not me. I felt unlovable and that it must be my fault. She would often tell me I looked so like my father. I was confused. He had dark eyes and skin as I did but so did my mum. My sister had fair skin, hazel eyes, and auburn hair like my mother's sister. Life felt so lonely, and I spent us much time as I could with my friends in the countryside building dens and wishing I could live there in the forest.

Morag progressed into jealousy over men when we became young adults. Every boyfriend that I had was a target for her flirtation and sadly most responded. I had my first boyfriend when I was 15. He lived on a local farm. I loved animals and we would spend hours in the countryside, spending most of our time together. One Saturday he was in the kitchen with my sister while I was upstairs studying. He was a regular visitor in our house. I remember hearing a song I loved coming on the radio. I started downstairs but stopped as I saw my sister lean in to kiss my boyfriend through the glass partition between the kitchen and the hall. He swore to me that she had been crying and he had given her a hug to calm her down when she tried to kiss him. I told my mum what had happened and she said it was my fault for leaving them alone together.. I felt there was nothing I could do to escape the continuous competition and I felt that I had to try and be as close to my sister as possible so that she would not want to harm me.

We started socialising together every weekend, but Morag regularly started using speed and cocaine and I was very uncomfortable. She would brag about it and call me a prude. One night we were due to head off to the pub and we had a whisky before leaving. It had sediment at the bottom of the glass but then whisky often did. On the way to the pub, I felt my heart racing far too fast, and I started to be scared. Despite my anxiety when we arrived at the pub, I stood for about 45 minutes talking non-stop to the bouncer. It felt so strange as I rarely spoke to anyone when we were out as I was so shy. When I sat down and said I felt worried and erratic. Morag started laughing and she said "I spiked your drink! You and your prejudice about drugs and you are off your face. It's hilarious" I was horrified that she would do that to me and so ashamed. I tried to tell my mum about the drug use as I feared the long-term effect on my sister, but she wouldn't believe it. I would search my sister's room and underwear drawers until I found the drugs and I would destroy them.

Over the years feeling second best became familiar and I would try my best to do everything right always looking for acknowledgement. I would talk and talk to my mum looking for her to want to talk back but all her friends would notice that she always interrupted to say "okay dear" with a side smirk to show that she was just tolerating her rambling desperate daughter. I was so embarrassed that my relationships kept going wrong as she would make me feel that I was letting down my family. After I gave birth to my first child Morag became pregnant too. My friends knew how nasty and jealous she was, and they said typical that she was even competing with having a child. When her son was born she seemed to be irritated and resentful of the baby. When he was little in his pushchair he would dangle his little legs and it would make it difficult for her to push. He would giggle thinking it was fun. One day she unfastened him and yanked him out of the pushchair smacking him hard. I was horrified and so upset seeing his frightened face and told her that she should not have hurt him but she responded, "just because you can't manage your own child". The little boy would look petrified all the time. If he spilled his drink when we were out having lunch, I saw him flinch and cower waiting to be hit. I found it so difficult to cope with seeing my nephew nervous and scared of his own mother.

Morag had gradually started using drugs and alcohol again spending most nights sitting on chat to my stepdaughter Susan and I while drunk telling us about men she wanted to have affairs with. She was bored with her partner and felt he was not intelligent enough for her. One was her university tutor. He was in a relationship, but Morag saw it as a competition and a challenge that she wanted to win. Susan and I felt awkward as we were both very fond of Morag's partner Steven. We tried to persuade her that she would be better concentrating on Steven, but he was never good enough for her and the drunker she would get the more determined to find a man who she felt would fit with her image of the perfect partner. As the drinking escalated it was obvious that she was again creating division between me and my mum, deflecting from her own behaviour by creating conflict and gossip about me.

One night my husband Chris and I went to Glasgow to see a movie and we travelled back on the motorway after midnight when the roads were quiet and peaceful. We heard a motorbike coming up behind the car very fast and loud. As it passed the car it shook with the force of the vibration and the sound was deafening. There was nothing there. We looked at one another in shock. The road was empty. For years afterwards we joked that we had passed into a parallel universe that night as everything changed.

The next evening Steven came round to see us in a very distressed state. Morag had returned home from a night out drunk. She was taunting him for being too scared to use cocaine while saying that she had been with two men in the toilets. Steven was in shock, and he didn't know what to do. He told me that Morag and my mum spoke about me and judged me constantly. We calmed him down and he returned home to speak to her when she had recovered.

The next day I called my mum about what Steven had told me. She told me she was so upset at the accusation that she was going for a drive up north. I telephoned my sister and she gloated that it was all true and my mum hated me. I went round to her house to confront her. As I walked in, she flew at me and grabbed hold of my hair to drag me back out of the door. I grappled with her to push her off me and managed to walk away into her open plan kitchen area. She ordered me out of her house. I lit up a cigarette and reminded her it was Steven's house too. She pushed past me as if to put the kettle on. I remembered seeing my cigarette flying through the air as I put up my arm to stop a wok hitting me full force on my head. She had calmly picked it up from the sink. I must have blacked out and when I came round, she was screaming at me that I was faking it. Steven had called an ambulance and I was taken away for tests. I couldn't move my arm and my head had a large lump on it. My legs were in agony and when I checked, covered in bruises. Steven told me later that Morag had kept kicking me when I was on the ground as she screamed that I was faking. The paramedic in the ambulance told me that if I had not managed to put my arm up, I would have been likely to have been killed, especially as my arm was so damaged and I was still concussed despite protecting myself. When I was sent home after a head x-ray and other tests my mother was in my house. She showed concern that the injury may flare up my lupus, but I think she was trying to minimise any future damage and ensure that I didn't call the police first or speak to them as the paramedics had called them. She explained that the police had been, but Steven had said the attack was in self-defence as Morag had threatened if he didn't the children would never be allowed to see him again.

Two nights later Susan went to Morag's house and knocked the door to confront her about attacking me. She could see through the glass partition that Morag was attacking Steven. Morag saw her through the kitchen window, and she came flying towards the door brandishing a rolling pin. Susan ran away very frightened. Steven later contacted Chris to say that he had called the police as Morag had attacked him and his face and neck were ripped apart with scratches from her nails. She had thrown a glass ashtray at him. Morag was arrested and taken away to the police station.

My mum was in my house to check up on me and she rushed off to find out if Morag was okay. I asked how she could still support her after what happened, and she said that Steven had said the attack on me was self-defence and that she believed him and Morag. I explained why he had to say that, to ensure he didn't lose his sons but my mum was adamant she had to go to her. She said to me "You have never needed me, and you have Chris. Morag has always needed me".

I didn't hear from my mother for many weeks, and I felt extremely upset crying often and still traumatised and scared Morag would come after me. I called my mother, and she told me that she would have to choose Morag and contact would have to stop as that was what Morag wanted. I was hysterical begging her not to turn away from me, but she was cold and emotionless. Chris took the phone and yelled at her how evil she was being. Afterwards weeks passed with nothing, and Steven pursued custody of his children. The boys spoke out to say that they had been mistreated by their mother and there was the record of Morag being violent. I gave a statement to protect the children. I felt awful and that I had betrayed my sister, but I knew the boys had to be more important and that she needed to seek help.

Four years passed and I spent every Christmas, New Year, birthdays, and achievements feeling bereft and distressed with so many times where I wanted to talk to my mum. One day I was driving home from work at lunchtime for a half day and I decided to stop at a garden centre. As I walked in, I met my mum coming out. I was shocked as she burst into tears. We went to sit in the car and my mum explained how much she had missed me but that she had been told over and over, consistently by Morag that I had attacked her, and she had defended herself with the Wok. I said "but you know that wasn't true. You saw my injuries and you know they couldn't have happened if I had been attacking her." My mum put her head down and said, "Morag needed me." I said

"Did you think I didn't? You were cruel to me. You turned your back on me. How do you think that felt?"

My mum was angry "you supported Steven. This was all his fault. I lost my family because of him"

"Yes, because Morag was drinking, using drugs, and attacking people. It was a child protection issue. Rather than report her I felt it was safer to just ensure the boys were looked after safely".

"He is just a liar" my mum said, "Morag has done nothing wrong".

It was like when we were younger, and my mum would never believe anything bad about Morag including her drug taking as a teenager. I gave up trying to convince her and we agreed to disagree but be back in contact.

Over the years it remained difficult as I could not just phone or pop in to see my mother in case Morag was there. She went on to marry a much younger strange looking boy with frizzy hair who dressed like a science teacher. He fitted her image of the intellectual partner. Christmases and New Year were hard as I would not see or hear from my mother in case it upset her. My aunt sided with Morag even though Morag had hated her and rather than try to tell her the truth which would hurt my mother I kept my distance. Losing my entire family all at once left me with a shell around me that I found hard to let go. It also created the emotional wall that enabled me to be able to withstand all that was to come.

The lady of the forest

I awoke from a dream in a pine forest lying on the pine needles like being in a soft bed. I sat up and looked around. Sunshine was coming through the huge pine trees to light the ground and giving shadows. In my dream I walked over to a tree lying on its side where a woman was sitting. She looked old and young at the same time as the light flashed over her face. I recognised my mother in the older woman. The younger image was so like her face with huge round dark eyes, plump cheeks, and beautiful kind features. The older image had tight lips as if to express pain and inability to show the suppressed emotions.

I sat beside her and said "you look sad mum what's wrong"

"I am remembering when I was young and beautiful when I was engaged to Ernest and full of plans being a teacher, him being a lawyer and a peaceful and happy life. It all went wrong."

"What happened?"

"Well, I decided I had to travel the world and have experiences before I was tied down. I went to America as a nanny and there I met your dad, and it all went wrong"

"In what way?"

"He seemed so nice and he looked after me but it had been strange how he contacted me as he had dated the previous nanny for the family I worked for. He wanted us to be serious so fast and wanted to marry me after only about nine months. It felt overwhelming so soon after the wedding I went back home. I soon realised I was pregnant when I kept being sick all the time and my parents realised I had married as my lost suitcase was brought back with my new name on it. I had to explain to Ernest what had happened, and he was in a terrible state. I realised I had let everyone down and I was so scared. Your father sent me so many romantic letters so I went back and you were born in America. After six months I was lonely and your father was trying to escape the draft so we returned to Scotland as a family."

"So, what happened next?" I said feeling shocked that my mum had such an interesting life.

"I realised he loved the attention of other women. He even made a pass at my own sister and there were so many situations where I realised that he had done that with my friends as they would suddenly not want to speak to me anymore and finally one told me. At the same time, he had intense jealousy and when men in his work would speak to me he would beat me when we returned home".

"Oh my God, he would beat you?"

"Yes so many times but then I had another child, and it stopped for a while. He went to train as a psychiatric nurse and for a few years we were happy. But gradually I realised things were going wrong again. I started a night class and you and Morag would scream and cry and beg me not to go. When I came home I would sometimes sense there was a smell of perfume. My neighbour then told me he was bringing a woman home."

"What did you do?"

"I confronted him but in those days, you made your bed and you lay in it. The beatings stated again. My mum died that year, and we were moved to another flat across the street. He didn't like me not giving him attention and the beatings became more violent. One day he smashed my jaw and I remember you saw me with blood pouring out of my mouth. I decided then it was over and I made him leave. In those days it was so hard to survive and we were always short of money and the stigma from being a single parent was huge. Over the years he would come back and go away again. I remember you and Morag being all ready to see him with your coats on, but he wouldn't show up. It used to break my heart."

"Sadly, you have often chosen men just like your dad. Morag would scream night after night and you were so withdrawn and always having sore tummies. I felt so responsible, but I didn't know what to do. Even being a teacher didn't prepare me. He kept trying to come back home but each time I would discover there was another woman. One day he was in the house, and we were planning our reconciliation. The police appeared at the door and said his partner Rose had reported him as a missing person. Realising he had been caught he fell onto the floor clutching at his stomach and wailing. You were terrified seeing your dad behaving in that way and that day I decided no more. He would come round still to babysit occasionally but one day you were crying constantly, and he said you had fallen off your bed. Later I discovered that you had broken a bone in your chest, and I was always suspicious about what happened. I couldn't cope with my children being so scared and confused.

Over the years I found it hard to trust again and I dedicated my life to my children but when you were a bit older, I met a new boyfriend. It didn't last as you were unable to trust anyone, and he was not good with children. I felt that I would never find happiness. Later in life I married again but he became aggressive in his manner after having strokes and I was on my own again."

"Why did you always choose Morag over me" I said, "especially after what my she did?"

"You never needed me. You didn't need anyone, and you were always so independent and inside your own head. Morag needed me always and I wanted to be there for her as it stopped me being lonely and afraid. Don't make my mistakes"

She stared into the distance changing to the younger vision as she danced off into the forest looking happy and carefree. I reflected on how different her life may have been if she had stayed with Ernest. The dream was comforting to me as it brought together many of the stories my mum had told me, and I felt some understanding.

The hidden monster

I had several relationships as I grew into a young woman and even a very short marriage, but none had connected with me in any meaningful way as I had grown used to living on the surface. On the final day of University, I went to the student union with my friends to celebrate the end of the exams. It was an idyllic beautiful day and we all sat on the grass eating pizza and drinking long vodkas. We were all becoming steadily drunker and more stupid as the day passed into night and we went back inside. I was ecstatic as I was surrounded by male attention which was something I craved in my early twenties. Kirk one of my classmates had not spoken to me all year but he would look at me with the type of stare that showed interest looking away when I stared back. Michael the younger guy that I would travel home with each night on the bus, was very drunk indeed and he was falling all over me while saying how much he liked me and trying to write his phone number on a napkin. Simon my best friend had started looking at me with "that look" as I told my friends, and he kept trying to sit close to me. Each time I went to the bar, fighting through the mass of sweaty students, I noticed a tall man with a slightly receding hairline watching me. He was dressed in Indie, but geeky clothes and he had a long face with large lips, sallow skin, and dark eyes. After I sat down, I noticed that my friend Janet was speaking to him, and they were looking over. When I came back to the table Janet said, "that guy wanted to know your name!"

The next time I went to the bar he came over and put his hand out to shake mine saying "pleased to meet you Danielle, I am James." I thought that this was in one way an impressive way to chat me up and in another way a bit weird. I said, "okay then" and went back to the table. Kirk finally came over to me and sat beside me. He laughed and said "how many times have we nearly spoken this year? I want to take you out if that is okay?" I said, "I know we have both been so massively awkward but yes I would like that". Kirk had to leave, and I gave him my number. In those days it was a house number as there were no mobile phones. I was so excited that we were finally connecting. Simon came over to speak to me and he seemed to be wanting to say something, but he was very nervous. I became aware of someone standing behind her and I realised James was standing waiting to speak to me. Simon realised too and he moved away to give James his seat looking defeated. James sat down and he asked if I had any Italian descendants. I confirmed that I did, and we chatted about Italian food. James had a Guardian newspaper under his arm, and he put it on the table as if to ensure that I knew he was intelligent and sophisticated enough to read the Guardian. I tended to read the Daily Record, so I was left feeling a little inferior.

We spoke for hours and then he moved in for a kiss and our friends had great fun taking photographs of us thinking it was hilarious especially as they were all now really drunk. James asked me to come back to his flat in the South side of Glasgow and I agreed as it would have been easier than trying to find a bus to go home. Janet was very worried and said "you will end up murdered" but I felt invincible in those days with the joy of being free from pressure, young and ambitious for a good life. The flat smelled of mildew and it was very dingy and run down but I was still drunk so I didn't care. Fortunately, I had my period so I was able to insist that nothing could happen. The next morning, he put on a second-hand charity shop three-piece suit that smelled of mildew to go to work in his part-time job in a book shop in Paisley. I went home and we agreed to meet for a date that evening.

I waited at Buchanan Street Bus Station standing trying not to look like I was waiting for a date in case he didn't show up. A very tall man came towards me from the distance in a light green oversized suit. He looked like a character from Miami Vice.

"Come on" he said "I want to buy you a present"

I was intrigued and we walked down to a book shop on Buchanan Street. He bought Martin Amis, Success. It appeared to be a way to impress but it was different and charming. We went to an Italian restaurant for a meal where he reiterated that he was very impressed that I was part Italian, understood the menu and he loved that I could cook Italian food. It all felt like the start of something wonderful. He explained that he had a holiday to Finland booked in a week so we would have limited time together before he had to leave, and he suggested we make the most of it. That week we spent every day together finding out about one another. When he left it felt like it was all too soon, and we agreed that after he came back, we would meet up again.

He was a quite strange when he returned but we were soon spending all our time together. In some ways it didn't feel quite right, especially his need to impress all the time, but I disregarded it as we seemed to have a lot of interests in common and I did like him.

James was very pretentious. He was ashamed of his family and his background. Before studying at university, he worked in a chemical factory. His father was an obsessive Rangers supporter with a sectarian attitude. He was always abusive and domineering to his wife. She always seemed very timid. James's father would criticise every meal his mother made. He would watch football with his father while his mother cooked and never defend her. After studying he would be seen to read the Guardian and surround himself with friends who were actors, musicians, or fellow students. He had a group of friends who would all have dinner parties in one another's houses. I hated pretension and dinner parties. I found his friends to be equally pretentious and I felt they always looked down on me.

I was due to go to America on holiday with my mother and sister. I had to choose if I wanted to keep my American citizenship. He was able to keep my mother's car to use to pick us up from the airport. While we were away, he had chicken pox and he was very ill. I wanted to come back to see him and ended the holiday two weeks early. We stayed in my mother's house together. He put on the film Blue Velvet. It triggered something in me, and I became very distressed. I told him about past abuse by my father but that I did not want to speak about it. He cried and told me he had been abused by his uncle and that he had not spoken to his dad for a year as he would not believe it. He said when he was younger, he had threatened his sister with a knife, set fires and assaulted his mum because he couldn't cope. I held him and said our shared past experiences would make us stronger.

The first big sign that all was not right happened one weekend when we went down to Greenock to visit his parents. We were not able to share a room, so I had his old room and he slept on the couch. We went out to the local nightclub with his friends. One of the girls, Julie was rude to me all night, challenging everything I said. She wanted me to feel uncomfortable and indicated that I didn't fit in. It felt really humiliating and James didn't intervene. When we returned to the house, I mentioned it and he became very angry shouting that I had made him embarrassed by not being able to build a friendship with his friends. I asked him to stop shouting and he pushed me against the wall then grabbed my arm and threw me on the bed. I was so shocked and upset, thankful that his parents were out at the local social club, and I told him to go away. That night I was sick into a bin in the bedroom feeling very scared about what had happened. I felt the need to look for clues to his behaviour and I quietly and sneakily started snooping in his room. I came across a letter in his desk drawer. It was from Finland, and I was confused as I thought the holiday had been alone. Looking at the signature it was from Mairi McNeil who I had heard of as James had dated her for six years from the age of 17 only breaking up with her not long before we met. The letter referred to him having been in Finland with her and her distress that they had not been able to work things out. I was horrified to discover he had been there to see his ex-girlfriend and that he had lied to me about it. It had now been three months since he returned and had not mentioned anything about it. I felt anxiety flood my body as I was with him in his home with his parents and I didn't know how to cope. I rummaged through an old desk in his room, and I found a diary of the trip. It was as if he wanted me to find it and it had been written for me as he almost wrote it to me and his new feelings for me. He was conflicted as he had been with Mairi for so many years. I felt very confused as it seemed so calculated to prepare for me discovering his deception.

The next morning, he was contrite about his behaviour the night before and when he discovered what I had done he was so panicked that I would leave him that he went down on his knees and begged forgiveness with tears streaming down his face. I thought his behaviour was very strange. I had never experienced such dramatic behaviour, but I thought he must really care for me, so I was flattered. I dismissed from my mind what seemed like out of character behaviour.

One weekend some weeks later I was alone in his parents' house for the weekend when the phone rang. I answered to take a message if necessary and man's voice asked for James. I asked what it was regarding, and he said my name is Douglas. I had not heard the name before, and I asked him if I could pass on a message. The caller said, "ask James". When James arrived back, and I asked him he crumbled in front of me. He confessed that while he was with Mairi for the full six years he had also had a relationship with one of his male school friends. He said the relationship had continued for so long due to blackmail as every time he tried to end it Douglas would threaten to tell Mairi and his parents. He went into graphic detail about what had happened between them as if he was trying to release it from his mind. He said, "by telling you I have freed myself and he can't blackmail me anymore". I was shocked and I asked if he was bisexual or gay. He confirmed that he was bisexual and acknowledged that could lead to concern about being faithful considering his past where he had already been. Instead of being concerned about continuing the relationship I helped him come to terms with what was in fact abuse, recognising it for what it was. I sat with him while he called back saying "I am with someone who loves me and who knows all about you so you can't hurt me anymore."

After around five months together he asked me to move into a flat with him in the South side of Glasgow. We were both returning to university. He had the last year of his Social Sciences degree and I had decided to study to become a professional accountant. The flat was over a rowdy pub with small market stall-based shops nearby with fresh fruit and vegetables. We shared with Clare one of his friends from work. The flat was a traditional Glasgow tenement with a large room, two bedrooms, bathroom, and a shared kitchen. The flat was within walking distance from the university meaning we could save travel costs and nights out were great as we could walk home drunk staggering about and laughing. The first few weeks were fun and all three of us would experiment with making meals are cheaply as possible which mostly consisted of macaroni and cheese with a treat of spaghetti bolognaise now and then.

At times it was claustrophobic being in one room most of the time. Studying was complex with both of us competing for times with no noises such as the television or radio. One night James was obsessed with watching football and he had the sound up very high. I was trying to prepare for an exam the next day and I couldn't concentrate so in a huff I went to turn off the television. The next thing I knew was being hurled onto the bed and punches were furiously rained down on my back. The pain was excruciating, and I crawled into bed rocking and trying not to scream. I looked at him in tears with my eyes red and puffy. He started taking photographs of me in distress. I crawled into bed in my clothes to escape him. This time rather than begging forgiveness he just said "well you know you wound me up. It was your fault. If you had not tried to antagonise me, it would not have happened."

The next day I felt feverish and unwell with severe pain in my back, so I went home and missed the exam. I had started to pass blood in my urine, so my mother called the doctor who diagnosed a kidney infection. I was given antibiotics, but I spent four days in agony until the swelling calmed down. My doctor sent me for a scan.

The radiologist was one of my closest friends from school. I hadn't seen her for a few years, so we spent some time catching up. I was so embarrassed about the circumstances that led me to the scan. I made up a story about falling. The results showed that my kidneys had been bruised. My doctor questioned me, but I was too embarrassed to say what had happened.

I was always more likely to accept that I had done something wrong, and I thought perhaps if in future I managed to quell my tendency to be determined to get my own way things would be better. From then I tried to be perfect in every way and things calmed down. I was unable to bring myself to have sex with him and I managed to disclose to my mother about the abuse by my father. She said she had always known. She explained that one night when my dad had stayed over I slept in the living room with him as my gran was over from America. She had my room. I had woken my mum up crying and saying my dad had hurt me. My mum had gone to speak to my dad and the strange things he said made her realise what had happened. She told me it was important that I dealt with it. She arranged a meeting with my GP. I was too scared to go and I stayed on the bus rather than go to my appointment. My mum insisted on calling the doctor to ask if he would still see me. The doctor was very kind and understanding but he arranged for me to see a sex therapist as I said I couldn't bear to have sex with James. The therapist asked about my dad. When I told her that he had been a psychiatric nurse who became a manager in a Glasgow psychiatric hospital she was silent. She commented that my name was unusual. She asked the name of my dad she told me that she had been in a relationship with him as they had worked together. I was shocked, horrified, and frightened.

Around two weeks later my dad called my flat. I hadn't seen him for two years and I felt sure he must have known I had spoken out about the abuse. I told my flatmate to say I was not there anymore. Whenever, I walked around Glasgow from then I was terrified that I would see him and be in danger.

James asked me to marry him, and I accepted thinking the problems we had were just a blip. We planned a quick and uncomplicated wedding, and I allowed his mother to organise it all, holding the reception in his parent's local social club. My mother was really annoyed at not being included and she was unhappy that all her friends would have to travel if they wanted to attend. The week before the wedding I collapsed in Edinburgh with severe stomach pain. On the day of the wedding, I felt more and more ill as the day progressed and by the time of the reception and the meal, I felt so dreadful that I had to stay in the toilets. James's mother came in furious that the guests were being let down and completely unconcerned that I was unwell. After a while and when my friends had arrived, I felt better and I proceeded to just keep drinking and sitting with my friends, ignoring James and his family. I realised that the marriage was a mistake and that my health was suffering from the worry of what may come next. We had our honeymoon in Paris and it was wonderful, so I thought perhaps I had overreacted. On the night that we arrived home we went up to James's parent's house to look at the wedding gifts as his parents were out. I asked where the wedding cake was and said "I hope your mother didn't forget about it"

"How dare you criticise my Mum!! He yelled.

He stormed off out of the house furious. I sat for a moment then thought I had better follow him. The flat we were now living in was about a 30-minute walk away, but I was unsure of the way to go so I thought I had better find him. I didn't want to be there when his parents returned. I started to walk down the steep hill to the town centre. In the daytime the hill looked over the water and there was a steep drop over the fence with gorse bushes and rocks. In the dark it was hard to work out where everything was. As I walked suddenly someone jumped out at me from the side of the path. I was knocked to the ground and dragged forward by the hair. My arms and legs were scraped, and I was terrified not knowing what was happening. I managed to stand up and I realised it was James who was attacking me. He was strangely silent and every time I tried to move away; he pushed me. A taxi driver stopped beside us asking if I was okay, but I was too embarrassed to admit I needed help. The taxi driver being there stopped him, and we walked down towards the flat. I was in complete shock walking in a daze. As we approached the flat, I saw a phone box and I jumped inside to call my mother. James begged me to come out promising it would never happen again. He promised he loved me. Repeatedly he begged until finally I came into the flat. As soon as the door was closed, he attacked me again. He dragged me into the bedroom and threw me onto the bed trying to force my clothes off with his other hand round my throat. He tried to force himself inside me managing slightly while tightening his grip round my neck until I managed to find the strength and I connected my knee with his groin. He rolled over off me in agony and I rushed to the toilet and locked myself in. I sat there shivering for hours until I knew he must be asleep and I came out. In the morning he did not mention anything, and he acted like nothing had happened. I looked in the mirror and I had bruises on my face and a black eye. James insisted we visit his parents "but look at me" I said.

"We are going like it or not" he said.

It was a bizarre experience as his parents had no reaction to my injuries, not even asking what was wrong. They all went through the presents and his mother confirmed that the wedding cake was in the freezer. I felt so stupid again and I felt responsible for what had happened.

The next few months passed with regular beatings usually happening when he felt embarrassed or awkward about something. One day we had booked to go and play badminton and I felt unwell on the way there. I had continued to feel unwell a lot. When I asked to cancel James hit me in the face with the back of his hand in the street saying that I was trying to embarrass him by cancelling. I went to the badminton upset and distressed but somewhere inside I found an inner strength and I managed to beat him in every game despite feeling ill. Adrenaline took over and the inner strength I found that day stayed with me though many future adversities. I never forgot the feeling of fighting back.

During the time I felt sicker and more worried that something was wrong. Tests showed gall bladder stones and surgery was arranged just before Christmas. A week before the surgery James insisted on a journey with his friend Andy to Largs. I felt so sick in the car and Andy was so kind. He offered to drive me to the hospital on the day of my operation. He looked at James as if he felt disgusted that he had forced me to go out.

I went into hospital terrified, a few days before Christmas. When I came round from the surgery, James was excited that he had been offered a job in the local council. He reassured me that all would now be fine. We returned to my mum's house for Christmas to recover. My wound became infected, and he acted irritated that my health issues were continuing.

Almost three months later after we had returned to Greenock the sick feeling was still there and I had strange growths in my vagina. I was sent for tests and was diagnosed with genital warts. I was devastated knowing that James must have been unfaithful. While they were doing the tests, they discovered something and asked me to get dressed and sit down.

"Did you realise that you may be pregnant. Have your periods stopped?"

"I thought it was my illness and then the surgery but yes my periods had stopped"

"You are three months pregnant, congratulations!"

I was so excited at the thought of the baby but so scared at having a baby with James. I walked home holding my stomach gently thinking of the baby inside and being determined to change my life. I called my father and Maureen his wife. I wasn't sure why considering how frightened I had been, but I felt like I wanted him to know I was moving forward with my life. Maureen was pregnant too and they were so excited to hear the news. We returned to live in Cumbernauld with my mother while we waited for a council house.

At around six months pregnant I was referred to a rheumatologist due to blood results. I sat outside the treatment room and overheard the consultant speaking to a heart specialist who said that I had a heart issue. I felt so scared and alone. The consultant told me that I had blood issues called thrombocytopenia which could be risky during childbirth. They said I also had lupus and anti-cardiolipin antibodies. The consultant handed me a leaflet, said I would probably be unsafe to have any more children, would be unable to work and would possibly live five more years. I was terrified. James told me he felt misled as he had married an accountant not a disabled person. From then he was cold and distant with me. When the pregnancy reached eight months, we were going to visit his parents and part of the way there I started to feel unwell so I asked if we could turn back. He was furious saying "this will be embarrassing having to tell my parents. We are going"

He grabbed hold of my hand and squeezed it until I was in so much pain, I agreed to go so that it would stop. When we returned home that night, he tripped me up on the stairs and I fell onto my stomach. I was terrified that the baby was harmed and lay crying all night particularly as the baby was not moving. Fortunately, the baby moved the next day and I felt even more protective.

Two weeks after my due date I started some contractions. We set off for the hospital and then realised that the car needed petrol. I realised this could be challenging as the pubs were coming out and the petrol station had closed the doors so there was a large queue of drunken revellers. I felt even then he had not cared enough to make sure the car always had petrol. I sat in the car as he waited in the queue watching him and feeling so lost and scared. We arrived at the hospital, and he went into the caring husband role to impress the hospital staff. They all acted soppy, and they fluttered around him making sure he had sports to watch on the TV. I remembered the assault over the football and felt the irony. The contractions had stopped so they decided due to the lupus, heart and blood issues that had been found in earlier months that they would have to induce the labour. The contractions then came fast and strong and I lay writhing in agony on the bed. James was engrossed in the sport, so the lovely Swedish midwife sat by the bed and soothed me by almost hypnotising me through the contractions. Hours passed and finally I was ready to push. It seemed like the room was full of medical staff and I realised how risky the birth was seen to be. A needle was inserted into me to take blood from the baby's head to see if he had the same blood disorder that could mean excess bleeding. The needle made my waters break but nobody told me what it was, so I was terrified that it was blood. They cut me to ensure that the labour would not cause the baby too much trauma and the baby was delivered. Through it all James was at the side of the room not participating.

All the family came in to meet the new baby and they all admired his lovely auburn hair and deep brown eyes. After they left, I lay and started at my beautiful son not wanting to lay him down and feeling the need to protect him forever. They took him away at one point through the night and I sat up waiting for him to come back.

When we were discharged from hospital my baby just wouldn't stop crying and he fed constantly as if he needed reassurance. I wondered if he was picking up my tension. James became jealous of all the attention the baby had and he threatened to throw him out of the window or smother us both when we were sleeping. I kept scissors under the pillow, and I kept my baby beside me in bed barely sleeping to make sure he was protected. Everyone commented that I would never put the baby down. My lupus had seriously flared up. I couldn't eat and I lost far too much weight to around 7 stones. I couldn't stand up holding my son and I had to crawl up the stairs. When the baby was around three months old, we decided to go out for the day to buy lunch and have a trip around the shops. As we left the street, I felt very ill and said I had to go back to the house. James was furious saying he would feel embarrassed if we went back in right away as if we had argued. He turned round in his seat and punched me. I said, "let me out or I will scream" and I crawled out of the car and grabbed the car seat rushing back to the house without realising that I was half lifting half dragging the car seat. I went into the house crying hysterically and my brother-in-law Steven sprinted out of the house to go and confront James. He had run off anticipating trouble. When he came back, he was even more furious that people now knew, and he threw me on the bed with the baby in my arms punching my legs from top to bottom. My sister Morag called my aunt to come round as our mother was in hospital having an operation. When she arrived, she told him if he ever touched her niece again, she would call the police. He stood like a passive child in the corner with his hood up as if to hide.

The beatings stopped for a while but when my son was a year old, we were offered our own house by the local council. I was terrified but excited at having my own home and for my son to have his own room I could decorate. The little house was a split level where the living room was upstairs and the bedrooms downstairs underground at the back of the rooms. The living room looked over a grass area and woods at the back and I would love standing at night in the dark looking at the silhouette of the treetops with the stars and the moon. I decorated the house spending hours travelling around DIY shops for the cheapest materials and charity shops for soft furnishings. I learned how to tile the bathroom and I wallpapered everywhere having learned many decorating skills having been raised in a one parent family. I painted a mural on my son's room, and I spent hours making it all perfect. I felt if it could all be the way it should then everything would be safe and all fine. After we had settled, we planned a day to Greenock to visit James's parents as his uncle was due to visit from Liverpool. That morning I felt unwell, and I panicked at the thought of James's reaction which made me more unwell. I plucked up the courage to say we couldn't go, and he went berserk worse than ever. He smashed my face with his head, and I felt my front tooth break. I felt dizzy and faint. After attacking me he ran out of the house, and I called my mother. She took me up to the nurse to check me for concussion and report the abuse and then she insisted on taking me through to Greenock with the bruises and broken tooth. On the way she said, "dear you have made your bed and you have to lie in it." The visit was strange as his family laughed at the little fight and ignored the bruises and they seemed not to even see the tooth. My mother was appalled and took me straight back home. When James came back, he was given an ultimatum to go to the doctor for help or be reported to the police. He chose the doctor.

He was offered counselling and for two years everything seemed to be fine. However, he kept receiving more and more work calls at home and he seemed to always be under work pressure that made him upset and stressed. He was working towards a planning degree to add to his other social science degree and there was a trip to Germany planned. He took money with him, which was a struggle for us, but it would mean more opportunities. When he came back, he was quiet and withdrawn. I took my son Thomas out a walk, and I put on James's coat as it was the first one, I could find. I put my hand in the pockets and felt paper rolled up. I looked at it and realised it was receipts for meals for two and photographs of a woman. I felt sick. When I returned home, I confronted him, and he confessed that he had been with another woman he had become close to, but he swore that nothing happened. I didn't believe him but for Thomas's sake I put my worries to one side. The woman started calling the house and eventually he had to admit that they had been having an affair. I decided to stay for the sake of my son but kept away from him and refused to share a bed. Following the event, he started acting erratically again and on one occasion he drove the car in a dangerous way with my neighbours' children in it. On a shopping trip round Asda my son was trying to touch things from the shelf and I caught James hitting him round the side of his head. That night I told him it was over and that he would need to leave immediately to go and live with his parents. He smashed a cup on his head and said he was not leaving. I realised I would have to go as it was not safe for me or my son and I arranged a privately rented flat. We moved out one day when he was at work. Finally, we were free.

The amazement of emptiness

I was so distressed when I split from James. I was in a very depressed state as I felt a failure for the family breaking up and my son having had such horrible experiences. He would go every weekend and James would continue to torment me by saying that he did not have clean socks on or that he said that he had not eaten breakfast as like most children he learned how to play one off against the other to have more sweets. I had a night out with my friend Jean to the local nightclub to relax and forget about the stress. Jean had become a close friend when James became so awful, and I would go round to visit her each night. We would drink coffee and talk. Jean was a single parent with two children one my son's age, and we all enjoyed spending time together.

We sat down at the only table with spare seats, where we were opposite three men. One of them was smoking and he took Jean's lighter. I said, "how rude" and he spoke in an American accent saying, "I enjoy being rude". We moved away to the other side of the nightclub where Jean started speaking to some men. I felt uncomfortable so I sat down. Suddenly another man sat opposite me. It was an ex-boyfriend I had lived with when I was 21. At the bar was another ex-boyfriend. I thought oh no this was the night of boyfriends past. The one sitting with me was drunk and he told me he had never managed to forget me. I squirmed in my seat wondering how to let him down gently when the man from earlier came and beckoned me from the seat while gesturing to my companion to apologise.

"Thank you so much" I said

He introduced himself as Wilson and explained he only sounded American as he had been living there for two years on a football scholarship. I thought it was weird to have such an accent after two years, but I accepted speaking to him as he had rescued me. He was stocky and a strange build, almost feminine with large hips and narrow shoulders bent over. He had long curly hair and eyes that turned down at the corners. He was not my type at all, but he seemed friendly, so I agreed to allow him to walk me home and we agreed to meet again at the gym. The ex-boyfriend who had been speaking to me in the pub had followed us and he jumped out from the tunnel beside my house. He begged me to consider taking him back. I had to let him down gently while asking him not to do anything to strange again. It was a surreal night.

For the next month Wilson and I would casually meet at the gym and then we agreed to go for a date. We arranged to meet at the train station to go to Glasgow. I waited for over an hour with no sign of him, so I called his house. His dad answered and he said he was still sleeping. It was 1 p.m. His dad woke him up and he said he would be there in ten minutes. It was not a good start, but we went home together, and he stayed for the next week.

Gradually I realised he was not going to leave. He went back to his parents' house, and he arrived back in tears saying they had thrown him out after a massive fight. I was horrified as I felt it was too soon after my marriage breakdown, but Wilson was great at stopping James bullying me, so I allowed it to happen.

He wanted me to have a baby with him and I refused insisting it could be a risk to my health. We had only been together for a month, and I felt it was part of his possessive nature that he wanted me to be pregnant so nobody else would want me. We were having sex with a condom and he ripped the condom off entered me again and came inside me. I was terrified and felt violated.

That Christmas we went round to his parent's house as he wanted to make up with them. I was shocked as he was treated like a child by his mum with a massive Santa sack, stocking and loads of gifts. My son was with us and at the meal he was made to sit by himself in another room. I was very upset looking at his face all crestfallen as he had been so used to being the focus of attention at Christmas. I felt it would be better to end the relationship. However, I had started feeling sick all the time and I discovered I was pregnant. We had only been together for three months. It had to have been from the time when he removed the condom. When I told Wilson he was abusive and cruel, and he told me I wasn't even a good kisser. He insisted that I have an abortion. I already felt love for my baby, and I refused. I pointed out to him that he had wanted me to be pregnant. He said he was too young and didn't know what he wanted. He walked out to go back to his parents, and I was terrified at the thought of being on my own pregnant with a young child. Two days later he came back after another huge fight with his parents where the phones in the house had been smashed and he said he had been rolling about on the floor fighting with his dad.

It became more and more apparent that he was really disturbed. He would burn his arms with cigarettes when we argued, and he threatened to take all my anti sickness pills having crumbled them into a glass of milk. He would have huge tantrums when playing board games if he lost. At one point he grabbed a pile of coins and threw them at me with force. They marked the wall behind me. He smashed my glass door and punched light switches. He would be jealous and possessive all the time. At one point when I was eight months pregnant a man touched my stomach and told me I was wearing a beautiful dress. He went into the bedroom and blocked the door and he cut up all my dresses. He would stay up all night playing the PlayStation and he would sleep all day. He constantly smoked cannabis and he could not sustain work as he always felt people were judging him. When the baby, William was born, I had to look after the two children on my own as he was always asleep. When my son was five months old, I started feeling sick again and I discovered I was pregnant. The relationship became worse as it went on. He would ruin every occasion, birthdays, Christmas, holidays and even days out. When I was six months pregnant Jean told me that he had asked to sleep with her. A month before Arianne was due to be born William fell down the stairs as the stair gate had been left open. Wilson blamed me and he flew back up the stairs battering me on the top of my head screaming at me that I was a stupid bitch. Shaking and crying I went to my mum's house with Thomas and William. I lay that night feeling my large stomach and watching my children sleep and thinking how life become this hard.

The evil that men do

One night when I returned home my five year-old son was sitting with his knees tight to his chest on a chair in the corner of the room.

"Why are you sitting in the dark?"

"He said if I spoke about it or told anyone he would throw me in the bushes or kill you mum"

"Who did?"

"Him. When I would go and visit him, he would hurt me. One time he was sick on my toy car, and he jagged me with a nail and then he threw a glass at me." I was horrified. I comforted my son and said I would make sure it could never happen again.

I confronted James by phone and he said it was lies and fantasies and I didn't know what to do. I couldn't prove it and if I stopped access my lawyer said I would be in contempt of court. Weeks passed and Thomas had constant upset stomachs every time he was to go and see his dad. I was told again I would have to send him to his dad or be arrested as it was legally agreed.

Then one weekend Thomas was at his grandparent's house in Greenock with his dad. He called me to say he wanted to come home. He was whispering and I could hardly hear but he said he didn't want his dad or his grandparents to hear. He told me his dad made his pee pee hurt but that he had told him the doctor fairy would make it all better. I was shocked and scared. When he came home, I asked him what he had meant. I remember I was in the bath with William. He stood awkwardly at the side of the bath and he told me his dad had touched him down below and hurt him while they were sharing a room. He said his dad then looked out of the window and told him there were "bad people in the world". I could see he was very upset so I didn't ask him any questions. I thought it was best to let him tell me in his own time.

I called so many helplines for advice. I didn't know what to do. I was afraid I could be wrong, and I could cause so much distress but I knew that I had to do something and it all tied up in my mind with the way he had been for months. I felt sick. I worried that I should have acted sooner. The helplines gave me the advice to phone the police. First, I called James at his work and told him what Thomas had said to me. He acted strangely and said, "don't use those sexual swear words with me". I was baffled as there were no sexual swear words and I realised that was for the benefit of his workmates. It worried me more that it was all true.

I called the police, and they came out with social work to interview my child. I was allowed to be there but not to speak. My scared little boy explained the room where it happened. He said he was asleep and then his dad opened one eye and then another eye and he touched him until it hurt, and he cried. He stopped and said the thing about the bad people. Throughout the interview Thomas threw his toys around and was clearly very upset. They asked if he had told anyone before about it and he said he told his gran. We found out later he had meant my mum but they thought he meant his gran on his father's side. They interviewed her later and she said it wasn't true. They interviewed James and said he denied it. They said because Thomas said he was asleep and he was only six a defence lawyer would pull things apart. The fact that his gran did not corroborate his story it made it harder to prove. It was not until a few years later when my mum confirmed it had been her. They said they were sure it had happened but there was nothing more they could do. I was in a terrible state, and I tried to at least find counselling for my son. I wanted to make sure he was never alone with his dad. Social work insisted on supervised access until he was 18. Thomas was not allowed counselling as social work were afraid, he would say something that would mean the case would have to be taken forward. James worked for the council and they were afraid he would sue as he knew his rights.

Thomas always put on a face that he was happy but inside he fell apart every day and he felt so awkward around friends and girlfriends as he wasn't ever able to really feel good about himself. As a six-year-old he said he wanted to die and that stayed with him throughout his life. He was involved with heavy drinking as a teenager to try and block out the memories and flashbacks of that time. He had very challenging relationships.

He went to my work for counselling but remained conflicted and confused, especially as he kept seeing his dad.

The hermit

As Arianne grew into a teenager her dad would give her his version of the past.

Time had ravaged his face; his teeth were blackened from years of smoking, and he was very overweight from many years of staying up late eating junk food. The man she knew rarely laughed. He would sit up all night and sleep all day and his life consisted of horror films and computer games.

"I met your mother at a time in my life when I was trying to find myself", he laughed.

"We were always trying to find ourselves in those days!"

"I was so unhappy at home as my relationship with my parents was awful. I was so young, and I met a much older woman who seemed to offer me a way out. She had a child but that was okay as children generally liked me. When she moved into her flat, I saw my way to escape. One night I turned up at her door with all my bags and stayed for four years".

"Did you love her?"

"You must understand sweetheart I didn't know what love was. I wanted a way out, some freedom from the constant judgement piled on me by my parents. Before I knew it your mum was pregnant with your brother, and I was trapped again. I was only 22 and it was hard to cope with."

"There are things I just can't tell you as you are too young to understand but the situations, we went through together are things that no-one should have to go through and it changed me, it changed who I was."

"Your mother was hard to be with. Her life was full of darkness. When we met, she seemed to be exactly what I wanted and seemed to fit into every aspect in life that could make me happy. We loved all the same things, and she would tolerate my tendency to be lazy and unable to hold down work. Through time I started to see glimpses of another person I didn't know, then after the dark time, she was never the same but in some ways I'm not sure I ever really knew her. No-one does"

"So why did you break up?"

"It's a long, long story"

"Please tell me I know what she has told me but there is so much about you hurting her and I find it hard to see you like that."

"I did hurt her, but it wasn't all me. When we found out she was pregnant with your brother I was terrified. I was so young, and I didn't know how to cope so I walked out. I told her I didn't love her, I said cruel things, but I came back."

"She became very ill when she was pregnant. It was dangerous for her to go through that with her illness and she ended up in hospital. I didn't know how to deal with it."

"Through the years we fought all the time often in a physical way, but it wasn't my fault. She was very hard to live with."

"I changed; everyone does when they are with her. She makes you not able to trust and she makes you angry. You can never understand who she is, so you don't know who you are with. I told her everything about myself and my family and she told me everything about herself. But I have a feeling she told me nothing."

Arianne pondered on that and said, "but she is so kind."

He laughed "everyone thinks that she will do anything for anyone but there is more than meets the eye. Those black eyes hide a lot. Like black holes"

Arianne grew angry "she is kind!"

"I am kind too sweetheart sometimes when people meet, they can be a catalyst in one another's lives for bad things and look at me know I have no partner and no real home. I can't trust anyone, and my life is you and your brother. I prefer to be here, it feels safer. Your mum lets you see the world isn't safe."

Love overcomes

I sat on a winter night casting spells by the light of the moon through the window. This was one of my monthly rituals when I felt life needed to change for the better. The whole family had been interested in mystical things for as long as I could remember and from a very early age I had dabbled with tarot and spell casting.

At times like that I would dwell on my life and the passing of the years, but many aspects were blocked out as if they happened to someone else.

There had been many challenges along the way and in some ways, life had begun anew with a new marriage to my soul mate and my career beginning to take off. The years to now had left scars that ran deeply through my being and as I had learned to do in childhood, I had reinvented a new person who fitted with the new lifestyle.

Meeting and marrying Chris had been the liberation from all that had gone before. We met when I was 17 at the local art club. Art was a passion for me, and the paintings produced over the years told the story of my life. Chris was kind and thoughtful and always full of smiles and chat to everyone young and old. At first meeting there was a connection, but the age difference was great, and he was married to a woman who I thought at the time was unbelievably stupid.

She was one of those women who would always call you by your name as soon as she discovered what it was, and she would be determinedly sycophantic. You were so pretty and so nice, but the eyes were full of disgust that you had to be alive. My feelings were that this woman was not to be trusted but then I had developed a teenage crush on Chris.

I remembered the first night I saw him. He was standing talking to two men in the art club. He was wearing a woollen smart blazer and he had longish hair. He looked mature and arty and very attractive. Despite all the years that passed I have never forgotten that night. I believe I knew then he would be important in my life.

Throughout the years we would bump into one another through all the changes in our lives and we would always talk deeply like old friends who knew one another very well. Then one day when I was leaving yet another relationship and moving into a new one, we met again. We stood talking and laughing and connecting through our eyes and then I walked away to start yet another life.

The grapevine was wild about a year later that he had discovered his wife was seeing another man and she had walked out and left him with three small children. There was a feeling of sadness but a strange elation even though the connections through the years had been brief and fleeting.

Soon after the birth of Arianne there was a call out of the blue to start running a new art project in the local school and the co-facilitator was to be Chris. I was very nervous as we only casually knew one another, and we would be working very closely together. Over the next year we worked together and created a wonderful experience for all involved. We started a new art club so were spending three nights a week together and the friendship grew and grew.

A friendship was all it could be until one day when we sat and talked in the staff room. Conversations had always been on the surface and about the work but somehow on that day we entered a space in time where everything else drifted away. He told me all about his life and the disaster that had been his marriage.

"Why have you never managed to be a famous artist?" I asked.

"There could be lots of reasons. I paint for me, for what I want to say in the world and not everyone may want to hear what I have to say. It's about us, our lives, about me and I didn't try to fit into any box or any fashion. Art is like the emperor's new clothes if you remember that story from when you were small. Some art critics will decide that an artist is trying to say something with his or her work, others will respect those views, and no-one will have the guts to stand up and say but it's a load of rubbish like no-one could say that the emperor was naked. It then takes the shape of fashion and it's not so different from the recent fads of reality TV. There will be a market and a populous and artists will paint for that market to find fame. They lose what made them want to be an artist and I will never be that."

"Why have so many galleries rejected your work it's so much better than the paintings I see there."

"I never had the opportunity in life to go to art school and achieve a degree. For some reason art became for the elite in society. When galleries ask for submissions, they ask for qualifications. Thirty years of being self-taught and learning your craft is not relevant to the art world. Look at the outcry about Jack Vettriano. The art world would never accept him. He was outside their world. No-one can teach the passion and expression that comes with creating an artwork. You can learn the techniques and in every new development in art it learned from the techniques of the previous generation of artists. So many students are another version of their teacher. I go my own way and if I end my life having painted for me, I will be content."

The conversation stayed with me as being the one that changed everything as we connected much more deeply than we ever had. I had so much respect for him. For the first time he drove me home that night and we sat in the car with what he later called the long goodbye. He told me that I looked like one of the actresses in Neighbours and I realised that he was thinking about me when we were apart.

The art club we attended each Wednesday was in the local community centre. I realised that if he didn't arrive on any night, I would feel loss and I would then call him. Chris later said sometimes he wouldn't turn up just so that I would call. I started to take more care over my appearance even wearing low tops and short skirts, although of course not both at once.

I would lean over the desk to talk to him watching his eyes trying not to look at my breast area. He was masterful at pretending not to notice and not to care. Over the next year we started talking on the phone weekly. Chris was lonely caring for three young children and the conversations meant a lot to him. I was at the end of my terrible violent relationship and was trying to persuade Wilson to move out, but he had no intention of doing so as he wanted to be looked after with no intention of working or being self-sufficient. I found that I was talking about how trapped I was and how terrible it all was to anyone who would listen but there seemed to be no way out. Wilson was aware of the friendship with Chris but he really didn't care seeing in one way that Chris was no threat and in another that even if he was he didn't care about me. It was the home and being cared for that he wanted.

One night Chris decided to invite me and my friend Janet up for a celebration evening as the club had finished for the year. He wanted me to have a break because he realised how hard the relationship was becoming. We all sat and talked while consuming large quantities of wine and as it was later and we were more drunk we decided to dance and Chris told me he was going to teach me how to dance in the way that some of the teachers had shown him. It was akin to dirty dancing, and I felt myself feeling really attracted to him. It frightened me and even more when I realised he was very obviously excited. I suddenly felt very sick with panic and said that I had to leave. When home I sat trying not to be sick and thinking what does this mean?

The next night I called Janet and said to her that I just couldn't stay with Wilson anymore. It was making me unhappy and was so bad for the children. I turned and realised Wilson was listening to the conversation. He was furious and went downstairs. I stood at the top of the stairs and told him that he would have to go as I couldn't take it anymore. He flew to the top of the stairs and threw me to the ground punching me. I ran down the stairs and out of the house terrified and found myself walking to near where Chris lived. I stood in a phone box and considered calling him, but I couldn't. I thought of calling the police but was too afraid of the shame. I walked back home and thankfully Wilson was on his PlayStation and he ignored me. I crept off to sleep in the children's room shaking and lay all night tense and terrified. It was combined with guilt as I could not stop thinking about Chris and I realised I was falling for him.

The next day we talked and finally Wilson agreed to move out. He went up into the loft to take down some of his things that had been stored there. A box fell out and smashed a hole in the bath and I said, "oh for goodness sake". Wilson went into a rage and he charged into the bedroom where I was sitting on the bed. He threw himself on me grabbing my throat and strangling me. I screamed and the children came running through. All three jumped on his back screaming leave mummy alone even Arianne who was only just under two years old. The children shocked him, and he let go but I could not breathe properly and my neck was circled by bruising. My son Thomas called his gran, and she came over having called the police. The police arrived and interviewed us both separately. Wilson admitted his actions and the police said it was a clear assault due to the bruising, but they encouraged me not to press charges due to the stress on us all and they said they would remove him from the house and tell him not to come back. I agreed as I was so ashamed by what had happened, and I did not want to have to deal with a court case. That night I felt upset and panicky, and I called Chris in tears. He was confused by the tears and asked if I was sad at the breakup.

"No" I said "but how am I going to manage as a single mum with three small children? How will I manage to go to work? Wilson's gran looked after the children, and I can't ask her now. What will I do if they are ill, and I can't care for them due to my lupus and infection risks?"

"You will be fine" Chris said "you were pretty much managing on your own anyway. Wilson was useless. I can't believe his gran had to care for the children when he was in all day"

"He used to sleep most of the day and then get up and obsessively browse porn sites. I had to ask his gran to help as I would come home from work and the little ones would be in nappies so wet they would hang right down being the nappies they had on when I left and they would not have been fed. If she hadn't helped, I would have had to give up work".

Chris was shocked as he had always dedicated himself to his children putting his own needs second. He worked in their school painting murals to stay close to them and he always felt a single father had to try harder to prove himself. He felt as they had been left by their mother, he had to be both mother and father to them. His ex-wife had left saying that she wanted freedom and that she did not want to push a pram every day of her life. She wanted excitement. Ironically, she had another child to her new partner within eighteen months and during that time the children didn't see her. The twins were very badly affected as they were so young, and they didn't understand where their mother disappeared to. Susan was eight when she left, and she was withdrawn and confused clinging to her dad and seeing every woman in his life as someone who may take him away. Clark was the image of his dad and he was a really affectionate and sweet little boy who wanted cuddles all the time. He cried very easily and was upset if he had to be away from home. Wylie was extremely quiet around adults but wild with his friends. I had known them over the years growing up and I felt love for them all and so much distress for what they had lost. I now reflected that would be the reality for my children. I was very shocked as I was told that my eldest son Thomas hated Wilson as he had always excluded him from everything and had punched him in the stomach the day before the assault that had him removed. I found out after he was removed, and I had felt there had been a lost opportunity to have confronted him.

Chris suggested that I should meet him in Glasgow the next day to go for a coffee. I was very nervous, confused, and excited all at once. I stood in Buchanan Street next to New Look where we had arranged to meet. Half an hour passed, and he still wasn't there. I felt agitated and nerves were now about him not coming. I started to walk away as he came running down towards me out of breath and apologetic.

"I'm so sorry my dad is looking after the children, and I was caught up speaking to him. I felt I couldn't just leave"

I was just so happy that he was there "its fine" I said.

We walked down to St Enoch's Centre nervously quiet and making small talk. We sat and had coffee and cakes in the café area. As time passed we talked more and more and the connection between us was tangible. Chris explained his lack of trust due to his wife. She had persuaded his to have a vasectomy as she did not want any more children. When he refused, she spoke to his father to persuade him, and he eventually agreed. Then she had gone on to have another child and if he was to meet anyone else, he couldn't have children. I was shocked at the cruelty. I spoke about how terrible it had been to be with Wilson and how in many ways I was relieved that the relationship was over. But finally, we spoke about our dreams and love of art and nature. It felt different for me from anyone I had ever met or even spoken to. I didn't want it to end. Finally, we had to leave, and Chris offered me a lift home. He asked me to come back for a coffee before going home. His children were with his dad and mine were with their gran so I agreed. When we had finished our coffee Chris laughed and put on a video of him dressed as a gladiator as a surprise for a teacher. Being the solitary man working in the school they would have him involved in many crazy stunts and flirtatious comments that were just a bit sexist. After we laughed Chris became serious.

"I hate seeing myself. I see myself looking so old and ugly"

"You are not ugly" I said "I have always found you attractive"

I gulped when I said it realising it was very forward and not knowing how he would react.

"Well come and kiss me then" he said

I moved over the room and sat on his knee. We kissed passionately and I had never felt so close to anyone, and kissing had never felt so right. We realised the children would be back soon and decided to meet again the next week when the children would be at school and nursery.

The following Monday I sat terrified about what would happen next. We hadn't spoken for a week, and I wasn't sure whether or not to go. I was doubled up with stomach pain and cramps. Finally, I pulled myself together and walked the long walk to his house. When he opened the door, he looked equally terrified, and he asked if I wanted a cup of tea. I stood in the kitchen as he made it shifting from foot to foot to try and ease the nervous cramps in my stomach. He stared into my eyes, and we walked towards one another and kissed. The rest of the afternoon was wonderful and passionate and like nothing either of us had ever known. He drove me into Glasgow as I had to attend a late meeting for work. During the journey it felt as each mile passed that he disengaged from me and I felt very confused. When I left the car, he barely looked at me. I went into work and had a massive rant to my manager about how confusing it all was. Karen was fantastic and cautioned me to take my time as going from one relationship straight into another was bound to create confusion.

That night I called him but he was dismissive and cold. That week I went along to the art club hoping he would be there and kept watching the door but he didn't arrive. I called him and he didn't answer. That weekend the children were all with their fathers, so I decided to go to his house to confront him. He maintained the coldness and just said "look it won't work. You are too tall and too young. The person for me is a middle-aged woman like one of the teachers. I don't want anything to happen between us".

I was devastated and I realised I was already in love with him and in a way that I had never been in love before. I felt humiliated when I started to cry. I went over and put my arms around him and watched as my tears stained his shirt. He pushed me away and told me I would have to leave. I walked home in shock disbelief and grief.

Two weeks later I decided to go to the art club but this time hoping he would not be there as I was so embarrassed. He arrived with all the children and spoke to me as if nothing had happened. I was so confused. When I arrived home, I called him and this time he answered. We spoke throughout the whole of the night watching the sun come up. He explained that he couldn't be in a relationship as he was too afraid to trust after his marriage. I tried to tell him why it would work. It became like a game back and forth as I tried to convince him, and he wouldn't be convinced. We laughed and battled but he wouldn't give in. The next day I went to work for a meeting in the local college where I could hardly keep my eyes open, and the rector of the college played footsie with me under the table pretending to keep me awake but being very flirtatious. I kicked his foot away and laughed at how

I could attract other men with no problems but the one I wanted didn't want me. The routine went on for weeks. I was more of a geeky dresser but found myself wearing revealing clothes to the art club which must have been obvious to everyone. He would then studiously ignore me and the game went on. I challenged him to make me a mix tape and was very surprised when he agreed. I walked up to collect the children from nursery and the after-school club listening on headphones shocked by the songs, most of which I didn't know but loved instantly. The first one was Secret Smile, "nobody knows it but you've got a secret smile and you use it only for me". Then Iris by the Goo Goo Dolls where the lyrics expressed everything about what Chris felt about himself and fear of going forward. Then Until it Sleeps by Metallica expressing a side of him that I knew was there, a passionate but angry side that was the depth in him that I found so attractive. All of the songs made me believe he was trying to give me messages and I felt so hopeful and wanted him even more as the songs were so much the music I loved.

The art project we ran decided to hold a party to celebrate it starting back after the summer. I offered to hold it in my house. Chris was first to arrive, and it was obvious when he came in that he was very drunk. The rest of the guests arrived too and the house was full of people with the children in one of the bedrooms to be part of the party but away from the drinking. Chris didn't like to drink and never did so he was acting confident and wild. He was dancing with one of the teachers in the way he had previously danced with me so I left the room. He followed me and we stood at the top of the stairs against the banister. He kissed me but Susan came out looking shocked so I moved away into one of the other bedrooms. He followed me and we kissed passionately again and again until my lipstick was all messed up. I was embarrassed at being seen by Susan and at the teachers being downstairs and I went into the room with the children. Susan was crying so I sat and cuddled her and told her not to worry I wasn't going to take her dad away.

The rest of the children thought it was so funny first that their dad was drunk and that their dad had kissed someone. Clark went downstairs and announced it to everyone in the room. I was so embarrassed, but I recognised that two of the teachers reacted with jealousy as they had seen him as the only man around and an artist so therefore, he was a good catch. They left soon afterwards, and the party was over. I did not know what it all meant.

Two days later he called me to say he was ready to try dating, but he wanted our first date to be an overnight stay in Loch Lomond. He was due to sell a painting the following weekend so we could go then. The trip was like the whole of the rest of our lives together. I organised everything so that we could stay in a lovely chalet next to a hotel but when we arrived, I was hit by my usual nerves. Chris then took over organising a more suitable room when the heating didn't work and then organising a meal for us at Duck Bay Marina. After the meal I felt ill as I was not used to different food with my illness and he looked after me all night. I realised I could trust him to protect me.

Two years later after supporting the children to adjust and with many arguments to fit into a pattern of being together we decided to marry after I proposed on the fifth tee of a golf course. After the game we went straight up to the registry office and arranged a date. The wedding was so suited to us. We held it at the local Brewers Fayre where there was a play area for the children then on to a hall in the local Indian restaurant with all our friends. The buffet had masses of Pakora. Afterwards we went off to St Fillans to play golf for a day. We had a week away afterwards to Thorpe Park in Grimsby with all the children.

I loved my three new stepchildren right from the beginning feeling so lucky to have them in my life and with such a protective feeling towards them as they had been abandoned by their mother. Susan was wary and distant at times wanting to trust me but unsure as she had already lost one mother. Clark clung to me always wanting to sit on my knee and be around me. Wylie always kept some distance as if protecting himself from further hurt.

I tried to encourage them to build a relationship with their mother taking steps to get to know Jan to ensure that she would make the effort to see them. It was strange as Jan wanted to befriend me, continuing to always call me by my name and acting as if she was in some way inferior to me. Under the surface it was obvious there was a hidden deep resentment and jealousy, but it was covered by an intense pursuit of friendship. I would receive emails and texts daily with new stories about Jan's partner drinking too much and being aggressive or news of angina attacks. Every detail of each day would be described with the protagonist of the action always appearing as a victim of the daily difficult events. It was arranged that the boys would have regular contact with her initially meeting in McDonalds to help them to feel comfortable. Jan arrived with a fridge bag containing pancakes and large bags of sweets. The boys were interested in receiving sweets as they were not allowed them at home other than as a special treat to help protect their teeth. I fought the urge to be maternal and take them away to be rationed.

Initially the visits were fine but gradually conflicts started. The boys were afraid of their mother's partner as he would play rough games with them but surreptitiously hurt them. When they told their mother she would not believe them. One Sunday the boys had asked to play in a football competition rather than go for their visit. A few days before I called to explain to be met with a venomous response which completely took me by surprise. Jan slammed the phone down and five minutes later her partner Rab called insisting that the boys would be coming on the Sunday. He was threatening and abusive to me and I was so upset I told him he had better leave me alone or else. On the following Monday I received a phone call from my work to say there had been an accusation of me being threatening in my manner on the work line. I worked from home, so the same line was used for both personal and work use. I explained the situation but felt so humiliated and embarrassed.

Some weeks later a newspaper covered a story for the Open University mentioning that I had achieved my degree while being disabled and raising six children. The newspaper contacted me to say that Jan had called to object to the article saying that the children were hers. The paper apologised for having to check it out but again it was so humiliating. The troubles with her continued with many conflicts including a time when her partner threatened Chris that he would stab him. When the police went round to question him, he thought it was Chris and almost attacked the police with a knife. He was arrested and at that point the children asked if they could choose not to go back as they were afraid of being hurt by their mother's partner and they felt that their mother did not protect them.

I was passionate about ensuring they would have a good home and life having such a massive loss and I became obsessed with being the perfect mother, cooking perfect healthy meals, making sure they all felt safe and showing them love even when they acted out with bad behaviour.

The boys had to go to court to ask not to have to see their mother again. I was very worried about the impact on them if they did and I spoke to them the night before to make sure it was the right thing for them. On the day of the case, they looked small, confused and terrified. The judge took them in to speak to them and they made it clear they would have still had a relationship with Jan but she had chosen her new partner and he was a harmful individual. Wylie climbed on to my knee and he sobbed uncontrollably. All the children could never understand why she couldn't choose them. Following the case Jan wrote to Chris to apologise for all that she had done saying that her partner was violent and controlling and that she had no choice, but he ripped the letter up and put it in the bin. He was finally able to move on without the stigma he had always faced. I felt glad that the phase of our lives involving Jan appeared to be over.

Outside influences

Sadly, the influence of Wilson never left the family. Arianne and William had contact with him on an intermittent basis but with more intensity when he had a sense that he could involve himself in family arguments. When they went through to visit he would encourage them to stay up all night as he did playing the PlayStation and watching violent movies. He would feed them sweets and junk food rather than healthy meals. Gradually they both rejected home cooked food and they would have tantrums when it was offered to them. It became impossible to set a bedtime routine and they would always try and stay up all night then being too tired for school. When I would try and put boundaries in place, they would call their father and he would come and pick them up meaning that they would be off school for days at a time. It all caused so much conflict as I would be stressed but scared to confront Wilson and Chris would be worried about the impact on me. The constant conflict made me start to become very ill. Arianne was being very badly bullied at school. She was targeted by a large group of girls who would follow her home from school throwing a full can of coke at her and calling her names. She arrived home unable to breathe due to running and panic. I was in constant contact with the school, but nothing was done to help other than isolating Arianne in a classroom away from everyone at breaks. I reported my worries to the community police officer in the school and some of the girls were excluded for a few days but they were even worse with Arianne when they came back. Arianne was very beautiful, and she found confidence from talking to boys online as they would tell her how stunning she was while on the other hand she was suffering bullying online from the girls at school. I was very worried about her safety and I insisted on having her Facebook account but as I monitored one another one would be set up and when I discovered that one another one up to seven accounts at one point. When I would restrict the internet Arianne would go through to her father's house to go back online as he would encourage her to do what she liked. It was frightening to think that my child was so at risk when she was insecure and confused. Many meetings were organised with the school but they were more focused on attendance than the trauma of experiencing bullying. We went to the doctor and a referral was made to the Children's Mental Health Team. They finally assessed her as having a school phobia but they couldn't give any treatment as it was not a diagnosed mental health problem. I felt our whole lives had been about not being able to find help and support. Because of the diagnosis the school then had to act but the solution was to take her out of school and send her to college. On the first day in her class was one of the main bullies and all the children were smoking and drinking at breaks. Arianne was quiet and as she wasn't part of it. She was excluded again with the bully gossiping to others about her. Finally, they decided that she should be allowed to study at home as it was making her feel suicidal to have to go and she was developing severe anxiety.

Alongside the bullying the online relationships were becoming more dangerous. Large numbers of older men were speaking to her, and some were sending naked pictures and encouraging Arianne to do the same. They would tell her they understood bullying and they were there for her. She was confused that all the nice attention she was receiving was about her appearance and she would work hard on that to find more acknowledgement. I explained to her that these men were predators and that it was dangerous but the feelings of being liked were too strong. When she was fourteen, I had become more anxious and I managed to find a way to access one of the other Facebook accounts. I was horrified as one of the older young men had been asking Arianne to send naked pictures and sadly she had after quite a while of saying no and that she was only 14. I contacted the police and the laptop was taken away for investigation. It was discovered that he was 20 and he was arrested with a trial to follow on some months later. Ultimately he admitted guilt but received no sentence. Arianne then became even more confused and she started a relationship with a seventeen-year-old strange young man. He became obsessed with her, and they would be together constantly. I was concerned and I tried to restrict the time they would spend together but Wilson would then allow them to see one another in his house. At one point I managed to access Arianne's Facebook and I discovered that Wilson had allowed them to have sex in his house. I was devastated and I realised that Arianne had wanted me to see the messages as she was confused and scared, wanting boundaries. I told her to end the relationship and she seemed relieved to do so. We were driving home one night, and we noticed that lots of cars had stopped below the motorway bridge. The young man was on the side of the bridge threatening to jump off. I called the police but Arianne ran up the hill to try and persuade him to come down. I was scared she would be harmed and brought her back down. The police took him to hospital and Arianne went home confused and upset. She felt so guilty that two days later she took him back and they went through to Wilson's house to be together. I contacted the police and he was arrested for having sex with an underage child. Arianne seemed relieved that it was over.

Wilson continued his negative influence on William. He would encourage him not to go to school persuading him that society norms should be rejected. William found nights sitting up playing PlayStation and eating junk food were more attractive than being "the bitches of society" as his father would say. He would spend hours discussing conspiracy theories with his father. I found a bag of some kind of substance. He said his dad had bought him it but that it was a legal high. I was horrified and I contacted the police. Later legal highs were found to be very dangerous but at that point the police did not know what to do. I had no idea how to tackle the influence of Wilson on William as he had worked so hard on him that he rejected any kind of boundaries. I was terrified of the future for my children. It felt to me like there was nothing that could be done. After Arianne finally settled down with her own children, she moved more towards me and didn't see much of her dad. William settled down buying his own flat with his friend. He also rejected the influence of his dad.

Bosnia

After many years working as a project worker and counsellor I went to work for a charity that worked in International Development as an accountant to enable me to achieve the three years' experience I needed. The people I worked with were very nice especially Jen the Finance Officer who became a good friend. Working in Edinburgh was exciting feeling the buzz of the capital every day. I went to lunch with my colleagues at least once a week in restaurants that were ahead of trends. One of the favourites was a Tapas restaurant. It felt like a large contrast with many of the areas the charity covered including Bosnia, Tajikistan, Kazakhstan, Eritrea, Pakistan, and Afghanistan. My colleague Cathy would write funding applications in the millions, and I would put together the budgets. The Bosnia project was a ten million project on its own. The American branch of the charity wanted to assess the success of the Bosnian Finance Officer with the possibility that they would put in an American worker instead and they wanted review the ability of the Country Director to manage the finances effectively with her assistance.

I was sent to Bosnia for five days to meet the local team and make an assessment while reviewing the accountancy files for the audit. I arrived in Sarajevo to meet my driver who was going to drive me to Tuzla. He held up a sign and introduced himself as Latif. At first, he was very quiet which felt awkward as the journey was to be five hours but gradually as I chatted he opened up and talked to me about what his family had been through during the war. He said how angry many local people were about interference from the USA and UK. He warned me I may not be welcomed by the local staff. We stopped for a drink in a bar and a large group of soldiers with guns came in. Latif bristled with anger and asked if we could leave and continue the journey. He was driving very fast and he explained that speed limits were not followed with lots of accidents. Service stations had bars in them so drunk driving was not monitored particularly when the police were in one drinking when we stopped to fill up the petrol tank. I was delighted that everyone seemed to smoke as at that point I still did. I really enjoyed spending time with Latif finding him warm and caring with very deep distress and grief a constant part of his life. There were large villages where all the houses were covered in bullet holes and previously beautiful houses were burned down. Some of the damaged houses were mansions with concrete lions at the end of the drive.

We arrived in Tuzla at dusk and I was dropped off at my hotel. It was up high in the hills above smallholdings surrounding it. The hotel owner did not speak English and I didn't speak Bosnian so I was awkwardly shown to my room. The room had a door that didn't lock in the bedroom that went out to a patio and the outside. It kept opening so I lay half asleep, half awake all night. The next morning, I went for breakfast and had a really tough time trying to make myself understood so somehow I ended up with an egg. Natasa and Lisa the Finance Officer and Project Manager picked me up after breakfast. They seemed very cold and rude to me but I had anticipated that there may be worries about my role so I just kept being pleasant and friendly. I joked about ending up with an egg. The joke was greeted with stony silence. We went to the office where they showed me all the financial systems. I was very impressed. We went on to the pub after work and gradually they softened towards me. Natasa explained how important the job was to her. She lived in Split and before the war her husband had a business with a boat to take tourists out. The business had to close with the war and Natasa had to travel to Tuzla for the week travelling back to Split at the weekends. She said without that she could not even afford shoes for her children. She was so frightened that her role would be replaced by an American worker. I promised to recommend that she stay. On the final night I looked down at a smallholding and saw a woman working in the fields bent over and sore looking with no shoes and obvious exhaustion. I had noticed that many Muslims seemed to be living in extreme poverty. On travelling home, I realised what an impact the journey had made on me and I resolved to come back soon. Two weeks later a Board meeting was held in an Edinburgh hotel. The American Board members came over too. Before the meeting was due to start the hotel staff suggested we come through to see the television. We stood in horror as we watched the planes hitting the twin towers in New York. The American Board members were in shock and they all started making calls to make sure people they knew were safe. We all felt sick and the Board meeting was abandoned with us all returning to the office to keep making calls. It felt like life would never be the same.

The chance came again two months later. The American Finance Manager had decided to go to Bosnia herself to make her own assessment whether an American should be managing the finances. The CEO of the Scottish Head Office decided I should go to gather the final information for the audit but that at the same time I should keep a close eye on the American Finance Manager to ensure that the process was fair. I asked if I could take Chris with me if he paid his own expenses to ensure that if any health issues came up I would be accompanied. It was agreed and we set off on a cold November day. After the events in New York air travel was tense and security was massively stepped up. My passport was in my maiden name but my ticket in my married name so I was not allowed to board the plane. The tickets had to be changed and by the time it was sorted out we had to book into a hotel in Vienna to wait until the next day to catch the connecting flight to Zagreb. We waked through Vienna at night ending up with a luxurious meal in the hotel. I always felt awkward with the wine testing formal meal process and we laughed about it in the room later. The plane the next day to Zagreb was low flying and it had propellers. We were slightly scared but excited as it was closer to the ground, so the view was amazing. We arrived at the airport full of attendants with guns. This time it felt more threatening. The driver was not as talkative and friendly and he swore at the guards at each checkpoint. We stopped at a petrol station and he stood having a drink before we headed back on the journey. Chris was shocked and I explained I had been aware of it the first time I had been in Bosnia. The hotel this time was in the centre of Tuzla, but the toilet was a hole on the floor. It was strange as the hotel was more modern but the facilities more basic. We met the Country Director, Mike who was really eccentric and fun. I met up with Anne the American Finance Director and Mark one of the Scottish volunteers. Chris, Mark, and Mike went off to have a tour round the area while Anne and I went to meet Natasa. The meeting with Anne and Natasa was uncomfortable and awkward as it was known by them all that the agenda was to take Natasa's job but we all acted dryly pleasant. After a few hours we all met up again for a meal. The men were all very drunk and Chris started accusing Anne of thinking she was above everyone. I dragged him back to the room. He said that he had been taken up into the mountains where they were joined by a Serbian General with a gun. They were stopped by a Jeep in front of them and it looked like there would be a confrontation, but the presence of the gun made them move on. They spoke to an old man who had been displaced during the war, having lost all his family. The project the charity was running enabled him to move back to his house to rebuild it with the help of microcredit. He was so humble and the General so rude to him. Mike explained that the American's wanted control of the microcredit as it was potentially a business and income generator. They stopped at a bar and as they had more to drink, they became angrier about the Americans.

The next day it was rumoured that Anne and Mark had disappeared off together and it was clear there was chemistry. It distracted us all to some extent from all the tension. We spent the next few days gathering all the audit information and Anne met with Natasa to interview her. At the end of the visit Anne said she had decided to recommend that an American take over the post. I made it very clear I would challenge it. I was shocked at my assertiveness. It was the first time in my career that I felt strongly about fighting against injustice. The visit affected us both very deeply. On the plane on the way home we talked at length about how the country was so beautiful and yet so destroyed. We felt fortunate to live in a society where people did not harm each other to that extent. Later in my career I realised the harm was just more insidious and injustice more hidden. When I returned, I managed to win the battle to keep Natasa in a job and I was linked to her on Facebook where I was happy to see she progressed in the organisation to more senior posts. I left the organisation soon after the Bosnia trip as it had been so difficult with the overseas travel having young children who were afraid of me going.

The light in the darkness

I had worked in many charities over the years and was on the Board of a charity that I felt very passionate about. The CEO job became available and I decided to go for it even though it was a drop in salary and a much smaller organisation than my current role. The charity had a special feel about it where it was focused on empowerment and community development rather than the model used by many charities working in the health field where it was almost like a social work or care in the community model. Survivors were part of the Board, the staff team and volunteer team. When I took over funding was very unstable and redundancies were imminent. The previous manager had been ineffectual and unable to understand the management of a charity. She had mismanaged the budgets not having a financial background and she had spent money that wasn't there. Staff did not have supervision which was not ethical for a counselling organisation and there were no policies and procedures. However even with all the concerns the organisation was so different and ethical in the work with survivors that I was highly motivated to resolve the issues.

Within two years the budget had increased by more than double, policies were developed, supervision was in place and financial procedures were developed. The organisation became Scotland wide, and it started to work with all ages rather than just over 12. After further time of development, we worked with early years and won a contract to work with all prisons in Scotland. As it became a larger charity some of the original team progressed into higher positions. I had a commitment to developing people and I realised that growth gave opportunity, but I arranged training for the new managers as they had service delivery experience but not service management experience. In the early days the politics that arose from working with abuse was not there. Confidentiality meant that cases were often not linked as cases were taken forward to the police individually.

After the Jimmy Savile abuse cases became public and the Rotherham situation was publicised the landscape for charities supporting survivors became very challenging. The local abuse charity in Rotherham was shut down as it tried to expose significant abuse cases and rings. Many charities were shut down across the UK. Abuse inquiries were started in England and Scotland with a great deal of anxiety from the authorities about what would come out and potential costs of litigation. Abuse organisations and abuse survivors were becoming a threat. A newspaper contacted me about the destruction of the field. I started to become aware that life was going to change.

The wisest man

Through my relationship with Chris, I now had two parents in law who I had grown to love very much. They were an inspiration in the way that they had grown despite significant challenges in life and they always stayed kind and positive, having accepted me and my three children without any judgement or reservation.

My father-in-law was a very determined and strong person but with a deep empathy and kindness rarely seen in anyone. He was small with white hair and pale skin having previously had the traditional Scottish red hair and the skin that went with it. He was strong and fit for a man over eighty. He would help us with anything that needed to be fixed and if anything needed built or renovated, he would come round, loving being active. He had recently been through a cancer scare but rather than hide away and be fearful he tried to fill his days with as much as possible.

Over the years every time I was home feeling unwell, he would somehow arrive for many different reasons but through time I became aware he was looking after me. He reminded me of my grandfather and uncle who had been such a positive impact on my life but who unfortunately had passed away too soon. The people I knew from that generation had been so determined and so passionate about making sure life was fair. The men I knew from that time were strong and respectful and I realised that was not always the case and how lucky I had been to know them. When I was lying on the couch feeling ill, he would have a cup of coffee and sit and talk to me. Sometimes I would have to go upstairs as my stomach was upset and he would show no fuss just understanding, sitting for a while to make sure I was okay then he would leave quietly. When we talked, he would always have something to say that would be relevant to my situation and it would all make perfect sense. At times if I put myself down he would give me a strong talking to convincing me that I was as good as anyone else.

He would tell me stories all about his life and the struggles he faced with years of family pain and fighting. His mother had never shown him love, preferring his sisters who would always try and compete with him, enjoying times when life had challenges for him. He lost other siblings at a young age and through the years he became estranged from most of his family. He worked in a job with terrible shifts to support his family and had the experience of losing jobs and being on strike. Life had not been easy as his wife's family were every bit as difficult, and they had been a team against the world. He seemed to recognise that at the heart of much of my illness was some of the same pain and distress. On describing his life, he could give me hope that even with the pain that could be there, with care and love it would all be okay. It reminded me of one day when as a child a friend had been cruel to me and I came home trying not to cry. I came into the house and my grandfather recognised instantly that I was close to tears and he lifted me up onto his knee where I lay against him and sobbed. I never forgot the feeling of safety and love as he told me to ignore nasty people and that I was worthy of being treated well. My father-in-law gave me the same feeling every time we spoke. I would tell him that I felt people always judged me. As someone who had grown up in a very run-down area in a decaying town I often felt somehow less important than the people I met.

"No-one is better than anyone" he said "you are as good as anyone else. Have your head held high and face anyone. You have the right to respect".

He was furious about the politics I faced every day both internally and externally and we talked for hours about why people try to destroy others. With the political system he could see how corrupt it all was and he would speak with anger about the things I was facing. The talks we had made me have the strength to keep fighting as I respected him and valued everything he had to say.

Gradually over the years my health started to improve through the times we spoke. He gave me the courage to try and go out or drive my car. At first, he would give me routes to work that would mean I would not have to go through a lot of traffic systems and the reassurance of having easier ways to go would help. He helped me with my golf swing so that I could build my strength by starting to play again as my health began to recover. I realised what an impact he had and that that was how having a father should have been. He gave me hope. He believed in justice.

The same ten people

I had started to realise that my choice of career was probably a mistake for someone with my past. It wasn't the people who came to the charity that concerned me, it was some of the staff. I had often thought that people are catapulted into ways of life where they are supposed to be rather than where they wanted to be. Somehow, I must have aspired to this, but I was never aware of wanting to be here, when it became so challenging.

Of course, helping people was a big part of my life and that was what motivated me out of bed every morning. But in some ways, I had felt that I would help by volunteer work or by monthly donations not from this all-consuming intensity.

Chris always said in life you will meet the same ten people and I continually laughed at that thought. It was true. We would talk for hours about who those ten people were. They had appeared in many guises in business literature, those who made up teams, and those who made good leaders. These stereotypes didn't fit real life. In team theory there were eight categories of what made a good team, solid stereotypes, and suggestions to oust the weak ones, the ones who would upset the success of the dynamic. In real life human frailty would be assigned to the dark recesses of the world of no achievement and no hope.

There were many stories of those who couldn't last the pace. They were those who had "breakdowns" and disappeared off the face of the earth to be discovered years later running new age businesses from home or in the world of consultancy. Those who had fought and battled to be someone and for who eventually the need to be eternally perfect became too hard.

The real protagonists in day-to-day life were the ones who led to the downfall of others. It was survival of the fittest, a primal urge to oust the weakest from the group and gain position. When the weakest was selected a frenzy would ensue until they were effectively destroyed. A while would pass until the new target was identified and it would all begin again. The pack would join in so delighted that it wasn't them being targeted. But in any group, there would be the ones who would fight the injustice, attempt to inspire others and try to make things right. They should be the natural leaders but, the leaders would often be the most destructive. I thought of some of the people I had met throughout life. Chris and I would analyse who had similarities in different situations, and we discussed possibilities while thinking well for some the ten people may be different, laughing at whether that made sense. I thought about my most relevant ten people. On describing it Chris laughed and said I sounded like I was describing a manual. I laughed and said as a business geek it is an occupational hazard.

There was always the office gossip (in other walks of life just the gossip). No-one would really know anything about them, but they would know everything about everyone else and they would then go on to impart this knowledge to anyone who would listen. They had an excellent knack of ensuring that if someone challenged them that it was someone else who told. The others in the group would develop a fear of this person's power of all that they held, and they would gain a position of power in the group. "No shit sticks to them" Chris would laugh, and it was true.

I described my same ten people to Chris, and he laughed "you don't half make things complicated and with lots of words. In my world it is much simpler, and it is so funny you mostly described work. You are obsessed"

"Well, who are your ten people then?"

"In my world it is simple, but one is my crazy wife who is all over the place"

It would depend on where we spent most of our time who we would include in the same ten people, and it would change for different situations. Those who would have the position of overall power in the group and whoever had the control would change the dynamics of everyone else.

"So, who am I in my list" I asked my husband. "I know who I am in yours ha ha"

"You are the one who thinks they don't have a category." He laughed. "You love observing everyone else and analysing them but you refuse to fit any category but that makes you the most difficult as no-one can fit you in a box. We are comfortable with what we expect to see."

"You have elements of them all and it changes by the hour."

I was horrified that it was possible to work with people in so much pain and distress and to be so lacking in empathy or care for colleagues. The workplace was like living in a bed of vipers with everyone biting to gain position. From my stance of being in charge it was possible to observe the worst of humankind in action without becoming closely involved. People would tell me parts of the story and through time I would piece it all together bit by bit until it was all visible in all its nastiness.

The passion would rise in me to make things right but every attempt I made just seemed to make things worse. It seemed to be a pattern. Was this due to the same ten people in different guises or was it due to my influence in the situation. It became harder to tell. The bile would rise every night as I digested the days and the unpleasantness that was all around.

Why did I go into every new situation in life with openness and trust in others? The trust was never rewarded and when I looked closer the real faces could be seen. It became a torture to see past the mask that people wore as the real faces were grotesque and bitter.

"How did we become like this" I asked Chris over and over as we digested the latest disaster.

"You are too open" he said "people see your weakness and they prey on it. I have told you over and over wait and find out who people are before you open yourself up. You never learn and time and time again you are hurt and disillusioned"

"But why do people want to destroy one another?"

"Why do they want to destroy me?"

"You are a chameleon" he said "no-one knows what category you fit into and therefore they don't trust you. You are something to everyone and you take on the shape of who you are with and then do the same with the next person. Even your openness isn't real. Your weakness isn't real. You deceive yourself and you deceive others."

I laughed at his recognition. It was the ability that had come from childhood and in some way, I felt proud of being able to keep my real self-hidden from the world. The world did not deserve to know.

The clients that came to the charities I worked for were the ones that the world considered to be dysfunctional. They were the ones who had been ousted from the group. The group was either the group of family, the group of friends or the group in work. Some had never been able to enter the group.

The aim of my work was to make people "well" enough to re-enter society or to be stable enough to not cause society any particular problems. The only problem with that was that many of the people I met were the most real and honest people I had experienced being with. Why did I need to change them? Why did I need to change myself?

This was never more apparent when the world fell apart in the space of a Friday afternoon.

Mob mentality

I had become very ill over a period of four years, and it was very serious and very distressing. My immune system was so compromised that I was afraid to be near anyone who had even the slightest infection. I was aware that a cold could become a chest infection which could become pneumonia and I would have no immunity to fight the infection. I became terrified of being in busy shops or in crowds of people. Along with the risks a condition had developed where my blood pressure dropped when standing and I had continuous vertigo and dizziness. I was unable to drive safely much of the time and had negotiated with my line manager to homework for safety.

The main problem with my condition was that I looked very healthy as lupus leads to redness in the cheeks. Whenever I would attend work the reaction from some of the team was obvious. I would walk into rooms and people would stop talking and when I explained how ill I was eyes would roll and looks would be exchanged.

In the main office there was an office manager, Isa who had always given me red flags as to her honesty and ability to relate to other people. Some years previously there was a young girl in the office, Mary, who had suffered significantly with health problems and Isa had a pathological dislike of her, continually grumbling and gossiping when she took time off work. She would embroil others in her gossip and disdain identifying those who were looking for a reason to be disgruntled. At one point there had been an anonymous complaint to the council about Mary being ill so much and I was convinced it had been Isa who sent it. The day after it was sent, she took six weeks off sick. On returning she asked for a meeting with her husband as a witness as he was a union rep. The unusual behaviour made me more convinced she was the author of the complaint. The council officer was shocked by the discrimination within the letter.

Isa was a complex personality who was hard to define. I often felt that people wore a uniform to define who they were. Isa would dress like a traditional office worker from the 50s with her long hair in a severe bun each day, smart skirt or trousers and a severely ironed blouse. In conversation she would exhibit a warmth and interest in everyone, but that warmth would not be expressed in her eyes or smile. The clients were hypersensitive to those who were not completely congruent, and they had a distrust of her and would avoid being engaged in conversation. I was confused. At times Isa would appear to be so understanding and she would tease out when I was struggling and offer empathy and care, but it always felt in some ways like she was trying to build a dossier of the weak points and sensitivities. After I told Isa that I was afraid of illness I would then be told "oh you better watch, there is a terrible bug going around. That would be dangerous for you. You would be better to stay at home".

I was confused about Isa's pathological hatred of people with health issues as she always seemed to be ill with various conditions that would change by the week. First, she had suspected heart issues, then it was suspected multiple sclerosis, then an undefined gynaecological problem, then anxiety and stress. Each time she would have weeks off and it was always the time a major report was due. Then she would come back with no issues found, continue her gossiping about Mary without seeing the irony of the situation. Isa discovered that I was seriously allergic to air freshener and if she realised, I was coming into the office would spray it everywhere then hide the can.

I was known in the office to be soft and easy to persuade due to my eagerness to please others. Throughout life people had taken advantage of my kindness and I would be hurt and confused that my nature would not just be appreciated and liked. Chris said "you are the boss; everyone hates the boss. It isn't personal". I didn't want to change to become tougher as I felt the problem wasn't being too nice the problem was those who would take advantage of it. In some ways I was not seeing the patterns where those who were power hungry or those who were dealing with their own complexities would use me to channel their frustrations. Some were intensely jealous of my position.

So, on a Friday afternoon in April came the shock that blew the patterns apart changing things forever. I had been on a call with one of my colleagues and my friend and deputy, Trudi had been trying to call me on the other phone over and over. At first, I felt frustration at the intrusion and gradually felt something must be wrong. I took the next call and was met with Trudi sobbing uncontrollably and unable to speak. When she managed to calm down enough to speak, she explained that a grievance had been submitted to the Board of Directors by fifteen of the staff team.

I felt my stomach tighten and felt the bile rise into my chest. It was overwhelming and I couldn't take it in.

"Tell me who" I said

"You don't want to know it's unbelievable," said Trudi.

She listed the people involved. I almost collapsed. Listed were people I had helped and supported, people I considered friends and who had told me I had changed their lives in positive ways. One of those involved had been supported for over a year when her husband had become ill, and I had listened for hours as she struggled with her pain. Others I had never met as they were based across Scotland and not part of my direct team. As Trudi read what it said I couldn't take it in and said, "send it to me, I need to read it for myself".

On reading it I read pages and pages of gossip, often in quotes as something I had apparently said written in a very nasty and vindictive way but clearly nothing to be concerned about as I knew I could prove it to be untrue. But then it came to the real issue where my health issues were challenged, and it was not believed that I had been allowed to work from home. I flashed back to a conversation I had with Sadie the manager of the children and families' service. One of the local council staff had joined the children and families team meeting to help them with some of the recent initiatives in children's services. A week before I had attended a meeting on Skype due to my health issues. Sadie told me that the meeting had deteriorated when some of the staff had discussed how recent funding issues could be resolved if I was to leave as I was useless anyway with my health issues. Sadie had said she had stopped the discussion but appeared anxious and quickly changed the subject.

After skim reading the document, I came to a section that shook me to the core. It was highlighted towards the end that my children had been referred to the charity saying that I had asked for them to be prioritised. That was not true but the realisation that now all the staff who signed the document and the full Board knew that my children were survivors of abuse was devastating. How could I tell them? I knew the effect it would have on my son as he was unable to cope with anyone knowing his past. Arianne's past exploitation as a teenager was part of it and she would be so embarrassed that people knew. I felt hatred for a moment before it turned back to distress and grief at the betrayal. I read the names over and over. Two I had promoted into better jobs and supported their development while considering them friends. One had almost lost her husband to complications of hepatitis due to injecting drugs as a teenager and he had been arrested for growing cannabis. I had provided countless hours of support and had cared deeply about the pain of my colleague. One had been a volunteer who was promoted to become a member of staff and who always treated me as someone that she valued. One had been part of a seconded project who I offered a chance when her other job ended. One was an administrator who I had helped to carry out her work whenever she was off, which was all the time. One was someone I had known for nine years and who I had offered numerous new posts to as others came to an end. One was someone I had rescued from another job where she was about to be dismissed. There was another who had been a volunteer and who I had given support to when her health was bad. A group of them had socialised with me on many occasions including in my house with my children. The rest I had never met which baffled me as to why they would have signed.

Chris arrived home and I collapsed into hysterical tears.

"I can't handle this" I said

"Why would people do this to us?"

Chris was furious and disgusted. He knew many of the people involved having been at many of our work social occasions, also knowing their husbands and children. Many had been to our house for parties, and they had built a relationship with my children.

"It is greed" he said "they know funding will be cut and they want rid of you and Trudi to save their own jobs."

The next few days passed in a fog of sleeplessness and conversations with the Board to see what the next steps would be. On the first night I sat up the full night writing a rebuttal to what was said in the document, gathering evidence against the allegations. One advantage that I had was I was extremely organised, and I kept everything filed and easy to find. By morning everything was written and referenced to numbered documents which I then forwarded on to the Board. I called Katy, one of the managers who explained that she had known about the grievance as Sadie sent it to her, but she had refused to sign. Sadie had then tried to persuade her for hours on the phone, but Katy had told her she was crazy. Katy wrote an open letter to the Board to say that allegations were nonsense as she had worked with me for years and I had been completely professional and decent. She was able to directly refute specific allegations. With the statement and the other evidence, it was compelling. Years later I realised Katy had been extremely ethical to stand up against her friend and without her it would have been very different. Katy told me that for months another member of the team had been reporting to her that Sadie had been using team meetings to make people join the Union and ultimately sign the grievance.

Ingrid, the prison manager, had been with the organisation since it started. She reminded me that the majority of the team were not involved. She wrote to the Board to say I had never been anything but kind and supportive to everyone.

The Chairperson, Pete decided it would be necessary to suspend Trudi as she had been accused of theft in the document, but I was expected to return to work and face everyone including those who had written the grievance. On the day I was to go in I felt close to collapse. My eyes were aching with crying and my entire body was in severe pain with my lupus. I struggled up the driveway to be met by the two young men in the office who looked at me with kindness and sympathy that almost made me weep again.

That day passed in a further fog of trauma and humiliation as I sat and presented my evidence to Pete and an external consultant and he grilled me on my version of events. Finally, he was satisfied that the evidence backed up my account and he reassured me that unless anything came up in meetings with the staff that there was nothing of concern but the same would not be the case with Trudi. Pete had never been keen on Trudi as she had pink hair, tattoos, and punk dress style. He didn't feel that she matched the corporate image. I defended Trudi as she knew that the situation with the money had been that Trudi did not have time to go to the bank as she had been ill. I had evidence that there was no theft, but Pete wouldn't listen as he was enjoying the chance to potentially remove Trudi from her role. He told me that I would have to tell Trudi she was suspended. I was very distressed.

"Why is Trudi being suspended when these people breached the confidentiality of my children and used my health against me breaching the Equality Act?"

It had not occurred to Pete that these aspects were so serious but when he thought about it, he realised how disgraceful it was especially the breach of confidentiality.

"I will have to tell the children" I said "years ago there was a potential breach within the prisons, and we were told we would have to tell prisoners if indeed their confidentiality was breached. Fortunately, it wasn't thank goodness"

Pete agreed and looked very upset as he knew my children especially my son and all who met him were struck by his naivety and trust in people due to the love and protection he had from his mother and stepfather. Despite his past he was now happy and hopeful about life.

I returned home exhausted and defeated where I called my children to speak to me. I told them about the grievance and then the worst bit that they had been mentioned in it. I watched the confusion cross the face of my children as they tried to register what they were being told

"How many people know" Thomas said

I could see the anxiety as he waited for the answer.

"Probably about twenty-two people" I said "but we can't be sure because we don't know how many people, they showed it to"

I recalled a time where a friend had threatened to tell others he had been abused and the fear and terror that he had felt at the thought of people knowing and I felt extreme guilt and shame at him experiencing this due to me.

He walked away silent which was something I had never seen in him. He usually talked and talked when he needed to deal with something. This was different and I realised this situation was going to be long term and awful but could not have anticipated quite how bad it would get.

A few days later Thomas came in to speak to me looking cold and stony faced which was not in character for him at all. He said "my friend at work has a flat and I am going to move in with her. I just can't deal with this".

Within days it was organised, and the moving van arrived. I sat in shock unable to deal with the fact that he would be gone. He walked out still with the coldness and with his face expressionless. Tears rolled slowly down my face as I was unable to process what was happening. Life had become unreal and so chaotic that nothing was really sinking in.

Arianne was angry and she did not hold back on her opinions on the people who had written the document. "I didn't trust that Isa woman anyway and I never liked Sadie. I always thought she was shady. She didn't like you, I knew that, but she always pretended she did. Can I not complain about this? This isn't right."

Thomas and Arianne agreed that they wanted to write to Pete to complain about being used in such an appalling way. They emailed him but I realised that the impact on both would be long term. Arianne found it hard to trust people through her past experiences and Thomas had trusted too much.

Years later I would come back to laughing at the grievance document as it was a ridiculous paper obviously pulled together by a frenzy of gossip and dragging out every situation that could be used while putting a spin on it to turn it into a grievance. The financial mismanagement allegation was that Trudi had money over Christmas that she was due to bank, but she had not and it was now February. Isa had raised the issue with me when Trudi was on holiday for her birthday. She said that she had asked Trudi about the money but she had said it had been banked when it hadn't been. I called Trudi about it and she went round to the office and sent a photograph of the money in the original bags. The money had been locked in her desk as she had been ill over Christmas and then had not had time to sort it out.

"Why did you not just tell Isa you had not had a chance to bank the money" I said.

"You know how long she has had it in for me. I couldn't tell her the truth. She would have accused me of being lazy as she always does. But now because of my mistake she is accusing me of stealing!"

"Just make sure you bank it tomorrow and keep the pay in slip with the breakdown as evidence. I will have to pass it on to the Board as it all must be investigated so they should contact you to set up a meeting. I will pass on the evidence."

That evening I was making a cup of tea when a memory flashed into my mind. I went back through my emails and found one from Isa about the same fundraising money. The email was sent in July and in it Isa said that she was going to bank the money the next day. This was the same money she said that she had found in the safe in December. I was shocked and wondered why she had kept the money. It had not been in the safe between July and December as the safe was accessed so often for checking petty cash it would have been found. Was Isa guilty of what she had implied Trudi had done?

Isa called me the day after I spoke to Trudi to pry about what had been done about the situation. I informed her it had been passed to the Board, but Isa was unhappy saying that Trudi should be instantly dismissed. She went through a large list of other issues she had with Trudi most of which were unfortunately administration tasks that Isa should have been carrying out. I felt it wouldn't be well received to mention that and she felt it perhaps was not the time to mention that Isa had the money from July as she was building herself up into a frenzy. I decided to use the technique of repeating the same response over and over to de-escalate the situation saying, "I understand your concerns I am writing them down and I will pass them to the Board". Isa insisted a meeting should be held where all the team could have the opportunity to complain about Trudi with Trudi present. I said this would not be ethical and Isa became very angry.

"My husband is a very serious union rep and I am going to get him to deal with you" she said "I am bringing a case for constructive dismissal"

"I have said nothing in this conversation that would lead to that being necessary" I said "I don't appreciate you threatening me with your husband"

I was really distressed by the conversation, and it played over and over in my mind. The strange unpleasantness was so similar to a previous occasion where Isa had changed in a meeting where she requested a pay rise to show such venom that I had realised how dangerous she could be, but she had instantly changed back to the intense eagerness to please on the surface.

I felt really concerned to the extent that I began to realise things were not right on a serious level. On the following day there had been a meeting of the managers. At the meeting Laurie from one of the projects and Sadie the other manager attended with Katy the other manager. It had been obvious that there had been a strong vendetta against Trudy where two of the other managers had said she was lazy. Katy had supported her.

I had realised at the time that this was becoming more and more messy and complicated. The vice chair met with Trudi and the evidence presented meant that there was no crime. Trudi told me that Isa had approached her in the kitchen while she was waiting. She gave her a hug and told her to come to her if anything was upsetting her. Considering Isa was one of the main instigators her behaviour was appalling. Trudi apologised to the management team for her failure to carry out her tasks as well as usual as the break-down of her marriage had a serious impact on her.

Laurie, another of the managers who was a main protagonist was a very unusual person and very hard to read but I had always liked her despite a few concerns. Laurie came across as supportive and empathetic, but I recalled one occasion where she was due to come over to my house for a meeting. I had woken up very unwell and I tried to cancel the meeting. Laurie and Maurie from a partner organisation had been driving and so they didn't get the message. I tried to fight being sick to speak to them to ask them to please just go and the look on Laurie's face was disgust and disdain. Laurie had a strange passive aggressive manner where she always appeared to be as obliging as possible but there was always a sense it was on the surface with real hatred underneath. I had so many emails and texts that said how wonderful I was and how supportive, but I was aware that in the background Laurie was trying to keep her project away from the rest of the organisation and it was obvious that her team were resentful about being part of the overall organisation. When I tried to broach the subject with Laurie it was clear that she no intention of changing her approach. I was afraid of forcing the issue and when I reflected on it I realised that I had sensed danger from Laurie.

Laurie always had some massive drama in her life which required me to support her and she would often call out with working hours to ask for help. At those times everyone would have to work hard to ensure she was not given any additional pressure and I would prepare her reports for her to ensure that she did not become too stressed. Laurie was happy to stab anyone in the back if it furthered her goals including Maurie a long-term friend where she made accusations to me that Maurie was using funding inappropriately. Isa and Laurie had a very intense friendship where Isa would support each of Laurie's dramas and then she would return the favour as Isa would also have regular dramas, meaning that she would have to be off work.

Sadie was a very complicated person. I had known her for many years as we had shared a workplace when I worked for an addiction organisation which rented rooms to the charity. We used to go outside for a cigarette, and we would chat each day. We became friends of a kind, but I was aware that Sadie would never talk about herself in any detail. We had compared that we both had six children, but the chats never became closer than that. However, I did learn everything about everyone that Sadie hated and learned every detail of the lives of those people. When the job in the charity came up, I told Sadie I was going to apply naively expecting her to be delighted but instead she reacted by putting her cigarette on the ground grinding it with her foot and walking away. When I started in my job Sadie suddenly became my best friend.

I realised that the sudden friendship was probably due to some form of ambition or sycophancy but one of my weaknesses was that I wanted to be liked as it made me feel validated. This was not a good character trait for a Chief Executive because everyone hates the boss no matter how friendly an attitude being presented. I always had a sense that Sadie was not trustworthy and that she would have no hesitation to destroy others to further her own ambition. It was obvious she hated Trudi continually undermining her with other staff and hinting to me that she was not being effective in her role but not in an obvious way so that it could not be seen as bullying. Trudi oversaw the administration team so everything the team did was wrong, but nobody was tackling it. One Christmas Sadie sent in a document criticising many aspects of the administration team and directly blaming Trudi. She then followed up by calling me at midnight. She was very drunk and therefore she did not filter the way she spoke. She accused me of liking Trudi better than her and said she wanted Trudi's job as she could do it better. She asked why she had never been invited round with her husband for an evening as she knew Trudi and her husband had been round. I was shocked at the blatant jealousy and no attempt to hide it. I promised a full investigation and took time to calm Sadie down after over an hour on the phone where at one point Chris had to take the phone as I was becoming stressed and upset.

When I was ill Sadie took over my office. She dumped all my books and paperwork into boxes and made the office her own. When I went in to collect a folder, I was devastated that it looked like she was ousting me.

The other main protagonist in the story was Aggie. I recalled the first time she had met her properly. She had joined the organisation as a volunteer and had always been fairly distant. Therefore, I was very surprised when on a fundraising night at a local social club Aggie tried to befriend me when we were both outside for a cigarette. I had a strange sense of disquiet from her that I didn't understand. The warmth she showed did not extend to her eyes leaving a strange, disjointed feeling. When a job came up in the children and family's team, I was happy that Aggie was successful as she had worked hard to show how committed she was to survivors of abuse and she would go out of her way to support all fundraising events even joining the fundraising committee. When I became ill she was empathetic as she was also disabled with an auto-immune condition. Her husband tried to befriend Chris asking him to play golf. Aggie persuaded me that her daughter wanted to date Wylie after meeting him at an event. Things started to be strange as I noticed on a night out that the daughter ignored him preferring to speak to her friends. After two months of dating, he came home very upset as the daughter had confessed sleeping with someone else. It was strange as Aggie never mentioned the situation to me despite many discussions. When Trudi's marriage broke up Aggie tried to befriend her. Trudi, Isa, and Maggie the other administrator all had regular nights out with Trudi where they would be very critical of Sadie making fun of her. I was very concerned at Trudi becoming too involved with them realising how vulnerable she was. I had a really strong sense that Aggie did not have good motives in being her friend, but I could not explain the feeling. Aggie became very close to Isa.

Maggie was a very quiet person who appeared to be vulnerable and unable to confront others. She accused Isa of bullying her and she asked for a move to the other office, but Trudi refused as there was no need for administration support in that office. She asked if Maggie wanted to make a formal complaint, but she refused.

On thinking about the grievance, it was so strange that they had all devised it together as they did not like one another. Sadie had always been scathing about Laurie and she did not want Isa to be included in management team meetings or an awards ceremony the organisation was attending. Maggie had complained about Isa being rude and power mad after she was promoted to manager, and they all disliked Sadie. Laurie and Sadie barely acknowledged one another. Sadie thought Laurie was disturbed and chaotic. I reflected again on why all these really distasteful people were working in the organisation.

The rest of those who had signed the document I either had not met as they were recruited by the other managers or I had not seen them over the past couple of years when I was so ill. One of them Carrie had been referred Arianne following her experience of online exploitation and bullying. I had been clear that if she felt it to be a conflict of interest or boundary issue she could say no or ask Sadie to say no on her behalf, but no issue was raised. I also made clear not to prioritise her. I had email evidence of it all. I knew that either Carrie had breached Arianne's confidentiality or Sadie had.

It was amazing how many of those involved had been offered help, the first step on their career or opportunities they would not have found anywhere else and yet they wanted to destroy the person who had given them those chances. Laurie had obviously had some story in her past as she had moved from being a manager in the financial services sector but she had a complete career change to become a counsellor. I had given her a chance to go back into management despite reservations that she was chaotic and often used clients to make her feel good about herself. This was something in counselling that always had to be checked out whether helping others was for their benefit or to make the counsellor feel powerful and needed.

Isa had come to the organisation as someone who strangely seemed to have no working past. She came in appearing needy and vulnerable and begging for an opportunity indicating that she had taken time out to raise her daughter. Throughout the time working for the charity, I would continually help her often catching up her work for her when she had been off ill. She was promoted to a manager post and given constant encouragement and support.

Aggie had been offered a paid job after being a volunteer and despite not being fully qualified as a counsellor. She had a disability and I felt it would be very positive to help her rehabilitate back into work, always ensuring that she took time off work when she needed it. I would write her reports for her because she knew she struggled with professional writing. I supported Aggie becoming a team leader.

Maggie came to the organisation through a short-term placement, and she came across as insecure and immature but I gave her an opportunity to stay on to give her a chance to develop into the role.

Sadie had been supported by me to become a youth service team leader and then manager of the children and family's team.

I loved giving people the chance to develop particularly where they had been through barriers, but my kindness had been seen as weakness and it had backfired in a catastrophic way.

I had email after email and texts where they all thanked me for my kindness or for the support to develop.

On reflection the manager's meeting had been a nightmare. The issue of the money was raised, and I explained it was to be investigated by the Board but that it would not be reported back how it was resolved out of fairness. Laurie and Sadie were very unhappy about it and said that many of the team had issues with Trudi. They wanted Trudi brought to a meeting for everyone to confront her, the same demand made by Isa. I asked who was unhappy and said the only way I could deal with anything was to know who was unhappy and what they were unhappy about. I reminded them both that professional managers have a role to remind staff about the appropriate grievance procedure. I informed them that I had been concerned about Isa's behaviour for a very long time as she had previously bullied the young administrator about her health and had then been insidiously undermining and bullying Trudi. It was a stressful discussion for us all, so we went into the kitchen for a cup of tea where Laurie hugged me. I read a note from Trudi where she apologised to the team for being less effective than usual after her marriage breakdown. Everything seemed to be resolved and Sadie texted me afterwards to say it was a good meeting. Katy supported Trudi but had stayed silent most of the meeting observing what was happening. I could not have foreseen what would happen only two months later with the grievance.

The warnings had been there that things were becoming nasty but the full force of it could not have been anticipated. The grievance was ridiculous in the allegations but those gossipy statements were surrounded by masses of legal jargon probably written by the husband of Isa although it was sent in by a union representative so it could have been written by him. It had been very strange that the union allowed and encouraged people to join to bring the grievance as usually people had to be existing members. In it were crazy allegations. As well as the allegation about Trudi and the petty cash there was a complaint that pay sometimes was put through a day or so early with a slant that this must have been as I needed the money early. This was just a situation where payday was a Sunday, so it had to be paid on a Friday. It became even more ridiculous where the Christmas bonus was criticised as if that was not approved by the Board and the extra holidays at Christmas were questioned. It was said that I had said "if I am going down everyone is going down with me" at the team meeting where I was on Skype even though there were many others there who knew I had not said it. It was said that I was friends with Investors in People and that Pete was like my father or best friend. I laughed at the allegation as Pete had always terrified me and made me feel intimidated. It was said that I had shouted at the other managers at the managers meeting demanding to know who feared me. It went on to say a child protection issue had not been followed up even though Aggie knew that it had as she had signed it off. Much of it focussed on my disability saying that I was saying I had permission from the Board to work from home, but they seemed not to believe it and referred to me having any kind of social life saying if I could go out, I should be at work. Trudi and I were both appalled by the vindictiveness and venom in the document but mostly complete stupidity as it was so easy to disprove it all.

The others who had signed the document were strange in the extreme. I had never met two of them and most of the others I had met a handful of times and not really at all in the last few years due to my illness. Two of the others I had known in the past and I had been concerned that they had been conspiring against me due to my health for some time. The previous volunteer manager had been very friendly with them. She was living with a mutual friend, and he had told me that one of them, Christine had been round visiting where she said they would have to be ruthless and ensure that I lost my job. Christine and her close friend at work, Sharon had remained close to the volunteer manager Jane, and she had always resented me due to my continued friendship with her partner. One day he had turned up at my house unexpectedly shaking and crying. He had found numerous texts between Jane and a work colleague, where they referred to meeting at a hotel and bringing bondage gear. This meeting had been part of a work trip away and I was very shocked. Jane left work soon after and she left him. I was aware that she kept herself involved in the work gossip.

A sixteen-year-old trainee had been part of the grievance which the Board had thought was disgusting as she should not have been put in such a difficult position. What was the same with most of them was that they had been given a chance by me or Trudi. I felt so betrayed. Due to the shock that they had all signed up I asked that the Board write to them to ask if they had signed it. I could not see how people I had supported or those I hadn't met could do this.

The Board arranged to meet everyone who had signed up and I was relieved that it would soon be investigated, and the waiting would be over. However, the night before the meetings were to take place an email was sent to the Board from the "grievance group" to say that they would not be attending meetings as they had no confidence in the Vice Chair as he was in a rock band, they all felt was inappropriate. They went on to say they would be reporting the grievance to the council. A week later a letter came from the council summoning the Board to a meeting. At the meeting it was insisted that a full investigation of the charity was to be carried out and they insisted that no-one involved in writing the grievance should be disciplined. The Board actively disagreed due to the breaches included in the grievance. The Vice Chair thought it was very strange that the council instantly seemed to be actively supporting those involved without checking out if anything was true or if in fact it had been in any way malicious. The council had obvious prior knowledge.

I contacted my union to ask for a representative to support me. It was not the first time that I had a strong sense something sinister was happening behind the scenes. The union initially avoided my calls and then when someone was allocated any conversations with him seemed to have a sub text and undercurrent. It was almost as if he was saying what he was supposed to say but he would drop in aspects to show a clearer picture.

"You would be wise to enable the council to carry out an external investigation" he said.

"But why" said I "this has all been bullying towards me and Trudi. Why should we allow the council to target us further?"

"You should be aware there is constant contact between the union representative and head of social work. In fact, a fax just came in from her before I called you".

I realised he was trying to warn me about something, and I felt afraid.

Corruption connects

I was sitting in my office going through paperwork when I came across the papers from a meeting which confirmed a very important aspect of all that had happened. For two years the charity had been managed by a seconded council employee and prior to that she had worked as a parent support worker where she had worked with many people who had reported significant abuse of their children and themselves. The previous manager had also been seconded by the council so effectively the council had managed the charity and the cases worked with since the charity started. I was the first external CEO. The abuse they discovered had been effectively covered up with very serious cases not reported. Trudi had reported to me when I started that she had been very unhappy that nothing had been done. She said at one point a woman they worked with had her nipple sliced off and sent back to her in a padded envelope with a warning not to speak. She was being abused by a paedophile ring who had abused her since childhood, but she was too afraid to break away. I was very concerned, and I wanted to contact the client, but Trudi could not recall her name. When the first manager had resigned, she destroyed masses of paperwork and files.

I had investigated the previous employee's manager reports to see if there was anything that would show she had reported these issues but there was not. Instead, I found a report that evidenced that the finances of the charity had been mismanaged with a £30,000 deficit in the core that had been covered by project funds. This was not okay in charity accounting. I discovered that the previous manager had been giving jobs to Sadie without any money to do so taking funds from other budgets to keep her friend in a job.

After applying for funding for working with sexual exploitation of children I was summoned to a meeting with various managers from social work and education. Sadie attended the meeting with me. Sadie seemed to be very nervous. At the meeting I was accused of carrying out work with children without the permission of the council. I was furious as my funding officer June was in the meeting and she had been kept informed about all the work. I pointed out that I had fully informed my funding officer and she reluctantly agreed that was the truth. The next accusation was that reports on the work had not been provided. Again, I was furious as they had been given to the funding officer regularly. Again, I challenged it and the funding officer confirmed that was true. In anger I said "why am I being interrogated in this way. The charity is now well managed. Under the previous manager when managed by the council there was a £30,000 black hole created where restricted funds were used to fill it".

The room went silent, and they brought the meeting to an end apologising for being misinformed. Outside the room the funding officer apologised with her head down but said "you should know one of the officers in the room was the manager's husband. She has it in for you already and this will not go down well". I was very concerned as I knew that the manager and the head of social work were very close.

I recalled the meeting that Sadie had mentioned following the staff meeting where I had attended on Skype. The previous manager had attended due to her role in child protection to educate the staff and the meeting had deteriorated. A few staff had referred to the staff meeting where I had mentioned funding cuts and they suggested Trudi should lose her job to resolve the funding issues and save their jobs. Sadie said she had ended the meeting immediately. After the grievance was received, I spoke to one of Sadie's team who had not signed it. She was very apologetic and confirmed that the meeting had involved saying Trudi should go and that I was expendable due to my health. She said that they were all disgusted that I had attended the meeting on Skype. She said that the council officer had not taken part in the discussion, but she had not ended it or excused herself. She said that the discussion was only ended by Sadie when the person I spoke to had expressed how awful she thought it was. The events were confirmed by another member of the team who said it continued into a visit to the pub afterwards where it deteriorated into a frenzy of how to depose me and Trudi. They discussed ways of inventing a grievance to make it happen. Both said that the council officer sat smugly through the meeting part of the day.

When reviewing Sadie's emails after she left, I found emails between the council officer and Sadie arranging meetings and referring to the internal issues. One meeting was arranged for the day before the grievance was submitted. I was told by the office finance officer that from then Isa and Sadie had been going round everyone in the office asking them to sign a petition to depose me and Trudi. He said that it was his impression that they had been offered jobs by the council if they took it forward and that was the reassurance given to everyone if it all backfired and they lost their jobs.

It was submitted to the council on many occasions that there were concerns about the conduct of the council officer and it was asked why she did not report to me what had happened at the meeting. Instead, she remained involved in removing funding from the charity and she wrote to all the schools and social workers to say not to refer clients. I realised there was something very corrupt in what was happening and I realised it was much wider than funding issues or a grievance.

Making the connections

The grievance was an ongoing concern within the organisation for a full two years after it was submitted and each week, I would feel it was the right thing to do to leave. I was offered two jobs, but I turned both down knowing it would be too hard for me to give up all I had fought for. The head of social work wrote to every funder of the organisation to tell them about the internal issues. I was very concerned about her obvious bias. Those in the grievance sent it to the government as well as the council.

The Board met urgently to decide a strategy and I was terrified wondering what would happen next. The Vice Chair was acting as Chair as Pete was ill. He decided that he would speak to a full team meeting, and he asked me to arrange one. On the day he was very nervous, and he sat smoking and then rushing to the toilet. He stood at the front of the room in an oversized suit with his hands trembling. The front two rows were taken up with people involved in the grievance sitting with notepads. He read out a long statement referring to his disgust and disappointment that people could raise a grievance, then be unwilling to meet to give statements. He referred to the document being sent to the council and government saying that he found that a very strange thing to do as it potentially risked the jobs of everyone. He let them know that one person had said they had no evidence, one said she had never signed it and one asked to be withdrawn from it. Those in the front row looked shocked at this news and they looked at one another as if to consider who had let the rest down. At the end of the meeting, I spoke to the group saying, "I don't even know any of you because I was ill and certainly didn't treat any of you with anything less than full respect so I fail to see how anyone could have an issue with me". Later that afternoon I received an email from one of the group saying that she had been asked to sign by her manager and acknowledging that she did not know me. She said that she was told she would lose her job if she pulled out. I reassured her that she wouldn't.

A week later Christine asked to speak to me after she had arrived at the office and made friendly small talk. Christine was tearful and she apologised to me for what had happened. She said that she had not seen the grievance and she had been told it was only about financial mismanagement. She said she was so sorry that my family had been affected and she acknowledged how unpleasant the whole thing was. She said it had become a frenzy where people were dragged in and afraid to speak out against the managers who were involved. I said it could be forgiven but Christine said we may have made a bigger mistake. She paused looking very worried before saying that the team had asked for a meeting with Bella from the government. I was shocked and asked, "what did you say to her?"

I was even more shocked because Bella had denied knowing anything about the grievance on several occasions. I was suspicious that there were very strange aspects of it particularly because more funders would have merely referred them back to their management team or Board.

Over the next few days Christine and two others withdrew from the grievance and one of those leaving wrote to apologise. The Board decided to discipline the two main instigators who could have breached confidentiality as they were the only ones aware that Arianne had been referred. Following the knowledge of the disciplinary meetings many staff put in resignations obviously afraid that they would be next.

I was excluded from the process but one of the Board members told me what happened later. It had been awful, and Sadie had been arrogant and defiant despite the evidence presented to her. The Board members involved had prepared a case, presented it to her with assertiveness and authority which caused Sadie to say she realised she was done for. Carrie had been more contrite but still she had an arrogance which was a trait common to them all they had spent so much time together building up a frenzy. Not long after Laurie had left, they all met to mark her leaving and those attending included all those who had signed even though most of them were now splitting apart. They involved Maurie too. They posted pictures as a group with a list of names on Facebook as a way of mocking and the childish frenzy was apparent. Sadie and Carrie took representatives from the group as their witnesses. They were belligerent which was a very strange way to be with the Board. It was as if they felt they had the support of someone more powerful than the Board.

The finance manager told me that they had been promised something to take it forward. He said that they had approached him, particularly Sadie and Isa to ask him to sign and there were continuous promises that it would be in his favour. A young girl in the office, said that they had been promised they could set up their own charity to compete or replace the current one.

I was on holiday in the Lake District when the Board sacked Sadie driving from Grange Over Sands to Bowness on Windermere on a beautiful sunny day. The call came through and the relief was immense. The Board had decided not to sack Carrie as there was evidence she had not wanted to sign, and she appeared to be the only one who was sorry.

On returning I was approached by Carrie to meet to talk. We agreed to meet at a local restaurant, and it was a strange meeting. Carrie always had a very obliging and almost crawling attitude but behind it there was clearly something dishonest. She was adamant that she had not wanted to sign the document, nor had her friend Yuna. They had been persuaded to join the union against their wishes. Carrie said she was sorry that she had breached the information about Arianne but said she had not wanted to work with her but had been too scared to say. I said but it was said I forced you to work with her. You knew it wasn't true. Carrie then became another one who said she hadn't read the document before signing. Following the meeting we parted on positive terms, and it was arranged to go for drinks with Yuna and Trudi to resolve matters further. We all met that night a hotel just outside the area and we were shocked at the misinformation from the main instigators of the grievance. They were both upset about the vice chair's band as someone had anonymously sent them details of it. Trudi and I agreed the lyrics and imagery were not a good match for the charity but we had not seen the video referred to. Each day became awful and each call or email led to enormous stress as I tried to manage it all. Carrie and Yuna resigned citing the bad press even though I was aware they had both been offered other jobs without interviews at another charity largely run by the council. One of the staff members who resigned was given a job with the government and then Forward Paths, a government quango. The vice chair resigned from the Board and gradually it all calmed down but I was left exhausted and confused. I could understand that they may have wanted to destroy me but to actively destroy a charity valued and relied on by people who had been abused was evil. Isa, Laurie, and Maggie had resigned at the beginning of it all so to go on and cause further issues showed them up to be vindictive and immoral. Right at the final few days of the deadline Sadie issued a tribunal claim.

Right after all the firefighting there was then the matter of the council investigation or as they called it a review. When issuing what they wanted to investigate one of the aspects was to examine files but the Board refused to agree to it, protecting service user confidentiality. They already had a worry that this had all been manufactured to gain information on what the charity knew about paedophile rings that had been covered up for years when the charity was controlled by the council. The reviewers were selected. One of the reviewers was someone I knew well which made the situation even more bizarre as he had been the person who had appointed me to my first job as CEO for an alcohol charity. I had worked fairly closely with him for almost five years and he had behaved inappropriately towards me on more than one occasion, including shouting at me in a public meeting and telling my senior colleagues he was going to "shag" me. When I refused obvious advances, he made he became more and more venomous. On the first day of the review, he told the marketing officer that "we all make mistakes" when I introduced him as the person who had given me my first CEO job. It was so humiliating to sit through meetings being interrogated by him. I answered well but the full document only included one quote from the meeting which I did not say. They refused to release recordings of meetings or notes. Throughout the process an obsession with accessing the files was the main focus but the organisation stood firm and did not allow it. Ultimately the refusal was used against us and the very unprofessional subjective report was appalling. It did not say anything that was serious or anything that showed bad governance but it was presented to a council meeting in private. The Head of Social work recommended in a report to council that our funding be removed. The organisation was told they were not permitted to share the report despite the fact that it could have evidenced we had done nothing wrong. That meant we were unable to publicly clear our name. However, the government had to admit there were no matters of concern.

Eva from the Board decided to attend a staff meeting to make sure everyone was okay after all the stress. The staff at the meeting were angry and they said the pressure to sign up had been horrible making them feel bullied by Isa, Laurie, and Sadie. Sharon stood up and apologised to the full team for being someone who had signed it.

Almost a year after the sacking of Sadie her tribunal date arrived. On the first day she walked past me saying hello in her usual arrogant manner. Over the week she stood defiantly while I sat in distress listening to what they had done. On the day of her evidence, she seemed to suddenly fall apart. She admitted breaching confidentiality was wrong. She admitted that most of the staff did not know me and said she only knew of one person who felt they had been bullied, Isa, but could provide no evidence of it. The judge managed to uncover that it was Sadie who had written the document. Eva as the board member who had carried out the appeal came across as measured, professional and ethical which showed Sadie up as someone who was malicious and vindictive. Some months later the decision came in rejecting her tribunal. The atmosphere in the charity was triumphant. The result commended the Board and made it clear that there had been no crimes committed and no evidence of anything unethical by me or Trudy.

My son Thomas, me and the Board had written to Laurie's governing body who had the responsibility to ensure she was working ethically. They decided to investigate her, and they decided there was a case to answer. As part of her process of making things right she was forced to come to see me to apologise. When she arrived at my home, she appeared to be very flat and she admitted she had taken Valium to be calm enough to face me. I made her tea and then said "why did you lie. You knew the bit about the management meeting was not true, but you signed it".

"I can't really explain" Laurie said "I can only say I didn't read the final version so I hadn't seen that part. I can only say I was stupid, and I am really sorry. I didn't know the bit about your children, and I didn't realise it was there."

"But you agreed to something that said I shouted at the management meeting and you out of everyone know that I was always kind. You knew how ill I was. You knew it was life threatening."

"Again, I can only say how sorry I am" Laurie looked to the floor, and she appeared like she wanted the ground to swallow her up.

"You destroyed a charity that help people. You must have called the funders?"

"No, I can only say that the government called me to a meeting, and they already knew about the unrest I didn't tell them. I think they had been told by the council as there were things going on there. When I met Bella, she offered me a job with the government, and it was implied that if I took things forward the job would be mine. I couldn't do it I still had some morals".

"How did it all come about? There were some people I didn't even know".

"It became a frenzy where everyone was caught up by some weird excitement. Isa was disgruntled by her relationship with Trudi and others were annoyed that you were allowed to work from home while we were losing funding and they thought you were faking so the union told them to gather as many issues and people as possible as it would cause maximum harm to the charity the more people were involved."

"Oh my god" said I "I knew the union were in it up to their necks and now I know for sure. No doubt their links to the local councillors who wanted to shut us down."

She went on to blame Sharon and Christine for starting it. They had apologised so I was very confused. Finally, a light had been shone on all the confusion and they could all be seen for what they were, just a bunch of gossips who had been used by those externally who were trying to destroy the charity for sinister reasons. The jigsaw was falling into place. I remembered that when Isa had written her complaint about Mary in the office, the council would then have had her contact details. This could have been happening behind the scenes for a long time.

Following the grievance, I met with one of our partner organisations in Airdrie. Ingrid and I went through together. At the meeting the head of the service told me she was sure we were being targeted due to our work and ability to expose high level abuse. One of our team, Sharon had been seconded to her service at the start of the new service for people abused in care. The service lead had asked us to take her back to our service due to very serious concerns about her conduct, backed up by others she had spoken to in the field. She was sure she must be involved in some way.

Moving forward

Following the grievance two new Board members joined who completely embraced the cause bringing extra knowledge and experience that gave extra strength to the Board.

Eva one of the more long-standing Board members had felt for a long time that it was very important to challenge what we knew about organised abuse. As a children and families social worker she knew that there was a real possibility that if abuse rings had not been stopped and people brought to justice that children would still be at risk. She was determined that could not be allowed to happen. She wanted to expose what had happened to the charity as she felt it was orchestrated to cover up what we knew. We all agreed that was the highest priority and the Board asked me to pursue contacts with the press. They asked me to see what other routes they could pursue and ultimately we met with the new Child Abuse Unit of the police. Eva, Ingrid, and I met them. We highlighted some of the cases we were aware of but the feeling we had that there was something much bigger being hidden. We mentioned the figures of multiple abusers and the strange behaviour of the council and government in trying to access our files. The unit were helpful and open to what we were highlighting but they felt that it all still felt too disjointed to take forward a full investigation. They felt the press were still the best way forward.

We all became very worried about the possibility of the files being destroyed or stolen and we discussed the possibility of ensuring they were stored in a secure environment. I felt very proud that the Board stood firm and together to take forward the concerns. At meetings we were determined to keep fighting and at no stage did we ever decide to try and play the game to achieve funding.

A new Board member Rena was actively involved in fundraising to try and support the organisation and she was fantastic at baking to raise additional funding. Everyone was obsessed with her lemon drizzle cake. Her whole family were involved in helping and her family and my family had a strong affinity. The whole atmosphere at the Board level was for the survivors, sadly in contrast to what had happened with the team. Fighting the situation had taken its toll on them all. Fay had to take some time out and Rena had become very ill with her immune system being affected extremely badly. However, she continued to fight despite her disabilities. Toni was diagnosed with cancer but again she kept in constant contact fighting for the charity. Eva was always supportive and Shona was there whenever needed. They were strong and courageous and I felt privileged to know them all. They were the ones who made it possible to fight and stay strong.

The corridors of power

The issue with the council was a strange surreal experience that lasted for over three years. In total it cost over £50,000 in legal costs with letters back and forth dealing with each new issue. After the grievance was submitted to them the council suspended referrals to the charity and wrote to all the funders to highlight that the grievance had been received. The Board were in shock and not sure how to respond so they needed the lawyer. They were aware the lawyer worked for the government but not the council and at that stage they couldn't see the links. The head of social work and the previous manager were at the heart of the process to destroy the reputation of the charity. A local journalist contacted me to say he had been approached by the head of social work to ask for a meeting also involving the head of the council. They told the journalist all about the grievance. He was shocked at the approach and said it was very unusual. I gave him information about what was included and he agreed to give the other side of the story. That week stories about the vice chair's band and his lyrics were anonymously reported to the press and the article had his resignation as a headline with the grievance publicised and the charity discredited. I spent the next month explaining to funders and having meetings to assure them that we could still deliver a service. It felt like a nightmare. The Board submitted a Freedom of Information request and in the response the head of social work had referred to the grievance and "how we can use this". She referred to the Board mentioning paedophile rings and her concerns that meant it more important to act. What was strange in the papers was that there were communications between the council and the government with them agreeing to carry out the review together. The Board were surer than ever that was what was really behind things with the council terrified of a Rotherham situation and the government concerned as we knew a great deal about abuse that had happened in care. As the previous manager had once managed the charity and had never reported potential rings she would have been scared of being exposed particularly now as she was a child protection officer.

While the grievance was going through investigation the council carried out a parallel process to remove funding from the charity. Elected members were in complete support of the removal and the Board wondered if that was due to a client mentioning local elected members as possible abusers.

One day a local MP attended a fundraising event at the charity. He went to sit in my office to speak to me off the record. He explained that an elected member had wanted a domestic abuse charity to be shut down as he had "beaten seven bells out of his wife". He turned to me and said, "why do you think he wants an abuse charity shut down?". I was shocked and horrified at the implication but I tried to keep an open mind.

I wrote an email to the provost asking to meet and I was surprised when he agreed. I gave him a folder with evidence of the respect shown to the charity before the scrutiny meeting including a glowing reference from their funding officer. He was shocked and he asked if the contents had been seen by the head of social work. I confirmed that they had. The provost continued to stay in contact indicating that he was trying to help once even meeting the clients but later it was clear that he had done so to keep me at bay while the funding was removed. I was very upset as I had always respected him.

After the funding was removed the council said they were starting a commissioning process to reallocate the funding and they said that the charity could apply and be part of the process. The Board were shocked to discover that the government had funded the process which had been a large contributory factor to the funding being removed. The Board submitted a complaint to the Ombudsman about the way the organisation was treated particularly as the grievance was proven to be unfounded. The Ombudsman came back to say they thought they couldn't investigate as we had a contractual relationship with the council. There was nowhere to go for justice.

Matters became strange in the extreme when it became clear that the person who would be paid by the government to carry out the commissioning exercise was another previous manager of the charity, Iona. Iona had her own issues. While she was manager at one point the Board had resigned due to financial mismanagement. When she left the team had to have a meeting to cry over what a bully she had been. She had left after a dispute with Pete and she did not have a good opinion of the charity. She had an added complication of being aware of rings being reported while she was manager and taking no action despite working as a social worker with the council and being seconded to the role as a council worker. She had been the manager who destroyed all the files. So effectively for thirteen years the charity had been run by the council with seconded workers. Iona came to meet me and Ingrid, the prison manager, to explain the process. She arrived with a confrontational approach going on the attack about the grievance. Ingrid questioned her knowing about it at all as she felt it would compromise decision making. I explained that it had all been unfounded but Iona questioned whether I should still have been working with a disability implying I should have given up allowing a healthier person to take over. She blamed me for not leaving early enough therefore allowing the grievance to happen. Ingrid had known Iona for years and they were friends but she was furious and she robustly defended me. As a disabled person Ingrid questioned that this attitude was a breach of the Equality Act. Following the meeting it appeared that Iona changed her attitude and she appeared supportive throughout the process. However, it was clear the council was supporting another charity to take over the work.

Just prior to the commissioning process the Board had written to the council to raise concerns about the level of multiple abuse in the area but the council ignored the letter. The level of animosity and venom led the Board to believe that the charity was a significant threat to the council, particularly what was held in the files and they wanted the charity to be shut down to seize them and destroy them.

Threats

One morning Chris had left for work and when I came downstairs I could smell burning. I looked around the house, checking the radiators in case anything was on them that could have been singed. I couldn't find anything. I opened the front door and there was a log burning on my doorstep. I put it out very concerned. I called Chris and he reassured me it must have just been coincidental but the worry stayed with me. I told the police but they reacted as if I had imagined it.

Around the same time I received a call where the caller said" I hope you have life insurance," It was an unknown number and the police said it could not be traced. Another caller told me they knew where my children went to school and I had better watch for their safety and stop doing what I was doing. The caller was very sinister.

I had several similar calls over the years. Colleagues were followed, phone calls echoed. The police could not rule out our phones were being monitored. It was a very worrying time.

Death and rebirth

I had been feeling strange since Christmas and I couldn't understand why I felt so restless. I had strange nightmares every night and my father was on my mind every day. I kept looking up his photograph on my computer and I was thinking about writing to him, although we had not spoken for almost fifteen years. One night in January I dreamt of a day we had spent at the Fintry falls, one of the only days I remembered as being content with my dad. The day was glowing in beautiful sunshine and we played in a clear stream with nets catching minnows. The waterfall was spectacular with a massive drop to rocks below. My dad had always been daring, often in a reckless way and he persuaded me to walk across the rocks with him under the water rushing down. I remembered the force of the water, the fear, and the exhilaration. Afterwards everything felt peaceful and content as we all lay in the sun snacking on our picnic. I woke feeling confused at the beautiful dream of summer, waking to an icy winter day.

My younger sister Gina was my dad's first child with his third wife. She was in regular contact with Clark often talking on Facebook through the night. She contacted him at three o'clock in the morning to ask if she could have my number to contact me. My dad had two children with his third wife, and they had all moved to America when I was twenty-five. We had been in contact for a number of years after I had my first child but had fallen out after a huge confrontation. I had Gina as a friend on Facebook, but we rarely spoke even though she did have some contact with Clark and Susan. I guessed what was going to be said but still when Gina said that my father had been ill since Christmas, and he had died I found myself unable to stop the tears. I had to steel myself to call Morag which was a very tense call. Morag just said that he had been nothing to us in life so why bother about him in death. Susan and Arianne came over to the house to make sure I was okay but for the next week I was in a daze and I kept trying to just go to work. The impact was so unexpected, but Chris said, "you are grieving the dad you should have had not the one you had".

For the next six months I found myself being unstable and crying without warning with heightened emotional sensitivity to every situation. Trudi lost her father some months later and I felt so strongly that all the normal parts of bereavement such as a funeral, sadness being acceptable and family pulling together had been stolen from me by who he was. I went out for lunch with my mother the week after it happened, and I had to pretend I didn't care while my mum released her anger towards him. For the months afterwards we didn't discuss it. I kept a close eye on Gina and how she was, but I decided that contact would not be good for either of us as we had different perceptions of our father. I felt that I had changed forever.

The birth of terror

One day I was sitting having my lunchtime cup of tea when the office put a call through to me saying they didn't know how to deal with it. It was someone who did not want to give a name. The caller described a situation that had been keeping her awake at night with worry and stress. She had been friends with someone who had been someone she had worked with as a health visitor. The patient had just had a child and she was traumatised at the memory of an event from her past. She had described that when she was around 13 she had fallen pregnant as a result of childhood abuse. The abuser was either her father or one of his friends as he had allowed several his friends to abuse her too. He had persuaded her to tell others that the pregnancy was the result of a teenage relationship. He refused to allow her to access medical care. Around the time that the baby was due he took her to Ireland. They lived on a farm, and he kept her in the barn. She went into labour and delivered the baby by herself in complete terror and distress with her abuser looking on coldly. Once the baby was born, he hit him on the head with a large stone and buried him. This was something I had heard about before as then there was no chance of DNA linking him to the abuse of his daughter.

The friend was horrified on hearing what had happened, and she begged for them to go to the police. The young woman was terrified and said that she couldn't as her father was a powerful man with friends who would cause her harm. I said to the caller that we could go to the police together to report what had been said and surely the police could investigate carefully and confidentially. The caller became very afraid and said she didn't feel she could do so, but she would speak to her friend again.

She called back two days later to say that when she had spoken to her friend about it, she became very angry and distressed. She had become so chaotic in her behaviour, threatening to kill herself that she had to drop the subject and promise not to pursue it further. I explained that we would have to do something as this was a very serious crime, but the caller persisted in refusing to give any details of who she was or who her friend was.

The case stayed with me, and I knew that I would never be able to put the images described to me from my mind. I felt something had to be done but that the police would not follow up an unsubstantiated accusation with no names or contact details. I called them for advice, and they confirmed there was nothing they could do. It left me with fear that the abusers would go on to harm more children. My work was very challenging in that often the abusers were not brought to justice due to the fear they instilled in their victims.

Death of idealism

I had always been fascinated by politics. It seemed to be the only area of life where people could shout at one another and be incredibly rude, but it was somehow okay and seen as debate. I thought there must be a better way. When I was a child, I was passionate about injustice and inequality and the thread stayed throughout my life. I remembered the time of the Conservative government under Margaret Thatcher and the complete defeat anyone from my background of struggle felt. I was raised in a council flat in an area of grey, damp flats with no heating and no hope. During the winter the wallpaper would have blue spores all over it and the Calor gas heater would cause water to run down the walls with condensation. This reality of life was not seen by the Conservative party. I felt deeply that there were some people who had so much but others who didn't know how they would clothe and feed their children. I spent my teenage years in clothes handed down by my cousins and I was terrified to have holes in my clothes and shoes because they could not be replaced.

On some level I believed in political movements to change things. As a teenager I was actively involved in campaigning against nuclear weapons, and I defined myself as a socialist as a protest against division in class and society. Over the years it became more confusing. The movement against the Poll Tax was won with enormous excitement that change could happen but over the years the destruction of the reputation of the main campaigner was gradual but complete. When the Labour party won power over Thatcher I sat up all night and I was filled with hope and celebration. I was not sure where my feelings of disgust at class prejudice came from but I recalled a day in the car with my mother and one of her teacher friends.

As a single parent despite being a teacher, which was seen as a middle-class role the family always struggled as most of my mother's friends and colleagues had partners who also worked and they spent their lives trying to impress one another with new furniture and fancy curtains. They had little time for the parents of the children they taught feeling that they were beneath them.

One such teacher was in the car and my mother had been discussing having to go into hospital to have surgery.

"Poor you," said the teacher. "I would hate to be in a general ward in Glasgow. You are likely to be in a bed next to the sort of person you would just not like to speak to or be near"

I was furious "who do you think you are. What makes you think you are better than anyone else?"

My mother was so embarrassed and upset that the conversation stayed in my thoughts as guilt at hurting my mother but an awareness that there could be class judgement even in those who were teaching children where they thought they were better. In reality those who really had money and status would not want to be next to someone so judgemental in a hospital bed.

In Scotland in 2014 it felt like life was changing and people were starting to question what we had always accepted. We had always been stuck with a right of centre politics that maintained division and the power of bankers and those who controlled the political process. The government had been implementing austerity measures to reduce a deficit in the country. I knew through my studies in economics that much of economics and so-called deficits could be manipulated to look like anything as much of finance was actually bookkeeping and skilled accountants could make it look good or bad depending on what outcome they wanted. The only way to reduce deficits was to grow the economy and stimulate new businesses and skills that could create innovation.

Austerity was like cutting back in a household to save money with refusals to move forward for fear of things falling apart and for children to not have opportunities to study and learn as to do so would cost too much. The resultant hopelessness would make the whole situation much worse not better. I knew through my work how much money was wasted in public services from layers upon layers of management with massive salaries and huge pensions of over 20% where the rest of the world had small pensions of 6% and some only in recent years. Those managers would spend their whole time at work in meetings that achieved very little, created more meetings, and justified existence. Huge amounts of money would be spent on feasibility studies, consultants, publicity, and away day events for large numbers of civil servants. Every time I would attend a conference in the same venue would be huge numbers of public sector managers attending another training day. In contrast the workers who were working on the ground never had training and they were treated disgracefully.

It appeared in Scotland that people did not believe in austerity, and they wanted change. The independence movement gave some the feeling that there was an alternative to the ongoing position of being forced to accept a Conservative government who were only relevant to people in the South of England. I was intrigued by it while still feeling sceptical. My son took me to events where there was much flag waving and Scottish music but not a great deal of substance as to how it would all work. I felt something had to happen to break free of a political structure that was not relevant in Scotland, and which didn't match the aspirations of most Scottish people. However, I was very wary of the SNP and did not embrace the anti-English sentiment.

The day after the independence vote many of the independence supporters were very distressed. My son joined the SNP despite major reservations in the hope that if they became stronger a further vote could be achieved. The party had a massive increase in membership so many others felt the same. My son asked me along to events and I still felt a real tension with the way that those in the party came across. It seemed for many it was about being Scottish rather than being about politics. It was clear that policy was set by those who were senior in the party and members were to then adhere to those policies and never be seen to question them. The atmosphere felt akin to a bullying culture where to fit in it was important to never question.

Through the problems faced by the charity I was thrust deeply into the world of politics. Through my time working for charities, I had realised the need to gain support from local councillors, MPs and now MSPs to help raise awareness of the needs of the clients I worked with. As the charity experiencing a threat of losing funding it risked closure. I went to see local politicians to gain support to save it.

Just before the grievance I had been encouraged by my funding officer to attend a scrutiny committee meeting which had seemed strange as that had never been suggested before. I was still very unwell, and I found the lights in meeting rooms and the need to sit in crowds of people very anxiety provoking, but I attended with Trudi and Sadie. Sadie left before the charity was discussed. Trudi and I were very shocked as the head of social work stood up to give a report on the charity. The list of other charities discussed had been straightforward and positive, but this report was different. It was reported that the charity had not been providing reports or justification for the funding. I had provided a report only the week before on the request of the funding officer with only notice of a week, but the report had been very comprehensive. It was strange that the funding officer was not there to present the report. I was not allowed to speak but sat furious as the lies being presented. It was suggested that money provided by the council was being used by the charity elsewhere and it was alluded to that cuts may be necessary. The committee asked for this to be explored further and brought back to the meeting. Trudi and I were in shock, and we spoke to one of the councillors after the meeting to express concern. Pete then wrote to her to note that the information provided had been false. Trudi and I sent a number of documents, providing evidence that the information had not been correct. We asked for a meeting.

Although very nervous I decided to visit the local MSP. I had met him many years before where I found him to be arrogant and with no real commitment to supporting those who were disenfranchised. His agenda seemed to be to further his own political career which had been successful as he was now a government minister. I put my doubts aside, deciding to give him another chance. He was actually strangely supportive and helpful suggesting that I go to see the local councillors as they were in control of the local decision-making processes being the administration. He also suggested contacting the leader of the main party in the council.

I researched who the members of the local administration were and I came across someone who appeared to be the contact for my area, attending her surgery in Asda. She was a tall woman with an air of impatience and aggression. I explained what was happening to the charity and I was met with a confusing level of dismissal. She said "I don't know what you want me to do. I am not the councillor for your area and you are not my constituent". I apologised for the mistake and asked for the name of who she should have seen. She swept away without further acknowledgement of my existence leaving me really confused at what I had done to make her so rude.

I recalled a previous email that had been sent to Trudi from the local provost and I wondered if that was why there was animosity. Some years before one of the fundraising volunteers had offered spiritual readings as a fundraising event and it had been publicised in the charity newsletter. He had emailed a strong email objecting to this and suggesting that the charity was promoting spiritualism to clients. Trudi and I prepared a response to apologise if that was how it appeared but stressing it was a fundraiser for staff. However, on discussing it we were really shocked at the blatant breach of equalities by showing prejudice towards the beliefs of the volunteer. I thought it would be straightforward to put right any misconceptions about the charity and move forward.

The following week I attended the surgery of our local councillor in a miner's club in an outlying village. Chris decided to go with me as he had been a colleague of his father many years before and the company union rep. It was clear that he was expecting me to come to see him and well prepared. I explained my concerns that if the charity was to lose money it could possibly cause it to have to close. The councillor said much as he wanted to be supportive the council often had to make cuts and nobody was ever happy about it and they realised they would have bad press but they just had to accept it as I would have to accept it now.

"Yes but that would be fine if our charity was not the only one facing cuts. It just seems strange for us to be discredited at a meeting then funding cuts announced when we are much improved and offering more than we did when it was run by the council. What is going on?"

He took time to answer "we have to rely on what is proposed to us by council officers and in this case the head of social work. I have always found her to be very helpful"

"I found her helpful too" I said, "this has all been so strange and we don't understand it at all".

"I don't know what you want me to do" he said

"You are our councillor" Chris said "we expect you to represent the interests of the charity and for people who have been abused. I know from my dad that you used to be a union rep years ago and he knew you well. Surely you should be used to fighting against injustice?"

"That all depends on what you think injustice is" the councillor said cryptically.

"Injustice is turning your back on someone who spend their childhood being abused and tortured" I said with angry passion "injustice is then spending their adulthood with mental health issues, physical pain, constant anxiety and being unable to trust anyone to help. Injustice is a small child being abused today because the abuser was never brought to justice. Injustice is that they can't receive the help they need because the council want to save money and they are expendable."

"Anyway, something about this whole thing stinks and we intend to get to the bottom of it!"

I left in tears with images of the people I had met and worked with. I recalled a child of only eleven who came to the service unable to look at anyone and so scared and tensed up. She had been removed from home as she was sexually abused by her older brother and her mother refused to make him leave while waiting for the court case to happen. The child was then placed in foster care and the carer had gone on holiday for a week and left her. She was placed in another foster placement where she was physically assaulted, and she was now in residential care. On her first visit she was unable to speak at all but her eyes showed some sign of interest at the room with all the toys and art equipment. Each week when she would come to see her counsellor, she became more animated, and she started to connect with the team in the office too. On the last day of her support, she came bounding into the building running around to see everyone, hugging the administrator with happiness shining from her. The child had always stayed with me in my mind and whenever I entered the toy room, I would think of all the children whose lives had been changed by that room.

"I need to keep fighting" I said to Chris "I just have to".

Wee grey cloud

One of the most complex people to understand in the whole work situation was Ingrid. When I started in the job Ingrid was talked about in hushed and anxious tones. She was a founder of the charity. She had been described as difficult and destructive. After her job came to an end, she had taken over a contract from the charity, but it didn't seem to have lasted long.

I had been at a meeting in Edinburgh with Trudi when a tiny grey-haired woman came up to speak to us. Trudi hugged her and introduced her as Ingrid. I, decided to ignore everything I had heard and find out all about her. Within minutes we had a rapport and we spoke with equal passion about services for people who had been abused. We swapped numbers and resolved to meet up later.

I contacted her about a week later and we agreed that Ingrid would come back to the Board of the organisation. She was very committed to the work in prisons, so when a manager job arose, she applied and was successful managing the work there and overseeing the prison workers. We became very close and always had a great deal of warmth with one another always ending texts with three kisses. I became very close to Ingrid opening up about my past and asking her advice when there were issues with the children. I told her all my insecurities about my health. Over the years I realised that the friendship between us was becoming stronger

Ingrid had been having some issues with the prisons. She was working in one of the prisons with a young man who had been part of a significant paedophile ring but as a victim as well as a perpetrator. He had been very distressed in the counselling continuously focussing on the fact that he knew it was still going on. The ring had been prolific in abusing children including babies of the friends of the perpetrators. They were caught by filming the abuse and sharing the images online. The main ringleader had been Chief Executive of a well-known charity held up as respected and valued by the Government. Ingrid had researched others involved in the charity as the young man had said that there was one more, the main instigator who had escaped being caught. He described him as "the man in the shiny suit". Ingrid found a video recorded in the parliament for an award to the charity, referred to by the young man, and she had been horrified to see sitting with the Chief Executive someone they all knew. He was wearing a shiny suit. In the next session with the young man Ingrid tried to discover if it was who she suspected. He described something the main ringleader would always say about travelling all over the world and the words were identical to something he had said to Ingrid. Ingrid also remembered him asking her for access to young male prisoners for a television programme. When Ingrid checked with them there was no programme. She was convinced he was dangerous, and she made a report to Intel. Her report became more serious as another prisoner had given her links to another very high-profile case involving murder and possible links to a child who was missing.

The person suspected was trying to gain access to the prisons to work and Ingrid reported her concerns not knowing the person she was speaking to was one of his friends. The next time Ingrid tried to enter the prison she was taken into a humiliating meeting and told not to come back. I called a meeting with the prison manager, and I was told Ingrid was a malicious troublemaker and she was not to return. One morning I received a call from the individual involved. It wasn't a normal occurrence for him to call me. He was unconsolably crying. He told me the government were planning to shut him down. I found his actions very strange and suspicious.

Ingrid was very vocal about the breach of confidentiality in the grievance and very understanding about the effect on the children and we both agreed that was the only important issue. She would say "the Board are not worrying about those weans". She wrote a statement to the Board to refute the allegations in the grievance, stating that I had always been a very supportive manager to all.

Ingrid was determined to prove her loyalty and she supported me in a complaint to the union. She was adamant that if the union helped close the charity her job would be affected too. We sat and devised a letter and waited for the fall out. The union came back to us and arranged a meeting to discuss their concerns. A worker from the union was brought in to investigate. He came across as part professional, part shady. He came in full of arrogance but working hard to appear very friendly. He explained that his role was to gather evidence and come to a decision. Ingrid and I explained that we were very concerned that the local rep had supported a grievance against another union member that effectively harassed her on the grounds of her disability and included a serious breach of client confidentiality. We raised our concerns that he had colluded with the council to affect funding and that he had recruited people to the union and then immediately allowed them to be represented even though the issue had predated their membership. We were concerned that the union rep was the leader of the local political party, and it was some of the local party who were trying to remove the funding for the charity.

We were not surprised when the complaint was not upheld as it was continually felt that everyone wanted this whole event to be forgotten.

Ingrid and I decided that the best way forward was to speak to Ingrid's local MSP as the routes with trying to achieve justice were not going to work due to everyone covering one another's back to protect their own position and to cover up what was at the root of it all. We were beginning to feel we would never find out.

We both kept thinking about the client we felt was at the centre of the issue and we felt we had to do everything we could. We asked to meet with the Public Protection Unit and two of them came to Ingrid's house to discuss the case. After raising the prison matters, they said that Ingrid should have extra security in her house so clearly, they were taking matters seriously. The head of the unit took the lead on discussions with his colleague taking notes where necessary. Ingrid explained the client's case explaining that it had progressed past the procurator fiscal but then had been dropped despite there being other witnesses.

"I have met the client he can say that everyone in the area has abused him" the officer said, "my other concern is that often experimentation in young men is seen as abuse."

Ingrid and I were appalled "he was seven years old when it started!" I almost shouted."

"We are really concerned that he wasn't treated with respect by the officers after he was assaulted."

"Well, you know sometimes victims can be an annoyance to the police we are all human and personalities come into it." He said.

He went on to describe a case involving a 13-year-old girl. He alleged that she had been grooming adult men and that they were the victims.

Ingrid and I were so disgusted that we looked at one another in shock but we realised we couldn't alienate the police officer if we wanted to achieve justice for the client and expose the ring. We told him that we found that perception to be of great concern.

"Please investigate the case again particularly the other witnesses. They are named in the file."

They left promising to further investigate it.

Months and years passed with further concerns being raised with politicians and the police.

Eventually things moved forward with press involvement.

Road trips

We received notification that the charity had won a major prestigious award and we had to go to London for four days for the ceremony and for a training event. I was still unwell, so Chris agreed to take time off work to go with me to manage the driving as I had been ill on trains since my illness started. We were excited but nervous as the journey was due to be over 7 hours. We headed off very early in the morning with the first leg of the journey to be to Gretna where we could stop at the outlet village. We had made CDs of music that would fire us up but make us reflect and remember who we were growing up and growing together. As we travelled down the motorway it was fun to see all the towns and village names that had been seen on television or spoken about. Passing through the Lake District made us want to come back and holiday there. We decided to stop off on the way back.

The smaller villages gradually changed to the outskirts of cities with signs showing Liverpool and Manchester. We stopped off in a service station and enjoyed browsing through the shops full of maps and travel paraphernalia. There were random items like cuddly potato cushions with faces and boxes of Edinburgh rock. Of course, there were the usual emergency phone chargers and medicines in amongst magazines for the bored passengers. Service stations didn't really do gluten free apart from solid baked potatoes with cheese strands like rubber. After chewing through rubbery cheese and almost breaking a plastic knife on a solid potato we set off again with strong coffee. The Birmingham outskirts were the worst with masses of lanes and complicated directions where there was a Toll or road without the Toll and somehow, we missed it despite searching frantically for change. We had decided to stop of at Northampton which was slightly stupid as it was only an hour from London. We arrived at the hotel and realised we were hungry. We drove all around the town finding nowhere to eat that had gluten free. The town was disappointing being unappealing with not much to do. We decided to go to Domino's pizza and we sat in the car eating them with me having a gluten free. Within half an hour my tongue was tingling and I realised there had been cross contamination. The next morning, I was so ill, but we had to be out of the hotel by 10 a.m. Chris drove and I spent the hour of the journey to the outskirts of London feeling horrible and nauseous. As we entered London excitement took over and I looked all around at the fruit shops at each block and all the frantic activity. We arrived at an area of large luxurious buildings and we easily found our pre booked car park. We walked to the hotel feeling nervous and excited. The hotel was an inexpensive one for London meaning expensive for Scotland and therefore fairly basic, but it was friendly and the rooms were pleasant. We tried to go for a meal in the restaurant but there was no gluten free. The same was the case in the restaurants all around so I had to settle for mashed potatoes kindly made for me for free by the chef.

The next morning, I went off to the training and Chris decided to go to see the attractions of London. When I arrived, I realised it would be difficult as I had to stand a lot and standing still made me weak and dizzy. The lights in the building made me feel ill. I stood talking to the organiser while feeling sweat cover my body as I tried not to faint. As the day progressed, I became weaker and sorer but I persevered loving the training. It was so inspiring and the people I met were too. They all seemed to have been through grievances at some point and in all cases, there were issues with funding cuts at the root of the problems. I was paired with another CEO from Ireland as a buddy, and we went for coffee. She had been through a very similar situation, and it made me feel so much better to talk to her as it had been resolved.

The next day I attended a training session with one of the main trainers from the awarding organisation. The training was inspiring and motivating and I started to feel like I could become better and find my way again. We went into a drama workshop next and that meant I had to stand so initially I was very anxious but as it progressed I enjoyed it and again felt maybe improvements to my health were possible. We went to meet all the winners from previous years and prepared for the awards ceremony that night. Two of the Board members and Ingrid arrived dressed in evening wear and looking fabulous. We all boarded a bus to the venue, the Science Centre. I had not been on public transport since being ill and I felt awful but managed to pretend I was fine. We entered a spectacular area where we gathered waiting to go into the awards. We followed a queue that seemed to go on for miles and then we were seated watching all the organisations shown on a video and then called up to give a speech. I was terrified but when I saw the video of the charity I felt so inspired I managed to do it. Afterwards we all went downstairs for drinks and we met a well-known TV presenter who was lovely to us. It felt wonderful and miles away from all the distress at home.

We progressed back in the bus and this time it felt fine with all the happiness from the night. At the hotel we sat in the bar with all the other organisations and the atmosphere was buzzing with excitement. They all continued to drink and Ingrid became very drunk and started fighting over a young man who played up to it, enjoying the attention. After a while Ingrid stood up to go to bed crashing down full force on her front. We all rushed to her but she seemed fine and she continued drinking. I didn't drink so I went to bed leaving them to keep partying. The next day we could not rouse Ingrid and we all panicked after her fall. Eventually after an hour she appeared looking awful but fortunately her daughter had arrived to pick her up.

Chris and I set off back home for the long journey. We played music and chatted for miles about all that had happened. Chris had loved going to see all the sights, taking photographs. We stopped at many service stations enjoying coffee at each to keep them going. We stopped at Kendal being aware that the journey was more than halfway over. Kendal was a small, charming town and we wandered around finding many small shops until we found one that sold Kendal mint cake to take back. We travelled up through the country roads parallel to the motorway stopping to look at the beautiful countryside and resolving to come back soon. Eventually we reached Abington services and it felt like we were almost home. We put on a CD full of rock songs and sang the rest of the way back only stopping at Tesco in Cumbernauld for food. As we arrived home we were stopped by the police who said there had been local burglaries. We laughed and said, "well it couldn't have been us as we were just back from London." The road trip had been an amazing experience and we were so proud of ourselves that we managed it. Even tired we wanted to try it again soon.

The opportunity came two months later. I loved the quiz show the Chase and I had auditioned to go on the show. I had been so shocked to win the audition in Scotland but thought it was probably because I looked geeky and a bit strange rather than due to my quizzing ability. I wanted the Governess as my chaser as she was my favourite, and I was such a geek I was part of her appreciation group on Facebook. The show was in London so we had to arrange another road trip, this time taking my son Thomas with us. Thomas was fascinated with everything all the way down making it all seem new and fresh. We all spoke all the way down until eventually Thomas fell asleep. We arrived in the outskirts of London this time and we went to find the hotel. We were confused when the booking didn't seem to exist but Thomas's did. We realised there were two of the same hotel and Thomas having booked later had booked a different hotel. He said it was fine he would check in and rest and we went off to our hotel to rest. The hotel was really inexpensive and really basic but it was still very appealing. The next day Chris set off to pick up Thomas for them to go to London centre for sightseeing. I waited with terrible nerves to be picked up for the show. I sat in the foyer and a minibus arrived to collect me and others. We started talking on the bus to break the ice and help the nerves. The show itself was an amazing experience and I was so excited meeting Bradley Walsh as I had always loved his humour. The Chaser was the Dark Destroyer and he was so nice and friendly afterwards that I decided he was my new favourite. I was completely hopeless as a quizzer. On the cash builder I scored four mostly due to the luck of a questions based on a film, the illustrated man that I had seen as a student. On the chase section I did not manage to answer any questions correctly which was embarrassing as it was multiple choice. We all did badly apart from the first contestant, a lovely older man originally from Scotland. He took part in the final chase but sadly he didn't win. We all didn't mind not winning as it was the experience that counted, and we all headed back to the hotel happy and buzzing. We had to travel back that night as we had work the next day and travelling at night was peaceful and relaxing. Thomas was so excited that he had seen the television studios and he loved visiting London with Chris. It was a happy journey back. We reflected on the fact that without the adrenaline from fighting the grievance none of the experiences would have happened.

The important call

It started as a normal day where emails were checked, appointments were set up and cancelled and all the staff carried out their regular duties. A call came into the office from Ailsa from the public protection unit for me, but the administrator took it as I was in a meeting. As soon as the meeting was over, she couldn't wait to speak to me.

"That was Ailsa from the public protection unit. She said there are 700 young men who have been abused and who they will be interviewing!"

I was shocked and I called her back instantly.

"I spoke to your colleague earlier" Ailsa said, "we have a case we are dealing with where we will be interviewing potentially 700 young men and we wanted to check we have the correct contact details for you in order to pass on any referrals or at least to give people information."

I was so shocked I wasn't sure what to say, "well perhaps some will already be in contact with us?"

"They may well be but thank you anyway."

The call was ended, and the staff and I were very shocked.

"I think she was passing on a message to us that they were looking into things" I said to Ingrid "it was strange to call as our details are on our website and they could easily access them."

It stayed with us all, but we heard nothing more.

Fighting for justice

We all felt too much time had passed with no progress after reporting the abuse rings to the press. We were aware there was a very high level of multiple abuse in our files. I had spent a weekend in the files cupboard looking through relevant files to assess what types of concerns were being reported. I was extremely upset afterwards. I spoke to the rest of the team about the cases they had been working on. It became clear there were several child abuse rings operating in the area. One was linked to an ice cream round. One was a report from three young people that their father had sold them to his circle of friends. They also had children and the children were forced to abuse one another while the men watched. They were severely traumatised. It had been reported to the council and the police with no action taken. I discussed it with the Board and we decided to contact the press. I called a journalist who had been supportive in the past. He had asked me for comments on the Dunblane case on a few occasions. I told him about the cases and provided email evidence that we had been in contact with the police. He was equally concerned that there had been no action taken. We knew the client had not been interviewed. We were sure the named perpetrators had not either.

The journalist asked the police for comment. He also asked the council as we provided a copy of the letter we had written to them to highlight our concerns. Prior to the article being published the police contacted me to ask if they could develop ongoing contact with us to look into these cases and others. Gray, the police officer was very friendly. He gave me his mobile number and said I could keep regular contact. He asked me to say to the papers that we would be working with the police. It felt like being handled but I agreed in the hope that we would be able to achieve justice for the client. Another newspaper contacted me. I provided them with the same evidence and they put out an article too. Gray asked me to promise to tell him if any other journalists made contact. He asked me to agree to co-ordinated responses in future. We started meeting every fortnight. I always took Ingrid with me as a witness. Gray was overly friendly. When we raised the issue of "the man in the shiny suit" he agreed with us that it was a very suspicious situation. He said that as the client who had reported him was in prison his testimony would not be taken seriously. Ingrid was furious. She said he was a victim too and he should be heard. We left the cases with Gray to investigate. He asked us about the clients on the database. He wanted names and contact details of the clients to "doorstop" them. We were horrified and said that could not happen as it would traumatise survivors who may not be ready to report. We were aware that he knew that could not happen. He wanted to be able to say in any future article that we did not co-operate. We made it clear that we wanted him to investigate the files we had been able to provide information on as they had already been reported.

Meeting the new enemy

In tandem with the situation with the council we had to deal with the government. After the grievance they had suspended our referrals while continuing to fund us. They said the reason was that they would be setting up a new service and our service would be ending. They said this had been planned prior to the grievance. That set off alarm bells for us. An external evaluation had been carried out. It was extremely positive. The researcher recommended our service model as one that should be replicated by all services. He highlighted broker models, later promoted as not appropriate or effective. I was mistakenly copied into an email where the government instructed him to change the report to make it less positive about our service. However, they met with our team to say the service would continue. Even if we tendered for it and were unsuccessful the model would remain and staff would TUPE over. We were happy that the clients would still have their service. The government held consultation meetings with survivors. In the initial meetings they mostly involved the survivors we were supporting. They were clear they wanted to keep their service. Two new staff were brought into the government team Jackie and Sue. They arranged a meeting with me and my colleague Talia, the manager of the service for people abused in care. They were aggressive from the beginning. Our last report had been commended by our previous government contact but Sue told us it was rubbish. She was a clinical psychologist. She would sign all emails with all her qualifications. She told me I was not qualified and therefore, the report was not useful at all. I said, "the report is the model given to us by the government to complete."

She said "I'm afraid I must be negative about my colleagues as it is not what I would expect. Things will be different now. We want you to go back and produce a new report to our requirements."

They said that at consultation meetings clients had been positive about our service. They had said that was what they wanted. Jackie said, "we have to give clients what we think they need, not what they want."

I said, "what was the point of the consultations if you were not going to take any interest in what was reported back."

Jackie presented a document with an illustration of a broker model. She said they were to present it to the final client meeting as the way forward. They were not being given a choice. The model would not provide services. It would instead broker services from the NHS. I was horrified. I said "there are no available services in the NHS. They are not trauma specialists and they refer trauma clients to us."

Sue said, "I don't believe you."

I said, "I will provide evidence."

I said "there are huge waiting lists. Our clients are deemed to be untreatable as they are often diagnosed with a personality disorder. Clients will die while they wait. There have been so many suicides in the past."

Jackie said "perhaps it will be necessary for clients to die for change to happen. Out of chaos comes order."

I was shocked and horrified. I asked her to repeat what she said. She repeated it three times. I watched my hand tremble holding my cup of water. Talia looked really shocked.

I said, "I'm sorry I have to end this meeting after what you have just said."

We stood up for them to leave. Jackie said "we spoke to Gavin, one of your clients. He said he often felt suicidal so you have clearly not cured him. I asked him have you not moved on yet."

I said, "you have just breached Gavin's confidentiality by telling me that."

She snorted and they left.

Talia and I were so seriously shocked we called one another that night and for the next few days. We felt we really had to take it forward. The clients reported to me that the third meeting only involved 18 clients. They said only 5 were in favour of the new model. Therefore, out of a consultation of clients when we were supporting over 1,500 only 5 supported their model but they went ahead anyway.

The tender was released with no service delivery included. We raised concerns that we could then not tender for it. I said it was a dangerous model creating a layer that was not necessary but with nowhere to refer clients to. The organisation who won the tender was the one that our referrals were to go to. The new service employed one of the staff from the grievance. We were instructed to "transition" clients to the new service and hand over the files. The clients refused to consent. They did not trust the government and they saw this new service as a quango. Our joint Board chairs met the government with the lawyer where they said they would not agree to taking away the client's control. They questioned the process as the organisation successful had been receiving referrals before the tender was even published. We were starting to understand why we had experienced the grievance from the government perspective. They wanted the files to establish what future litigation costs may be if they overturned time bar or what may be a cost if redress went forward. We knew of some high-profile cases that may also concern them.

The inquiry

I wrote to the inquiry about my concerns regarding the tender process and the new model. They agreed to meet me. I submitted a long paper with evidence against broker models and with evaluations from our clients. I raised concerns about the treatment of our service. I had the meeting with senior members of the inquiry team. They grilled me but ultimately were very supportive. They were very concerned about what had happened. They said that in a month or so they would call me to give evidence. They would try and do so as soon as possible due to the pressing time concerns. They asked one of my colleagues in the field to come and also give evidence. She said she backed up my account. She said the team had taken it very seriously and they wanted her to give evidence too. We were delighted at the progress.

A few weeks later the chair of the inquiry resigned. This was followed by two other members of the inquiry team, who had met us, resigning too. They cited government interference. I was later told by a legal firm the interference was from Jackie and her team. The chair was discredited in the press. It was said she made inappropriate comments. The person raising it went on to be offered many contracts with the government. A new inquiry chair was brought in. She had no interest in meeting me or allowing me to give evidence. I was told by some of the inquiry team later that they were told not to speak to me. We repeatedly applied for core participant status as we had worked with more in care survivors than anyone. We were turned down on four occasions, despite strong legal arguments. I became very concerned at how big this issue was becoming. It felt overwhelming as I had never faced anything like this before.

The chameleons

Right from the start of the funding issues Ingrid had encouraged me to go to see the local MSP for her area. He was a very jolly and friendly looking man with a kind face and empathetic manner. I found it impossible not to like him but I always struggled with trusting anyone involved in the situation. He was friendly with the other local MSP which felt strange as they were so different. I thought maybe it was good cop and bad cop.

From the beginning he seemed to want to gather a great deal of information not giving much back at all. Ingrid and I explained all that had happened with the council but also with the government and the removal of the longstanding service for people who had been abused in care. He was sympathetic and he said that he could try and help with the issues with the government. He said that he would try to arrange a meeting with one of the important government ministers. Ingrid and I were very excited taking the suggestion at face value and hopeful that now we were being listened to.

We explained to the MSP all the facts that we felt were behind the issues we were facing. We were convinced that the client's story had started off the issues as the timescales matched. The client had taken part in a DVD where he talked about being abused by a paedophile ring in the area. The DVD was on the charity website and within weeks the charity was broken into. Nothing valuable was taken apart from a cheque book. Later the cheque was cashed by someone connected with a well-known local crime family. The most worrying aspect was that the main filing cabinet was destroyed, and all the files were scattered on the floor. Years later the public protection unit told Ingrid the robbery must have been carried out by a paedophile. We mentioned the concerns we had about the client mentioning the "man in the shiny suit". We mentioned the ceremony in the parliament that had been online. After the discussion the video clip disappeared. We mentioned the possible links to international abuse and the child who had been abducted. We explained how we could not put it all together. The statistics showed many cases of organised abuse locally. We explained that we had raised the issues concerning organised abuse to a local councillor and she had advised us not to report it locally but to report it out with the area. After appearing supportive she had spoken to another supportive councillor, knowing that he was supporting the charity saying, "distance yourself from them the government has plans for them".

We could not understand why the government would want to destroy us so we could only presume it was due to the grievance or they had been misled so the chance to meet the government minister gave us a great deal of hope. We were sure when he was aware of everything that had happened and how unfair it had been he would intervene to make things right. We were sure someone as senior as him would want to do the right thing. Ingrid and I had reported to the MSP that Jackie had said it was okay for clients to die to bring about change and that she had asked a client "are you not over it yet" when he said he felt suicidal. She had repeated this conversation to me and my colleague Talia as a way of illustrating that clients had not been "cured" and therefore there was evidence it had been said and that the confidentiality of the client had been breached.

For weeks before the meeting I prepared a paper to be taken to the meeting. The meeting was cancelled twice, and I became more nervous. On the day of the meeting, I was afraid not knowing what to expect. The MSP met me at the entrance to the parliament and we went upstairs in a lift to deep inside the parliament. The area upstairs was not as I had expected. There were open plan areas with many workers who I presumed were the assistants to the government Ministers. We sat in a waiting area, and I spoke rapidly about what had all gone wrong to make sure it was all clear in my mind. The MSP told me it would all be fine but I would only have 20 minutes so I would need to be concise and to the point. We were taken to a grand room with furniture that was luxurious, and it probably cost more than the entire assets of the charity. The government minister sat at the top of the table with a stony expression shaking my hand without a smile. I handed over the dossier I had gathered, and he wrote down the names involved. When I referred to the meeting where it was said clients should die, he pretended not to know who the civil servants were. I found out some months later that they were friends when I found pictures of them on Twitter. He was non-committal and cold which I found confusing as I was still in an innocent mind-set where I felt I was raising awareness of a serious issue the government would be glad to know about so that they could resolve it. In my mind the MSP had felt it serious enough to arrange a meeting at the most senior level. I found my throat was becoming so dry that my voice had a strangled gulping sound. I had a strong awareness that this was not as expected and I was suddenly aware that it was information he wanted, not to help. Chris said later they will put what you have provided to their lawyers and if they say there is nothing you can do then you won't receive a response. He ended the meeting suggesting a meeting be arranged with another minister with more relevance. When we came out, I said to the MSP "that was awful".

"You appeared very nervous" he said "we will just have to wait and see. At last, you have the chance of a meeting with the other minister".

Each time anything new would happen I would add it to the dossier, and I would inform the MSP by email. When major issues happened, we would request a meeting. The meeting with the minister was moved at least three times. In the meantime, I met with the Convenor of the Cross-Party Group about our concerns. I reported what Jackie had said and that services for survivors were now to follow a medical model and largely be provided by the NHS. This is what survivors had particularly said they did not want. She suggested I raise the issue with the Cross-Party Group as it was following straight afterwards. When I mentioned my concerns, the group were appalled and they insisted that a motion be raised to ask the Minister for a debate to consider all the issues.

The debate took place before I could meet with the Minister. I was invited to attend but that day I was very unwell. I arranged for two of the more experienced counsellors to attend in my place. I was able to watch the debate live online but I watched feeling afraid and tense as I somehow knew that nothing would change. As the debate began most of the SNP MSPs left the debating chamber, including the First Minister leaving mostly opposition MSPs. A Labour MSP read out the motion and then other MSPs followed with their own submissions ending with the Cross-Party convenor. The minister was then to give his response.

He appeared nervous and unsure when reading out the civil servant prepared response. It would have been Jackie who wrote it I thought laughing. He spouted out information on the plans for mental health services and additional resources for survivors being dedicated over the next five years without answering any of the points. He looked unprofessional and aggravated at having to be involved in the debate at all. Instead of explaining that the way forward was not to be based on a medical model he justified the use of medical approaches. Following further debate, he agreed to engage with members of the Cross Party Group to find a consensus. Many months later it still had not happened. After the meeting the two counsellors questioned him robustly, but they reported that he was unable to answer any of their questions. One of those attending was an abuse survivor and she had found the event so upsetting that she dissociated and became very distressed. One of the counsellors spent time with her grounding her and ensuring she was okay. One of the oppositions MSPs had seen her supporting the survivor and how effective she had been in keeping her safe and he asked if they could meet at a later date to see how he could help.

In the meantime, I was at last offered a meeting date with the Minister. I spent ages preparing for it completing a dossier of evidence, an index of the main issues and a paper outlining the main concerns. When I arrived, I was horrified to find that Jackie was there as his advisor. I refused to go ahead on that basis and thankfully she was asked to leave. I presented all my concerns giving a timeline of events feeling that he must be shocked and horrified about how corrupt it all sounded. I was sure that now things must change as it was all so obviously wrong. He was aggressive to begin with and he answered many of my concerns dismissively but as the discussion progressed there was less opportunity for him to justify matters. However, the attitude of underlying frustration was there. He said that he would respond to all the concerns including the one about Jackie saying clients should die. I reported to him that government reports showing how positive our service model was had been changed on the insistence of government civil servants. I provided a folder of evidence.

I waited for a response but in the meantime a letter came in for the Board saying that I should stop saying what Jackie said as it wasn't the view of the Government. It was clear that it was not a good idea to raise issues as this was a direct threat which clearly hoped the Board had not sanctioned the raising of the issue. They said take it to the press. I was asked to respond to it, and I said that this was a concerning response to what was a whistleblowing complaint. Following that letter came another one from the Minister which was approaching aggressiveness in tone and referring to the other letter. It dismissed all complaints and did not accept any of them. There had always been some hope that we were wrong about whether we would be listened to, and the full team felt distressed and let down. I wrote to the original MSP to express my distress and disappointment, but he just wrote back a cold response to say there was nothing more he could do. It was suddenly so obvious we had been played to ensure we would not cause any trouble as the new model was forced through. It was so disappointing as we had trusted him and we realised that nobody could be trusted in the situation.

Weeks later the Scottish election was approaching, and the organisation held a Hustings event. The MSP agreed to attend much to the surprise of us all. At the event he said that the Minister was willing to look again at funding for the service. He said they would also look at core funding. We were all so happy that finally it looked like something would be done. Following the event, he gave a press release saying the same. As soon as the election was over, we made an appointment with him to take forward his promise and he informed us that the Minister had been moved to a new post with another Minister brought in so they could not be held to the comments. This was the most shocking development of them all as it showed that they would be capable of a direct lie and false promises to be elected.

Many weeks later I asked for a further meeting with him as I felt I needed to have one last chance to reason with him. He reluctantly asked me to come to his office in a small village outside town. It was difficult to find it and I was late and very nervous as this felt like the final opportunity. I started by saying "I don't see how the health minister leaving means that all his work stops with him. If I left my job someone would have to take over my responsibilities. This is not right"

He agreed that perhaps that had not been fair or reasonable.

I said "I want to trust you, but you must see that this all looks very suspect. He made a promise through you and then suddenly he is gone. For you all to care so much about keeping us quiet and making promises to keep us from fighting back there must be something major you are hiding"

"Do you think I am the one covering things up" he said, "is it me that you think is hiding something".

"We trust you. We just think that you are being used as a pawn in this too. The other MSP was rude to me when I met him. He called me a conspiracy theorist and raised his voice to me. There is some way that we are creating anxiety and there must be a reason behind that".

He just put his head down.

"You know we have reported to you that the local paedophile ring case involved babies and we don't know if they are still alive. We know that a case came out in the prison that highlighted international abuse at the highest level. The fact that the government will not work with us to resolve it raises questions as to why".

He promised to go back to the government minister to see if anything further could be done. He said perhaps a further meeting would be helpful.

"I won't hold my breath. It may just be another attempt to stall us"

"I promise to respond in the next two weeks".

When the inquiry chair resigned citing government interference and I was asked to go on television to give a comment. I texted the MSP to ask what I should say, and he responded to say just say that it should be investigated. It was weeks later that a response was received and then only after press attention. After the final response he gave a cold response to say nothing more could be done. I realised I had been manipulated for over a year to ensure any threat from the charity would be held back.

Holiday hurts

It had been a common theme throughout life for me to struggle with holidays. I would become so excited about going but then on arrival I would realise that all the coping strategies for dealing with my illness were gone and I would feel like someone hanging onto the edge of a cliff. My condition meant dealing with daily pain and nausea and for someone afraid of being sick that would require strategies such as lying down in my room near the en-suite toilet away from everyone to enable me to distract myself from the feeling safely as being around people when feeling sick would send me into an intense panic.

Car journeys were not good but trains and planes were out due to the dizziness so I would be the driver as much as I could to avoid car sickness on top of everything else. Therefore, getting to a holiday and getting back would be the first fear. Then throughout the holiday I would analyse every single symptom to check out minute by minute if I was becoming ill. The thought of being ill in a different environment felt like torture. Therefore of course being in that constant state of fear I would be ill. My lupus was delighted by tension and would strike.

Holidays should be fun I would grumble to myself. Looking back the memories would edit out all the anxieties and pains and all that would be allowed through would be beautiful walks, waterfalls, lovely little craft shops, historical venues, and romantic cuddly times. But each time I would arrive the last experience of being so ill would flood back into my mind. The first few days would be full of the excitement of having new things to do with planning each of the days. Then thoughts would come into my head of not being able to eat outside just in case or use public toilets just in case. I would start to count the nights passing congratulating myself for managing to stay another day.

On a number of holidays, I would take ill after one or two days as the frenzy of nerves would become a strike on my body. I would endure the discomfort and then say to Chris we have to go home.

I would arrive home the tension would dissipate and I would kick myself at ruining yet another holiday as it became apparent that I had made myself more ill. Through life I had so many amazing experiences but each one had its shadow side of fear and distress. Each time I would resolve not to let it happen again but what if would always creep back into my mind.

This holiday while the tension was rising was no exception. We would go to the Lake District every year and this year we decided to book a holiday cottage for a full week. The cottage was a beautiful country house split into flats with a beautiful garden filled with wildflowers and ivy growing up the walls. It was on a working farm and there was a camping area onsite. The farm was in between Penrith, a busy market town and Keswick where there were a wide range of eating places and pubs.

I had decided to treat Chris to a visit to the Open Golf championship as it was something he had always wanted to do. It was mad as I had booked it to go to Troon on the second day after arriving in the Lake District so we would have a journey back of almost four hours and then we would have to return the following night. It was exciting and we were full of anticipation on the journey up, passing through many small villages, somehow without the charm of the Lakes and we discussed how Scotland could be better at tourism. We arrived at a massive car park, and it was so well organised as buses were waiting to take people to the venue. It was spectacular with massive hospitality tents, although most of the tents were only for those who had paid more. We were able to go round and watch being very close to the golfers and it felt strange seeing famous golfers they had seen on television. We had a wonderful day walking from green to green and sitting in the stands at the fourteenth hole and then the eighteenth where we sat looking over the sea and the hills in the distance watching the final golfers walk up the final fairway. We travelled back down as it became darker feeling content and excited for the rest of the holiday.

On the next night we travelled through to Keswick. It was the night of the Solstice, and it was a full moon and we planned to go to the standing stones. First while it was still light we walked down to the lake watching as the light changed to dim and pink skies predicted sunshine for the next day. We travelled to Castlerigg standing stones arriving in the moonlight. When we walked up, we realised there were many people there. Chris walked around taking photographs and I sat on a stone reflecting on my wishes and dreams. An older woman came over to speak to me and she asked Chris to explain his camera technique. A family of two parents and two children were running around in the moonlight the mum stood on top of one of the stones reaching for the moon and Chris photographed the scene. We talked to the children about orbs on the camera and told them about mystical beliefs and traditions. We returned to the cottage feeling blessed at the beauty we had experienced and we sat outside in the garden area.

The next night we decided to go and find a waterfall out in the countryside. It had been a really warm day and I always suffered in the heat but at night it was cooler and more comfortable. We followed the Satnav which went through the smallest country roads and we were between feeling nervous at not knowing where we were going and in awe of the beauty of the scenery. We stopped at the top of a hill looking down into a valley and wondered why this beauty was not everywhere. We drove into a very small village that only really consisted of a hotel and a local shop. We decided to stop at the side of the lake where groups of people had parked and we stood looking at the sky as it turned pinker and then darker. The sun behind the clouds as it descended made them look like they had a silver lining.

I had spent the last couple of nights unable to sleep through worrying about work and my fights with the government and I thought maybe there was hope. We were shocked to realise we had stopped exactly at the entrance to the walk to the waterfall and we climbed up a hill in the forest until we heard voices. When we followed the sounds of children laughing we found a series of waterfalls flowing down through the forest. It all felt magical and we drove back as it became dark feeling peaceful. That night I twisted and turned with dreams and worries as I reflected on some emails I had sent for work before the holiday being terrified of what response I may receive.

The next day there were explosive thunderstorms following the heat the previous day. I felt very anxious and I could feel the impact of the extreme heat the day before on my body. The nausea led to anxiety as expected for a holiday situation and I stayed on the couch all day as Chris painted outside in the garden. He managed to create a beautiful painting of the cottage. I was delirious but I was determined to stay and enjoy the holiday. The effort not to run was very difficult. I would always feel that I wanted to be alone and that was impossible in a small holiday cottage. The fact that Chris was outside painting helped. Gradually the pain and nausea subsided, and we decided to go for a walk through the farm to let me gain strength in my legs. As we reached the top of the hill the iPhone received the emails and there was one from Alex from the government asking to meet up when she was back. It was in response to an email I had sent to express my serious concerns about everything that had happened. The email was not the horror expected so that night I actually managed to sleep.

We decided to travel next day to another waterfall called Aira Force which sounded romantic and it was highlighted in the tourist guides as a place to visit. We drove down past Ullswater and we found the car park near the walk. We walked up the hill which was a real achievement for me after being so ill and we were delighted to find a massive spectacular waterfall into a gully with places all around to look at it from all angles. The force of nature relaxed us and made us feel we were somewhere that meant something. We then visited Wordsworth's house in Grasmere and I was completely immersed in the feeling of the life of a writer knowing that is what I wanted to be. We walked round the village reflecting that it was the most charming place we had ever been. We both felt that to have the opportunity to live in amongst all the beauty would be perfect, but we realised it was probably something we could never afford to do. Chris joked that we would have to win the lottery.

On the final day we found a small nine-hole golf course just outside Penrith and we realised it was somewhere we could have been every day as it was a similar course to the one at home that we played every weekend. Chris said, "that's it its perfect here!"

We travelled back on the almost four-hour journey feeling relaxed and content at the beautiful holiday and we resolved to come back soon.

Public servitude woes

On the drive to Edinburgh, I felt the tight pain across my stomach worsen like a vice as I thought about the meeting to come. We arrived at the Dean gallery to attend the Surrealism exhibition but realised we were in the wrong place, and it was the museum of modern art. We walked across to the other side of the road and with each step I felt the pain worsen. I felt complete awe as I walked through the rooms and corridors looking at the paintings with their commentary on the society of the time expressed with passion and the subversion of reality into something dreamlike. By the third room I felt overwhelmed, and the nausea rose up and rose up until I felt I would have to run from the room. The intensity of the work and the beauty of the creations made my feelings of hopelessness more intense.

"Why did I agree to this" I said to Chris "it is pointless".

"Just get it over" he replied with kindness "just think of being back home and relaxed. You can do this. You have been through so much up to now and you are still here"

We left the gallery resolving to come back on a better day and drove into the centre of the city parking at the castle terrace car park. We walked across the park and up into the part of the city with large glamorous buildings and expensive shops. We found the street with the café on it amongst a number of bohemian style restaurants and cafes. We had arrived too early so we walked around a bit just killing time nervously. Gulping and then social awkward as ever I went inside to see if the government civil servant had arrived. She was not there yet so I wandered through the restaurant awkwardly not sure what to do. The waiter rescued me finding me a table saying that he would escort my companion through when she arrived. I ordered a pot of tea and sat waiting in dread not knowing what was coming.

The civil servant Alex arrived and at first, I was startled as she looked so much like the other one who had been so rude.

"Oh my god they now all look the same" I grumbled under my breath

Alex was dressed like someone about to head off on a hike and she looked poised and confident, ready for her mission.

I was sitting at the back of the table but Alex insisted on scrambling past me to sit on the left side of me saying that she had an ear infection and that was the best way to hear. I thought am I being completely paranoid or is she wearing an earpiece or taping this conversation. Well let's really give her something to tape. I doubt any of them have ever heard the truth. I doubt if they care.

The pleasantries then awkwardly took place feeling disjointed following the conflict that had taken place by email.

"So how was the Lake District" Alex said with a false smile that almost seemed to crack the tension in her face.

"Wonderful" I said, "it is always sad to return".

"So anyway, I thought we should meet to .."

"Well yes my ranty email"

"Well yes, no I thought it would be good for us to meet to plan the way forward for the transition to the new service" Alex looked smug at the word transition.

"I understand that you are here to manage me following my email" I said, "but as I said we have very significant concerns, and they have to be addressed".

"My plan is for us to discuss this then I will write up a minute of what we have discussed and email to you to agree then send out. Would that be okay?" Alex said.

"Yes of course I would be very happy for all that I am about to say to be fully recorded as I feel transparency has been lacking" I said looking Alex straight in the eye. There was no reaction not even a flicker of recognition.

"I would like to start from the beginning of this situation. The removal of our service and government involvement in an internal grievance".

Alex interjected "I was not here when all that happened it isn't really relevant to me".

"The context is important as it is all connected so bear with me".

"I met with Laurie recently as she was told by COSCA to come and speak to me as part of her process of reflection for signing up to a malicious grievance with breaches of the equality act and client confidentiality. You should be aware that I am significantly disabled with lupus which has been life threatening and was at the time of the grievance. The writers of the grievance referred to my disability to say why do I need to be home based when I am able to have a social life. It was disgraceful. Laurie told me as part of that process that Bella had contacted her to come for a meeting not that she had contacted Bella and that she already knew about the grievance even though it had not yet been submitted. Laurie was then offered a job with the government as an incentive to take the grievance forward".

"Well clearly if that is true it doesn't sound very good" said Alex "but it is still not relevant to our meeting. My purpose for being here is to manage the transition to the new service which should be starting in September".

"It is relevant as the grievance was the reason why our funding was removed and for the government to remove funding due to a grievance that was malicious, full of gossip and hearsay and constituted disability harassment was a disgrace. The government denied having seen it, but the union confirmed under oath in court that they had. It had ridiculous things included like I paid people a day or so early and I awarded people a bonus because I was skint and needed the money. It said that I had said "if I am going down everyone else is going down with me". Other people there said that was nonsense."

Alex laughed at the ridiculous nature of the content. "I have certainly not seen it" she said.

"I should give it to you for bedtime reading you would have a laugh".

"I think life is too short for that one" she laughed.

"Sadly, it was serious as it breached the confidentiality of two survivors".

"Yes, that is of great concern" Alex said showing warmth in her eyes for a second.

"Then to make matters worse an investigation was forced through with one of the investigators not being independent. The Board wanted the care commission as fully independent but that was ignored. Instead, they recruited someone who had sexually harassed me".

At that time, I fought and fought against it but burst into tears with the sudden realisation hitting me that what had happened had been so disgraceful and bullying. I was flooded with vulnerability.

"Even worse on the first day he arrived I introduced him to the marketing officer. I said this is the person who gave me my first CEO job. His response was well we all make mistakes".

I was so upset at becoming emotional and so flustered at being emotional in a café that she started trying to pour more tea. Then she tried to put hot milk for the coffee in the tea. Alex tried to give me a glass of milk with a look of panic at not knowing what to do. I gathered myself together and took a deep breath.

"I'm sorry I didn't expect that. This whole situation and the past two years have been horrific".

"I can see that" Alex said.

"So, our funding was removed following being summoned to a meeting with Bella where our Chair felt she was treated appallingly and rudely and despite the Chair making it clear the breaches within the grievance. She denied that she had spoken to anyone involved but we discovered later that she had met people involved. There have been so many lies in this situation. The next thing was that you came to see the full team. We all liked you and we thought perhaps things would be different"

"Thank you," said Alex.

"Yes but you and I both know you then lied to me on the phone to say that conversation didn't take place. The lack of honesty in this situation has been awful. You told all staff the service would be the same. You told Christine that at a meeting as well. They were all confident that jobs would be safe and if we did not keep the service, they would all TUPE over".

Alex just nodded looking worried but making a point of saying nothing.

"Then when we met Jackie and Sue in August 2015 they said that the new service would not have any counsellor posts so staff could not TUPE over. We were shocked"

"Yes, I could see how that would have been of great concern" said Alex.

"The whole meeting was a disgrace. We had provided a report and Jackie and Sue said it was rubbish. We explained that it was a format Bella had given us and Jackie said that Bella didn't have a clue and she was much more experienced, and she would give us a proper report format".

"Oh, how nice" said Alex.

"They went on to describe the new service which gave us huge concern. This was not something that had ever been discussed in the consultations and had not been anything clients wanted. I had remembered that in the report by Theo in 2011 broker models had been seen as outdated with our model being one that was recommended not only for our service but a model of good practice for all survivor services. Jackie said clients should be provided with what they need not what they want or think they need. She explained that services would be provided through the NHS. I said that the NHS referred to us. Sue accused me of lying when I said that. She was aggressive in her manner. I said I would provide evidence and she grunted. The confrontational way they spoke to us concerned us. I said that one of the clients had been told he was untreatable. He said he was suicidal, and the NHS said, "well that is your choice." I said clients could die through this proposal. Jackie said, "well maybe it is necessary for clients to die for change to happen" I was shaking so much I looked at the cup I was holding and watched my hand trembling I was so shocked. I checked what she had said three times and she said yes only by chaos does change happen. I said, "well that is so unethical I will not tender on that basis."

"Did Jackie and Sue agree a minute of that meeting" Alex said.

"Of course, not but you can be clear I would not breach my ethics or affect my professional reputation by saying something that was untrue. Nor would Talia. We have been completely honest. I raised it with two government ministers, and I am really concerned that she still has her job when the chair of the inquiry was forced to resign over saying something not great but not on that scale. Two clients complained as she told a client had he not recovered yet when he said he was suicidal and her version was accepted over theirs".

"I can see how all of that was not great" said Alex but there is nothing I can say or do as that is not my area. I am just here to manage the transition."

"I feel you are here to manage me and there will be no transition we have told you that. It is the choice of clients what they do when our service ends."

"But even when the service ends you will be offering a service to some clients."

"Not on a unit cost basis. That would put the team on zero-hour contracts and that is not a fair system and very distressing for staff. Therefore, on that basis we will be ending the service."

"So, what will happen when clients transition then? Will you hand over their files?"

"Clients will not "transition" we keep saying that."

"So how will clients know about the new service?"

"We will of course tell them about the new service, but it will be their choice if they go. That is why transitioning is a terrible term. Clients were transitioned from one care home to another in childhood."

"So will you hand over the files?"

I was shocked at the insistence about the files being so obvious that was the main agenda.

"We have an agreement with clients when they come to us on confidentiality. We sign it and so do they. If a client wanted their file, we would give it to them, but it would then be their choice what to do with it. Some clients may want us to keep their file. This concerns us as again an agenda to seize the files. This was the same in the review. It was mostly about financial mismanagement, but all the reviewers wanted was the files. We were so concerned that it was to do with the paedophile rings we had been aware of with 367 clients in our files having been abused by multiple abusers. This could confirm what we were told off the record that the government wanted a record of all clients to assess the potential litigation when time bar is overturned, and the new service is a way of showing that damages were mitigated."

Alex looked worried "no of course that is not the case. Well, if your organisation will not be funded by us how will you receive your funding. Remember the service intellectual property is owned by the government".

"Well, no actually I disagree with that" I said "our lawyer said we would have a very good case to say the intellectual property is ours. The contract was put out as a grant application which I then developed a service from and submitted it. The fact that the other main organisation developed a totally different model evidences that the model was mine. I developed the name, the logo, the website, and the helpline as well as the model of work. Therefore, it is ours."

"Well, you need to send me evidence of that so our lawyers can look at it."

"I will send you what my lawyer allows" I said.

"Well perhaps that is the way forward. Rather than confirm the whole conversation I will email you actions like the intellectual property action as I already have your emails with your concerns."

"I am so happy for you to record all that I have said" I said "it needs to be recorded and dealt with. The Board wish to go to the anti-corruption body or the press to highlight these issues as they appear like corruption. They need to be investigated. Please confirm in writing by the end of the week that the service will be on this zero hour's basis so that we can manage endings with clients and notify staff. You may also want to remind David that he promised the service would continue but it would be funded by the new providers rather than the government."

"I can't do that by the end of the week" said Alex "I am going on holiday from Thursday, and it will be Jackie who would have to confirm this."

"We need an answer. It is not fair to clients or staff. The uncertainty is disturbing them. They didn't feel they were consulted. We have worked with over 1500 clients and in the consultation process only around five supported this model with it only even being discussed at the final meeting with only eighteen survivors present. I have the minutes of the consultations and it was not discussed. We were told it came in through postal consultations but none of our clients received postal invitations to comment. At a meeting with 50 survivors none of them wanted the new model in fact they were very angry about it."

"I was at a couple of the events" said Alex "Anyway how did that meeting you referred to come about?"

"Well, you will know then that only one or two clients were in favour of an approach like this."

Alex sighed and acknowledged that was the case.

"You know the meeting was us being transparent and informing clients that the service would be ending and a new service starting. Did you want us to keep them in the dark with no knowledge?"

Alex shrugged and nodded in a way to say no.

"I will take the objections to the model and the request for confirmation about the process of payments for clients to Jackie for a response but that is all I can do" Alex said.

"Well, when you speak to her please tell her I think her conduct and attitude to survivors is disgraceful and she should not keep her job. We are aware that she slated our organisation to senior prison staff and that she funded psychologists to compete with us even though there should not be duplicated funding and we hold the prison contract."

"Perhaps you could also remind David that around four years ago he called me to a meeting which two of my staff attended to question if I could still deliver the service with my health issues. Perhaps you could remind him that is a breach of the equality act."

"I know nothing about that. I can't comment" Alex said angrily.

"Regarding the issue of the reports and the very rude email from Vera in your department I informed the Board as the Company Secretary. The Board were very concerned and wanted to complain. The Board made it very clear that client information would not be individualised. To clarify we were asked to give information of a client's area, gender, and age. There will not be for example more than one 55 year old male client in Ayrshire so that client will be identifiable and the only way that would be okay if we did not give any more detail. If we were to give individual CORE scores that would then give further information that clients have not agreed to. This would be a breach. As you are well aware the Board were very clear they would not sanction that. We provided what we said we would provide. We will not accept any more bullying behaviour. Vera was aware I sat up all night writing the report and that it was a final version".

"I can't comment on the actions of Vera" Alex said.

"We feel we still need to pursue a complaint that we were misled in the tendering process" said I "we were told it would not recruit counsellors as I said earlier but now Jackie is saying it could provide counselling. She said the new organisation could refer to themselves but told us that support services would not be part of the contract. We were misled and I know the ombudsman can intervene in these matters as we were not allowed to previously pursue a complaint. It was clearly a prejudged process as we were told contractually to refer to the new provider prior to the tender even being released."

Alex became quite agitated "but the ombudsman couldn't even do anything."

"Yes they could make you start the whole process over again. What about the prejudged process."

"Well, there are very few specialist providers in the field so it wouldn't be unusual for that co-incidence."

"Oh, come on they are not specialists in the field. They are a mental health organisation not trauma specialists and they have very limited experience of providing services to survivors. They also rejected the model and said they wouldn't work with it.

Clients have been to them and complained they were not fit for purpose."

Alex sighed again aware that her prearranged excuses were not being accepted.

I said "I am not the only one very concerned about all this. I have many professional friends in the field who are very concerned. After the provider event we were all not happy with it and went for coffee afterwards. The event was supposed to take two hours but took one as it was in disarray and those presenting the new model were so nervous, they had to sit down. When we start questioning and pursuing this it will be a Tsunami as we all feel very strongly about it. We are passionate about the needs of survivors and the right support for them. In the government civil servants have no knowledge of their policy area but they make significant decisions. We are experts in the field with years of experience, but we were not asked. I know the survivors personally. I have worked with them and know them, and I won't accept them being sold out."

I felt myself ready to cry again so I stopped.

"You had better get to your next meeting" Alex said.

"I am aware you have managed me in this meeting" I said, "this situation cannot be managed it is too important."

"I realise you will all think I am crazy and over the top and I don't feel comfortable with that. Bella said I am defensive well people are generally defensive when they are being attacked."

"Fair point" Alex said "It goes both ways. We don't think you are crazy."

"I am sorry if I have seemed less than friendly" I said "I hold no animosity towards you as it is a business thing whereas I like you personally. However, this is an extremely important issue to ensure the best for survivors."

We stood outside awkwardly funding it hard to end the conversation positively and then we both walked off in opposite directions.

Mr Michaels

Over the years of working with people who had been abused in care there was a rather worrying person who would call repeatedly calling himself Mr Michaels. At first, he seemed angry and confrontational but more recently as me and my project manager Talia had been challenging the government publicly he seemed to be warming to us and trying to help. He would give instructions and then would always add that he was going to follow up to see if the instructions had been followed.

Worryingly he had discovered that I had called the local television news and that they were considering pursuing a story. It had always seemed almost surreal the level of information that was leaked throughout the survivor and survivor organisation community and very impressive. Mr Michaels asked me to explain what my worries were.

"The government are demanding we hand over the client files or at least provide individual client information. They have not agreed to that, and we can't do it, but we are being bullied and told we won't be funded if we don't".

"Do not hand over files" he said angrily "if you do you will be breaking the law and clients would have a case against you. They want you to do it so that they can then shut you down by doing something illegal."

"Or unethical" I said, "We won't."

"You need a lawyer to represent your clients. If they go to the inquiry, they would then be able to access legal advice free to them."

"But would the government be paying for it? Surely that is a risk as how could that be independent legal advice?"

I worried about what he was about to say but spoke anyway "if the new support fund mitigates the damages suffered by clients does that not mean they will then be unable to pursue legal redress? I am really worried they then won't be able to achieve justice. I am worried too that is why they want individual information from our files to see if clients became less ill and therefore entitled to less damages but in all reality the situation for any client can change from day to day. One day they could not be feeling suicidal but the next a memory could be triggered unexpectedly; something could happen like a bereavement and the client would be even more at risk. Support will be lifelong as the impact of the trauma will always be there even if we can keep people safe external circumstances can take over".

Mr Michaels paused and then spoke as if he did not hear what had been said "there have been several cases that we have highlighted. The scale of abuse in Scotland is huge and disgraceful. Look up the three articles I want to give you one about the abuse of children in a psychiatric hospital, having been put there for being badly behaved teenagers to be kept there for 45 years. Then look at a case of forced drugging and experimenting on children. There was another case about a paedophile ring being reported by a teacher, but his equipment was then seized by the police, and he was chased out of his job."

"Yes, and all of the former children should have justice" I said "all the government are worried about is the cost. I was thinking about £135 million."

"More like billions!"

"I don't know what to do" I said, "Our lawyer is now the law company who are representing the government for all their legal matters"?

"Find a good civil lawyer and ask them to go through the government for being retained to support your survivors."

He said "a lot has still to come out. The chair of the inquiry and the other panel member who resigned will be giving evidence to a committee where they will give their version of events What will come out will embarrass the government as it will be clear they interfered in the inquiry. What was that all about that trauma clinic writing to say that the chair had made inappropriate comments? Did you know her service put in a bid to provide the new support fund? It was worth 3.5 million. When it all comes out the government minister will have to fall on his sword. It will be October so sit tight."

"I can't believe she was removed for making allegedly inappropriate comments, but we reported to the Government minister and the health minister that Jackie said clients should die but she still has her job".

"She was torn apart at a meeting a week ago for being completely inept in her job. Just watch this space."

After the discussion I left the office and I felt unable to breathe. It was all so corrupt, and I felt panicked that underneath the surface there was so much horror and that the horror was being covered up rather than accept that so much wrong was done and do the right thing to give compensation and acknowledgement of the harm done. I decided to drive home on the motorway to drive fast and blast a CD but I ended up stuck in traffic for over an hour sitting dwelling on what I had been told. Any left innocence was finally gone. I sobbed for a second then swallowed it down. I put on the radio playing the song that had been the one that gave us courage throughout everything "Read All About It" by Emile Sande. The song had a line which referred to giving "our version of events". Over and over, we said it was time for the truth and for justice.

Media moments

I decided that something really had to be done and I emailed STV not thinking that anyone would return my email. I explained that the government wanted the client files and I explained that the service would potentially be ending which was causing great distress to clients. I received a call within ten minutes from a reporter. He explained that the news was not the best place to cover such a complicated story, but he said that if there was anything that developed to keep him in mind and update him. I later discovered that he was the chief reporter, and I was shocked.

Some weeks later I discovered that the issue with the registration with the new service and the issue with the files was potentially more serious. On thinking about what could be achieved from accessing the files I thought about the potential that the whole reason for a support fund which was "to put clients back to where they would have been if they hadn't been abused" I thought this could potentially avoid clients being able to access future damages through civil cases when the Prescription and Limitation Act was to be changed to drop the three-year restriction on bringing claims often called the Time bar. I emailed the reporter back to say could that be what it was but acknowledging I didn't really understand the law. I asked why spend salaries including one at £61,000 and to a total of over £400,000 when this was much higher cost than our service as a way of saving money.

The reporter called me back and I gave him the full story. He listened seeming shocked about the civil servant saying it was okay for clients to die and amazed at the level of salaries. He wasn't sure about the legal issue, but he said he would check. He decided to speak to a campaigner on abuse issues for many years and she expressed similar concerns. No answers were given to clarify the legal issues. He asked to speak to some clients and one agreed to talk to him.

Some weeks passed and then he came back to say he wanted to film. It was frightening but exciting that at last something may be done. The reporter explained he would have to show both sides and be balanced so I joked that they would portray me as mad. He said it would be more likely that they would try and say they had not asked for the files so it would be my word against theirs. He filmed in the office and then went to visit a client group where he stayed for over two hours. The clients liked him, and they were all full of hope. They wondered if anything would come of it.

The crazy week

I had been corresponding for weeks with the journalist from TV about the issues faced by the charity and the government trying to access the files. I had become convinced that the files were an ongoing obsession with the government so there had to be something major behind it. It could have been that the files contained information on abuse at the highest level which would cause anxiety or that the files would contain evidence that could support future civil cases. I had some memory of my previous law training including law of damages. I remembered that there was a requirement to mitigate damages if possible and to consider mitigated damages in any claim. I started to wonder if what was behind this was that the new service would keep records of people having improved lives which would mitigate damages and any future claims. I had asked the journalist to find out if that was indeed true. He had finally decided to run a story about the issue with the files. The week before he had filmed the group sessions talking to four of the survivors and he had filmed me speaking about my worries and concerns. At one point I cried in distress and desperation about what was happening but I was assured it was off camera. Over the previous week I had spoken to others in the survivor community about what was happening and they all had similar concerns about government officials.

The crazy week started with contact from the journalist to say he would be running the story on the Tuesday night. I was terrified as I did not know how it would be portrayed and I knew there would be a comment from the government that would attempt to discredit me or the organisation. The journalist phoned and texted all day on the Monday to finalise the story. On the Tuesday the whole day passed in a blur of nerves waiting to see what would happen. I left work and was driving home when the phone rang. It was the journalist saying that at 5.15 a call had finally come in from the government to say that they had not asked for any confidential information and that the charity had not engaged in the new service. I angrily said you have seen the emails you know that is not true. The journalist told me that another charity had tried to discredit ours saying that it was all about money.

I arrived home and I felt very apprehensive when turning on the television. It felt surreal as I watched one of the team taking a group with people I knew so well and watching myself on screen. The scene with me crying was there and I cringed with embarrassment worried about family and Chris seeing it. Even the awful comments by the other charity and the government felt surreal as they were about our charity. The world had not felt real for so long and now it felt even more bizarre. I cried as I watched the survivors speaking realising how much the service meant to them and feeling so useless that I couldn't fix things. I was terrified about what would happen next now that I had challenged the government suspecting it was not a wise thing to do. The phone rang and it was my mother and father-in-law. They were like my own parents they were always so supportive, and they gave their unreserved support to me for the action I was taking saying to keep going and be strong. For the rest of the night there were phone calls, Facebook messages and emails offering support with nothing negative at all. I received an email from a very senior person in the local authority offering support and I felt very humbled. The most important thing was that a survivor contacted me to ask to come for counselling as she realised, she could trust the service.

The next day I headed off to Ayrshire to visit another charity and the mobile rang constantly the whole way down. When I listened to the messages they were from journalists asking me to call back. One was asking for more information so I promised to email it as soon as I was back. The meeting was so positive with us all being of the same principles in our work and I managed to relax to some extent. On returning I was hit by many issues going on in the office about setting up a new service so was late in returning calls and sending emails. Finally, I managed to speak to all the journalists and deal with all the chaos in the office. I was due to go to an art exhibition with Chris that night and I had to insist to my workmates that I had to leave as they all wanted to speak to me. Just as I was leaving I was called into a meeting about the new service with one of the new staff who was sitting like a rabbit caught in the headlights as two of the other managers tried to work out her hours. It was becoming more and more unreal that the general office chaos was still going on as normal while there was massive interest externally. The office staff had been taking calls of support all day many with people saying thank you for maintaining trust. On the way to the art exhibition every inch of my body was sore as the lupus decided to respond to the hectic nature of events. We arrived and Chris's painting being in a prestigious Edinburgh venue made everything just feel even stranger. We raced around the gallery and then just headed back for home as I was just so sore. Chris asked me to go for a coffee and I snapped at him for not understanding my illness even though I knew it wasn't true and he was just trying to relax me. We went to Tesco on the way home as we hadn't eaten so we bought food and then on the way home the mobile rang again. All the way home I spoke to another survivor organisation. When I arrived home the home phone rang, and it was Ingrid wanting to go over again all that had happened. I fell into bed exhausted.

The next day I reviewed one of the articles which was very positive for the charity and I spoke to another journalist correcting all the inaccuracies in the government response. The lawyer emailed just highlighting the link. There had been concerns with the lawyer as his firm had been given a contract to work for the government. I made sure he knew about all the support we had been given. It had all been coming clearer that he had often seemed to be discouraging me from arguing with the government. The other article came online after lunch, and it was even better. The day was equally chaotic and the television journalist kept texting me to ask if everything was okay. On the way home I went into the pet shop to buy cat food and the cashier said "I saw you on TV. Good on you for what you are doing"

The customer next in the queue agreed and they both keep urging me to keep fighting. For people who knew nothing about abuse to give support felt fantastic and made me feel it was important to keep going. On returning home I checked my emails and there was one from the MSP with a letter from Government minister. The letter was rude and blunt telling me that Jackie had done nothing wrong and that I was to stop denigrating her and affecting vulnerable survivors. I was upset and angry but I felt that I would need to take time before responding. I went over to collect my grandson to take him for a walk and spent time playing with him to relax. I called Ingrid and we had a long rant about the injustice. At midnight Arianne called me crying uncontrollably as her partner had told her she was fat after they had been arguing. I rushed round to her flat, made sure she calmed down and told her partner that it was time he grew up and never to speak to Arianne like that again. I went back home and collapsed into bed.

I woke up at 5 o'clock in the morning with thoughts running in my head about how to reply to the government minister. I couldn't sleep so I decided to just go downstairs to write notes of what I was thinking. It became a three-page letter which seemed to just flow out of my mind as if it had been playing over in my dreams. At 6.30 Chris came downstairs and I read it to him. He said, "Oh my God that is the best thing you have written yet". He went to work and I called Ingrid and read it to her. Ingrid agreed with Chris that it was powerful. I realised it was now almost 9 and I rushed off to work. Not long after I arrived Mr Michaels called. He told the administrator that the government minister would be attending a meeting with survivors on Tuesday, and he would be critical of the charity. Mr Michaels said that they would be supportive of the charity but that the journalists would be there so the government minister may make a negative statement about us. I read him the letter I had written and he said I had to send it immediately to the journalists. I was terrified but he asked me to press send while on the phone so I did. Later I was having training to use my computer equipment hands free for my bad joints and I saw emails pop up from two journalists. I couldn't open them as the trainer was there and I spent the next hour almost doubled up with stomach pain needing to know what the emails said. The phone rang and it was Arianne crying hysterically to the extent that I could not understand what she was saying. Her partner came on the phone to say she was saying she couldn't cope. I said I would be coming straight home. The trainer was okay about me leaving to sort things out and I raced off after reading the emails which suggested pursuing a further story. When I arrived home, I went round to try and give support to Arianne. I went home and corresponded with the journalist offering to meet on Monday. I went back to see Arianne and we hugged and talked. I went back home again to burnt food as I had left it on when I left, and Ingrid called. She was on the phone for two hours.

The weekend was a way to wind down and I took my son Thomas and Arianne out for the day. We were driving off to the beach and we decided to go to the Sea Life Centre. We walked around, three adults amongst families with children looking at all the tanks and doing all the things they would have enjoyed as children. We went for lunch and we discussed the depression that Thomas and Arianne were dealing with in different ways. I felt again how surreal the week had been sitting in a restaurant surrounded by all types of marine life talking about the depression of my adult children while young children ran around us.

The plot thickens

On the Monday following the crazy week I had the meeting with the journalist. I was ill with an upset stomach all morning and was unsure if I would be able to go but the adrenaline and determination took over. I dressed in a flowery dress and strappy sandals trying to look professional but summery and not trying too hard. The image with journalists was important. Too professional and they wouldn't understand the passion of the work and too much like a flowery counsellor and there would be no respect. I always analysed how to dress as a way of easing the tension and nerves.

By the time I arrived at the offices of the newspaper I was calm, and I sat outside catching up on calls. The newspaper offices had a circular seat surrounding a statue and it felt peaceful sitting out in the sunshine. It was the first time in a while that I had been able to reflect during the chaotic working day. I looked at my pretty dress in the sunlight thinking of when I was younger, and all of this would feel like an unrealistic dream. I went inside and waited for the journalist. I had googled him, so I knew who he was when he came towards me. He suggested we go to a café to meet as the meeting rooms were not helpful which was surprising but I decided to agree anyway.

We walked through Glasgow and I broke the ice "I contacted you as Mr Michaels asked me to. I wrote the letter to the government minister and miraculously Mr Michaels called as he always seems to when something is happening. We all laugh about it in the office as he always knows our every move and he is so mysterious"

The journalist laughed "I know him, and he calls me too, sometimes several times a day but I always tell him that I can't do a story on cryptic messages. When I go into meetings with politicians and survivors I know he is probably there but he never identifies himself."

The conversation broke the ice slightly but we were both still a bit wary and the journalist took us into a café round the corner. He took us to a table next to a man who was sitting reading a newspaper. In my paranoia I thought it may be a set up to ensure that I could not back out of the story or change what I had said with the other man being a witness. I laughed to myself thinking maybe I am becoming a conspiracy theorist.

I started to speak about the complaint I had submitted to the government minister a year ago describing how we had been promised the project would continue but then Jackie came in with her colleague and became confrontational from the beginning.

"I felt that she took a confrontational attitude in a way to start off by making me feel off balance. Her colleague called me a liar as I said most of our referrals came from psychology."

"She actually called you a liar?"

"Yes, but I sent her the proof later and she only replied noted."

"Jackie told me she was developing this new broker service and referrals would be made mostly to the NHS, but I told her the NHS were not equipped to work with complex trauma. Most of our clients were rejected as untreatable as they had borderline personality disorder which I personally feel doesn't exist as it is a made-up condition. One of my clients said he was suicidal and was told that's your choice. I explained this and said the services were not there so clients would be at risk and could die. She said maybe it would be necessary for clients to die for change to happen. She also referred to a conversation she had with a survivor when he said he still felt suicidal and she asked was he not over it yet."

The reporter was horrified "but the head of the inquiry had to resign as it was made public that she made comments nowhere near as bad as that! I have heard so many complaints about Jackie her name comes up over and over again and she was the person who the previous chair said was interfering in the inquiry. Oops I shouldn't have told you that! But I could never find a story as no-one would go on the record, but this will now give me a chance".

I said "I am committing professional and organisational suicide by giving you this story but ethically it must be made public as she is destroying the trust and confidence of survivors. I feel it is due to power and control."

"But why do you think they are doing it?"

"It is one of two reasons. The first is the information we hold in our files. Some very senior people have been implicated. The other is that when survivors go for civil cases in the future their damages would be mitigated if the new service cured them."

"Do you not think it is purely financial and your service is just too expensive as it works with people for a long time?"

"Well, if that was the case why pay the head of the new service £61,000 and each of the POCs £36,000 up to six of them. With other administrative posts the cost before they even see a client would be around £500,000 and our service is only £200,000. I only earn £37,000 and I manage a service with 44 staff and 30 volunteers and I'm not paid to run the service so I have to work on it in my spare time working 60-hour weeks. I have refused a pay raise for ten years."

He wrote down the salary as if it was significant.

"So do you think short term work is not enough?"

"Can you imagine being taken away from home maybe because there was abuse at home or a bereavement to be placed in a strange place and then abused again often for years. It takes maybe even a year to build trust and then to work on the effects of the abuse. Cognitive Behavioural Therapy will not resolve the issues in twelve sessions."

"So, what is CBT and how does it work."

"Well imagine you couldn't walk outside as you had been assaulted in the street. I would work on you being able to be on the street and you would be able to do so again but we would not have worked on the assault so you would find another coping mechanism as we would have taken that one away. The next one could be more challenging like drinking or self-harm. We work with the issue that had caused the coping mechanism but not right away as if we go straight into the work then we can do harm rather than help someone".

"I get that" he said, "but still I think that is what the government want to promote and you are stopping them".

"I know I sound like a conspiracy theorist but speak to the Board as we are all of the same mind that something has to be done".

The journalist agreed to speak to the Board, the client who had made a complaint and Talia.

I returned home to call Eva from the Board who agreed to confirm they were backing me. I called the client and he was very excited that things were moving forwards. He had been such a fantastic campaigner and it felt so important that his actions were making a difference. He had an email from the news reporter to say he would still be pursuing the story further.

I then called Ingrid finally relaxing at about 9.30 in the evening when I begged Chris to go for ice cream. I reflected how each time more information came out. Soon all the pieces of the jigsaw would be in place.

Leading child abuse expert

After I had started raising awareness of childhood abuse publicly one of the main newspapers in Scotland ran a story calling me the "leading child abuse expert". My colleagues found it very amusing and they had a t-shirt printed for me saying "leading child abuse expert". I was proud of the first article as it challenged cognitive behavioural therapy as an appropriate approach to support survivors. Trauma affects the instinctive part of the brain so any therapy working with the pre-frontal cortex would not be effective. Dissociative or hyperarousal responses are a coping mechanism for trauma. To remove those coping mechanisms could be very dangerous if the trauma had not been dealt with. As the press started to notice I was willing to speak out I was asked for quotes for many newspaper and television pieces on child abuse. When the scandal of abuse in football was publicised, I was regularly on television news giving my views. I was asked to appear on a late-night programme to debate with a politician on the abuse in football and whether there should be a government inquiry. I felt the government should intervene and carry out a full investigation but they did not agree that they should.

I was regularly asked for quotes about whether the inquiry should be open to more than those abused in a care setting. Only 10% of those abused were abused in care. I was very open about my view that to uncover the scale of abuse, including organised abuse the inquiry should involve all areas where children are abused. I was soon quoted so many times on the topic of abuse that I was being recognised as an expert in the field. I was asked to the late-night programme asked me on again to debate a case where a trainee dentist had abused a six-year-old child but had been given a full discharge to enable him to pursue his career. I was very clear that I found the court decision appalling. The debate with a senior member of the legal establishment was heated. It ended up with many hits online.

I was so pleased to be able to raise awareness of abuse and the survivors I supported were thankful. However, suddenly I was not approached by the press for comment again. It was very confusing. One journalist told me they had been warned off and told that they would not receive quotes from senior politicians if I was used in stories. It was all very strange and confusing.

The child within

Gavin, one of the clients had asked me to accompany him to the inquiry. I accepted realising that it could be rather awkward as I had raised so many concerns about a new government model. On arriving it was a luxurious hotel room with tea, coffee, and shortbread on offer. It was bizarre with all the aspects of a conference in place, but it was held in a room which they had managed to ensure felt private and comfortable. They were wary of me being there but obviously keen to discover what I knew and what my plans were.

Gavin described the effect the abuse had on him throughout his life and the aspects such as shame, inability to trust, severe anxiety and attachment issues. I had heard about his life many times but somehow hearing it in this place where he was so vulnerable was harder. He described the night where he attempted suicide describing it in detail and I wanted to cry and give him a cuddle to make him feel safe. He ran outside and I followed him. We stood in the car park, and I held his arm guiding him to breathe deeply into his stomach to calm down his panic.

We went back inside, and he spoke passionately about how the government were going to take away his service which he said had saved his life and gave him back feeling human. He said he had never felt so valued and part of things. He spoke about how important it was for people to acknowledge him if they saw him out with the service as he had been through many situations where a professional would act like they didn't know him if they met in a shop or in the street.

He asked me to explain about the situation with the records and I spoke very strongly about the fact that no way would I pass over records so now, as clients had to be registered with the broker model to receive support, that many people would now not be able to have support as they would not want to. I spoke of my concerns that a record of support given would risk future compensation through civil action. I insisted all these aspects should be given formal written responses before any new service could move forwards.

The inquiry lawyer offered to have a meeting as soon as possible to further explore these issues. I was delighted as it seemed at last someone was listening. Gavin felt so excited afterwards that he had managed to achieve some actions that might improve things for all the clients. He was motivated to keep fighting for justice.

Sadly, the next day I received an email from the inquiry saying that a meeting would not be useful at this time and that I was just to supply a written submission. I was really upset and didn't know how I was going to tell Gavin they had been let down and misled again.

Gavin was really upset, and he told me to say that he had been there to witness what was said. He asked me to please come to his next meeting so that we could challenge it. I felt so sad that again the survivors of abuse were being lied to and let down.

The Justice Tree

Chris and I had a favourite place. Cumbernauld Park and Glen was a place we had both been going since childhood. The fields at the top were where Gregory's Girl was filmed. The forest below was magical. It was full of pine forests with streams running through them. The paths to walk along initially ran close to the stream and at one clearing there was a mysterious large piece of rock which was hollowed out. Many thought it was a wishing well. Chris and I would take coins with us on walks to throw into the stone wishing well. Slightly further along was a small bridge over the stream with a winding steep path up to the top of the glen.

In February 2014 two months before the grievance, Chris and I had gone for a walk to deal with the tension I was feeling about strange behaviour from Laurie, Isa, and Sadie. I had a sense many things were not right, but I couldn't find anything concrete to tackle. We walked down on a Saturday afternoon and the full forest was covered in snowdrops. We walked down the steep hill to the foot of the glen listening to the strange silence that can only be heard in winter. The trees were bent with knobbly branches waiting for new buds and leaves. We walked along to the part of the glen with the wishing well. The water was flowing fast following rain and it was far up the side of the rock structure. I threw a penny, and it landed successfully in the hollow of the rock. I wished for those who would harm me to please go away. I did not wish any harm to them only that they would not be able to cause me any problems.

We then climbed the steep hill to the top part of the glen where it looked over the massive expanse of Cumbernauld fields. We walked along the path and noticed a tree that was bent over surrounding snowdrops underneath it. It felt peaceful and beautiful and I thought this would be a good place and removed a small jar from my bag with a trowel. I had learned from studying the power of the universe that to put the names of your enemies in a screw top jar and bury the jar then the power of the enemies to cause harm would be stopped and they would go away. Chris found a spot where the snowdrops had a clearing, but they surrounded the area and he buried the jar.

Within days Isa had handed in her resignation. I was shocked at such a fast result. I joked with Chris that only two more to go having no idea the real result would be the grievance. Many times, afterwards when we returned to the glen I would speak out to say to the universe "I get that you are trying to teach me lessons but how about easing off a bit now". I realised that unintended consequences would always come from wishing for something always remembering to be careful what you wish for,

After the grievance we went to the glen most weekends to revisit the wishing well and the place where the jar was buried. We realised that we had watched the seasons passing for two long years. We watched the bluebells appear after the snowdrops. The forest was full of them and the whole place glowed with the purple blue haze. It was my favourite time with spring being rebirth and with the feeling that anything was possible. The summer would see a mass of greenery with wildflowers in amongst it. New ones would appear every year and we would comment that each year even some weeds would be stronger than others. During the second spring we found another area that somehow meant something. In a clearing of the massive pine trees in the depths of the pine forest was a tree that had fallen over but it was now lying across the clearing like a seat. In winter it had water gather like a shallow lake and I buried another jar to be covered by moss and pine needles beneath the flood and under what we then called the justice tree.

Each week we would return to the justice tree writing the word in the snow at winter and wishing for justice for the survivors and for us. Sometimes we would walk on to the historic dovecot that we remembered exploring as children and which had stood in the forest for centuries. The forest was the most magical place we could ever imagine, and we would joke that our weekly visits would reboot me to enable me to face the next week knowing that each week would have massive challenges but accepting them because there was always the return to beauty and peace at the weekends. Two days before Arianne lost her baby the glen was full of robins chasing us as we walked along and afterwards whenever we would think of the baby a robin would be there close to us and watching us.

It was by the escape into magic each week that we would survive the coldness and corruption that was all around to fit into the working life. It didn't fit with working for a charity that helped people and it all felt wrong. It felt so wrong that people who worked for the charity could create massive conflict through greed, prejudice, and ambition. The council and the government felt like a bad dream in the bubble of tranquillity that was the forest. It would soon be time for autumn and the beauty of the leaves becoming a mass of oranges and reds eventually falling and forming a carpet of beauty to walk over. I always feared the winter due to my health but the beauty of the entry into it and the peacefulness of winter in the glen made it feel comforting this time. I always had thought justice would come and two years later it felt strange that nothing was going right. My belief and faith was so strong that I could not conceive of it not turning out successfully.

As summer came in we decided to try a spell on the tree itself to make it more powerful. We took with us some spell powder from the Green Witch in Aberdour, paper to write on and a long handled lighter. We waited until there was nobody on the nearby path and I wrote a spell repeating what was in all my wish boxes. I realised I was asking for many resolutions but that they were things to put right what should never have happened. We were not asking to be wealthy or to be powerful we were only asking for justice and for all that had been so wrong to be equalised and resolved. For me it was very important for my reputation to be restored and even improved after the very public humiliation that I had suffered unjustly. I wished for the charity to be safe and for those who had been abused to find justice from those who were trying to destroy the organisation with sinister intent. Mostly I wished for good health and happiness for me and for all the family. We sprinkled the wish powder on the tree and burned the paper over the powder until it all became a small fire turning to ashes. We sprinkled the ashes beneath a pine tree and walked back to where the jar was buried to ask that those within could no longer cause harm.

As we walked back along the path from the tree, I was aware of footsteps behind us and I had a sense of a person following. Presuming it would be dog walkers I turned to look and caught a flash of the image of a woman following. I had a clear vision in my mind of a young woman in a grey box shaped jacket and a powder blue skirt. The style of the outfit was from the 40s. Each time I turned round the woman would be there, but she would then vanish making it appear that she was purely imagined. As I relaxed in the car returning home, I realised the vision had been my grandmother. It made me feel safe and protected.

The night of wishes

Chris and I came home from a night out at a 21st birthday party. During the day we had been through to the seaside new age shop as it was always a good way to feel relaxed and to find a way forward. We bought a small spell bag called an emergency wish spell. So that evening once we were settled and relaxed, we played some music and then set out the spell. It contained paper to write the wishes on, a small crystal, some incense grains, and some bay leaves. The sequence of the spell was to burn the incense and cleanse the crystal in the smoke and then write out the wishes. The final part was to write a wish on each of three bay leaves and burn them in a metal tray.

I focused hard on what I wanted to achieve. As with most times I wished restoring my reputation was the most important personal wish as was for my health to be improved. I always wished for funding to be restored to the charity and for the family to be healthy. The final wish was always justice. It was important never to wish harm to anyone. I always burned a candle, and the flame would add to the feeling of peace.

After completing the spell, I reflected on how many of the wishes had already come true and I thanked the universe for what had been gifted to us. I did not want to be greedy just security and for things to be right for my work. Helping survivors of abuse was so important I could never understand why things had gone so wrong and I begged the universe to put things right.

I realised that many people did not understand my beliefs thinking they were somehow wrong. I had always believed in the power of nature and the universe to out things right and to give positive outcomes if the wishes were for the right reasons. Going back to wishes and spells had always enabled me not to be led into wishing harm on those who had caused me hurt.

I sat again like I had done practically every weekend since the start of the troubles and watched the flickering candle flame as it burned brightly on the fireplace. I thought this was the time that it would happen and things would be right.

The darkest hours

I woke from a night of dark and awful dreams that were disjointed and seemed to make no sense. There was a man in amongst them who seemed like a giant with dark hair and almost black eyes and the feeling of him stayed in my mind. The dream passed over years in a number of places but the strongest memory was a town full of a mix of industrial wastelands, rows of council housing and countryside rambling away into hillsides that seemed to go on forever.

In the dreams I saw me bent over and in pain and shrinking in distress. I shrank into a tiny child who looked about four or five. I sat in the corner of a room in a house decorated in 70s patterns with a brown swirly carpet and orange and brown walls with large motifs in the wallpaper. The windows were open and the curtains blew into the room. Everyone was crying and the child looked scared and blank faced like someone who had already learned not to feel other than the feelings of anxiety. Everyone passed round a photograph of a beautiful woman with almost black wavy hair and beautiful round soulful dark eyes. A man who seemed to be around fifty held his daughter as they both wept inconsolable.

The child shrank further and disappeared and reappeared at around six years old locked in a dark cupboard. In the dream I took the form of the child feeling what she was feeling and experiencing. The cupboard was long and thin like a small room but with no windows and coat hooks along the wall. The child sat under the coats with the coat tails brushing her head as if the feeling gave her comfort in the darkness. The cupboard was so dark that the contents appeared to take on images like figures which terrified the child. The time passed so slowly until there was the sound of a man and woman speaking outside and then the door was opened by the giant man from the start of the dream. The man was the child's father.

The child was aware that her mother had returned, and she felt safe again but confused. She had screamed and cried when she knew her mother was leaving for her night class, but it made no difference. The child had found a lipstick on the floor of the bedroom and hid it as she felt it may upset her mother, but she was unsure why. I felt the confusion of the child and the fear of the darkness that had stayed but I knew there was more to face, and an intense nausea took over.

Time raced forward to another flat across the street from the first and I stood at a door afraid to open. I heard the sound of children laughing and opened the door. The man with the dark eyes was playing with two children. One was sallow skinned with dark hair and dark eyes and the other very pale with auburn hair and blue eyes. I was aware that the girls were sisters but so different. The man was playing with them by lying on the floor with his legs at an angle so that the children could balance on his lower legs and be held up. They were so excited at the game and fighting to be the one involved in the game. I became aware that the man held the touch on the girls a bit longer and a bit more intimate as time went on. The girls became quieter, and they looked anxious and embarrassed but still giggled as they felt they should.

The man told the dark-haired girl to sit up on his knee. He placed her hand on his crotch and touched her in a way that made tears run silently down her cheeks. The other little girl went into a room at the side but showing no reaction. I became aware that this game was one that had been played out many times. I was shocked at how much the girls wanted to trust the game and to believe that the man was not bad. The child crawled into the other room to join her sister. She climbed into a large toy box and sat with her knees to her chest silently rocking so that the box moved from side to side. She sat there until the room started to turn dark and cold and then she rocked the box forward until she fell out lying staring up at the darkness and the shadows as if they were ghosts coming to take her from the pain. None of it was real and from that day she shut herself off from feeling, learning to show only false feelings to the world.

Over the years the incidents became worse and more frightening. The most horrific always happened when she was ill but that was because that was when she had to be looked after by her father as her mother worked. It gave him the opportunity. The first serious incident was one day he took her to the dentist. She was put to sleep and the dentist removed eight milk teeth. She woke with blood pouring from her mouth and her father forcing himself upon her and pushing himself into her mouth. She was sick and blood poured all over her pillow. She screamed in terror not knowing if it was from the blood or from what was happening to her, but it all became confused in one memory.

On another day she had been at a party for a friend's birthday and had overeaten which made her sick. She did not make it to the bathroom and was sick in the hall. Her father was enraged in a way she had never seen him before, and he threw her across the hall before hitting her, making her hit the wall and then pushing her again. She was terrified by the onslaught and confused as her father had never hit her and had always spoken about his hatred of people who harmed children. Her mother was later to tell her that following that day it had been discovered that a bone in her chest had been damaged but that her father had said she fell off her bed.

She knew that her father was not like other fathers like the ones she had met through her friends. It was as if there were two different people. On the one hand he was loving and sweet and so much fun and then his eyes would turn black and expressionless, and the other side would appear. One night he was looking after the child and her sister, and they both had a stomach virus. He was trying to make them laugh to cheer them up but it was making them feel afraid that the laughter would make them sick or to have the runs and they begged him to stop at first laughing but gradually becoming nervous. As he saw the fear his eyes changed and he started to tickle them becoming more and more aggressive in the tickling until he was causing them to become ill. Both of the children spent the rest of their lives being terrified of being sick or having an upset stomach and were scared of having anyone around if they did become ill.

The incidents continued through the child's life until she turned 11. Her grandmother had come over from America to visit and the sleeping arrangements had to be changed to give her somewhere to sleep. The child slept on the couch in the sitting room and her father slept on the floor. The child lay tense and afraid and aware that he was lying naked under a blanket. She became aware of him making grunting noises and rhythmic movements and she felt uncomfortable and ashamed feeling like she should not be in the room. As if he became aware that she was not asleep he stood up and came over to the couch standing in front of her and making her touch his erection. She was deeply ashamed and afraid as he lay on top of her so that she couldn't breathe and felt smothered and crushed. She blanked out with the next thing she remembered going to her mother's room to say she was ill with a sore ear and could she sleep with her. Her mother gave her the bed and went into the sitting room and she lay all night with the pain that had become real in her ear. The next day she woke to the smell of pumpkin pie and blueberry muffins baked by her Gran. The smell made her feel nauseated and it disgusted her and from that day forward she could not cope with the smell of blueberries or pumpkin pie.

Some weeks after that day he appeared again at the house in a terrible state saying that the police were looking for him as a woman he had been involved with had reported him missing. The child realised that her mother had started a relationship with him again and that he was afraid that the police would contact her and his other woman would be exposed. He rolled about clutching his stomach and moaning in pain and begging for forgiveness. From that day on he was not allowed back into the house.

Years later the girls were sent to visit him at his home for a holiday. They were to be there a week. They sat in the car tense and silent travelling through. By now they were teenagers, but the usual teenage insolence was absent replaced by uneasy respectfulness. He had married again, and his young wife was beautiful and lovely to be around. She made the girls feel special and they thought she would make the holiday bearable. The house was large and spooky but with a beautiful garden with fruit bushes and large berries. Much of the garden needed large weeds removed and the girls helped feeling unexpectedly relaxed. Following an active and busy day he made them spaghetti with meatballs, showing them how to cook. Night fell and they were to sleep in the corner of the bedroom shared by their father and his wife in sleeping bags. The child lay tense as she heard the sounds of sex leading to the usual feelings of embarrassment and intense anxiety but now made worse as she felt the shame of her father's wife as she protested what was happening with the girls in the room. The day was spoiled.

The next day the child was sent on an errand with her father's friend from work Matt. The car was plush and like nothing she had seen before with a smart dashboard and all sorts of lights and dials. The car was a Rover, and the child knew this meant expensive. Matt began to ask her strange questions like if she had a boyfriend and when she said no "you must have, such a beautiful girl with such pretty eyes". He was an old man and it felt uncomfortable. He kept staring and she felt herself sweating and very scared. The rest of the journey was blanked out completely and the next memory was back home in the safety of her room.

As the child grew, she was always aware that there were parts of her life and memories missing and much of her life was spent in continuous anxiety and tension with days upon days of being bent over with stomach pain. For the rest of her life certain places or smells or even the way that people looked at her were enough to make her panic and run. I was disturbed at this view over a young life in its distress and torture and in the knowledge of who the child was.

The big lie

I sat on a Saturday afternoon watching the television and reading a magazine at the same time. Multi-tasking was not difficult as there was not much in the way of challenge in either medium and anyway the magazine I was reading was telling me that women were fabulous at multi-tasking.

The channels had a mass of repeats and reality programmes. I flicked through to try and find something bearable that would pass a rainy afternoon. I came across a day-to-day blow by blow account of a so-called celebrity and stuck with it for a moment or two. I thought why do we want to watch this? The woman fascinated me. Her eyes stared out of the screen with blankness that could only be attributed to a deep pain and yet she was living the life aspired to by hundreds of teenagers. Her body was distorted and adapted and almost every aspect of her personality was fabricated for the cameras.

It was disturbing to watch looking into another person's life but not a life. It felt voyeuristic and pretty sick to be part of creating a reality that wasn't real. I grasped the remote control and continued to browse. In small screen the woman continued with her performance shedding a few tears from empty eyes to satisfy the public desire for second hand emotion. I felt her pain should not be a public sport she needed real help.

Next was a DIY programme, renovating the house of someone who had recently been through a trauma in their life. A new kitchen was going to make it all better. The enthusiastic and empathetic team of people smiled for the cameras as they changed a disaster into a beautiful creation, and all was right with the world. I was not so sure of the green colour as I thought that would be sickly after a while but at least the woman can use her cooker when she is having her next bad day. I felt I can relate to this a bit. My credit cards show all the changes to my environment when I've had a bad time. I laughed as I thought we certainly fall for this one. Years of smart flowery designers making life all better stops us asking too many questions.

Life was created and designed through magazines, newspapers, and television. Now that there was the internet the propaganda was all around and unavoidable. I remembered being 17 and going into a garage and insisting that the magazines be removed from the top shelf showing women as bottoms thrust in the air or sections of bodies contorted into painful positions. I was laughed at, but the feeling stayed with me that women were shown as objects for sexual gratification and that young men were presented with unrealistic images of women.

Now there was a reality TV show for everything and the Jeremy Kyle show to make us all have the chance to laugh at and judge others on a daily basis. Reality TV in all its forms was to give us the opportunity to see the weaknesses and challenges in the lives of the new TV stars. Was it a way of making us feel superior, a desire for gossip to take away the daily drudge or a desperate need to find some understanding of the world through watching others play out the daily dances of relationships and desires. Twitter let us more and more into the lives of celebrities and the weaknesses they had were there for everyone to see and enjoy or they were fabricated to achieve the next huge headline. I thought about why we want to watch distress and why we want to find weaknesses in those we place on a pedestal. Was it to make us feel that they were like us and that therefore anyone could achieve fame and fortune?

Tension building

The weeks were becoming stranger. I decided for the fourth time to go for another job interview. I had been offered two jobs previously and turned them down. Katy had laughed when we spoke about it saying "Looking for jobs is your coping mechanism. It makes you feel it is okay to go through this madness as you have an escape route, and you keep checking out that it is there".

I realised that was true but in some ways this job felt different as it was something I could believe in as it was for dads to be more accepted as part of the lives of their children and it related to the situation Chris had been in when we met. I arrived in Edinburgh on a blistering hot day and had to rush around trying to find the building. With my usual chaotic and terrible planning, I had not thought to download a map or even spend any time finding where it was. After the old-fashioned way of asking people as I didn't know how to work my phone navigator I found the building and dashed in with perspiration making me feel very uncomfortable. The normal overheating was exacerbated by the menopause hot flushes that regularly hit unexpectedly. I felt flustered and uncomfortable while feeling slightly faint with the heat. I was given a test to do and I managed to gather myself before being taken into an extremely grand board room with glass windows to the floor and a glass table with four interviewers sitting around it. They all seemed really nice and enthusiastic, and I felt comfortable and I was direct and honest. I felt it had been positive and I was confused as I then felt conflicted about the job with how much my own job meant to me. When I arrived home a call came through and it was one of the panel offering me the job. My instinct made me accept which then led to panic and a night with no sleep.

The next two days seemed to be set up to make me doubt further. They were hectic, Katy was belligerent and moody and I felt very unwell much of the time. I had a letter insisting I make a written submission to the inquiry. On the Friday the craziness seemed to build further. I woke in the morning with the thought of finding an email which Theo sent where he was asked by the government to change a report that looked favourable for the charity to make it less positive. I was initially shocked as I couldn't find the folder named Theo but then shock changed to a strong feeling of unease as I realised that all emails relating to Theo had completely vanished. I called the IT company on arriving at work and called Chris to say how scared I was suddenly feeling. Straight after calling Chris, I received a call from the lawyer. He said, "I am just being nosy wanting to know what is happening?"

"Well, you know how hard we fought to not breach confidential information. We have to stick to our ethics no matter how much it makes the government hate us".

"Yes, but how have the other funders reacted?"

For goodness sake I thought he is trying to freak me out. "Fine actually in fact if anything very positive with a very senior person sending a message of support and wanting to help".

"But what about the charity regulator?"

I wanted to punch him through the phone for trying to worry me even more.

"Why would they be bothered our core values are openness, transparency and confidentiality and that is what we are keeping to"?

"How do the Board feel?"

I was now in a complete rage where it took a massive degree of restraint to stay relaxed and friendly.

"The Board wrote to the press to say they support my stance, so I am sure they are fine."

He seemed disappointed and I realised that meant the Government had probably reported me.

"Well, I am having to field a lot of journalists" I said.

"That is great that you are being so measured in your response and not being carried away."

I laughed thinking he must be either very stupid thinking I wouldn't realise he was double dealing or he knew that I knew and was playing the game as I was playing the game not letting him know that I knew.

Someone arrived at the door to meet Katy. It was a funder she had arranged to meet in Alloa, and the venue had been mixed up so I had to wing it and meet him for half an hour while Katy travelled over. It was stressful as I was aware he probably knew I had no clue what was going on. Katy arrived and I went into a meeting with a client and then another meeting with another client both of which were really emotional. The day made me realise why I loved my job. It made my decision so much harder. I wrote the report for the inquiry and then continued writing it into the night to be able to send it as soon as possible.

The big reveal

I was completely exhausted. On the Sunday night the alarm company called at 12.30 to say the alarm had gone off. Chris and I went through to the office to investigate. There was no evidence of anyone having tried to break in but there were some signs that someone may have been there. We returned home and there was another call at 3 a.m. We drove through feeling awful and this time we noticed that the security light was on. When we walked up to the door, I heard a noise at the side of the building but we just reset the alarm and went home rather than investigate as we were both tired and a bit afraid.

The next day I contacted the IT company regarding the missing email folder. They said that it was very possible that my email had been hacked and they reset my password. Matters were feeling even more sinister. After work I decided to try and have a nap, but an email came through for a survivor organisation with an attachment showing the front page of the newspaper. I couldn't see the small text but I could read enough to see that it said a civil servant was accused of saying clients should die and I saw my name and Talia's. My heart speeded up and I felt nauseated. A couple of hours later the full article was available online and I felt shocked and afraid. It mentioned my complaint and named the civil servant. However, when I read on it was clear that other complaints had been made from other organisations and a survivor. I was even more shocked that none of the complaints had been followed up.

"She must be untouchable" Chris said, "she is acting for someone higher up and they are protecting her as she is carrying out their troubleshooting and was picked because she really doesn't care!"

"She will really be out to get me now" I said, "at least the Board wrote to confirm they asked me to contact the press or I would have been personally sued!"

The article was posted on Facebook by one of the team and those who were still awake reacted to it by saying that it had to be done to ensure justice for survivors.

The next day I was still exhausted with the impact from the alarm call out and the other survivor group called twice being on the phone for over an hour each time. He was really happy it had been progressed and he said that he had been told by the journalist it would be fully investigated. After work I took my grandson to give Arianne a break and he cried for two hours only stopping when I danced with him on my hip. After I took him home Arianne called in a panic because he wasn't breathing normally. Chris took them to hospital, and they said that he was trying out his breathing for fun. We were all relieved and they thought he was a little character. On the way home in the car they called me and I was so happy hearing him singing the way a five-month-old baby can along to the car radio.

The next day I was looking for the article and I saw that there was another one printed. It confirmed that the government were going to investigate the civil servant fully. I wanted to feel triumphant but I couldn't with the knowledge of how I felt during the grievance. I knew it was necessary and I was thankful it was moving forward but it felt uncomfortable. I knew the civil servant would have gone on to cause so much more damage to survivors and survivor agencies if she had not been stopped. I had calls all day wanting to talk about the article. The television journalist emailed to say the government minister had agreed to an interview the next day. I was excited and scared all at once. Ingrid called and she was very excited that the civil servant was being exposed due to her interference in the prison project. One of the other campaigning organisations who had also exposed things the civil servant said called to speak to me. He said that there had been all sorts of cover ups over the years with the government meeting with the establishments who had abused children in a friendly and collusive way. I noticed that the phone had the same strange echo as it always did when I spoke to Ingrid. As I sat with my head in my hands reflecting on how it had all ended up so uncomfortable and corrupt an email came through. It was formally offering me the other job. I was so confused. The job was more money, so much easier and home based much of the time. I emailed back saying that if I could stay one day in my current role I would accept. It felt frightening and exciting, but I was so exhausted I could barely decide which had priority.

On the Thursday I received an email from the journalist saying that the government minister had been negative and insistent that the government had done nothing wrong. He denied they had tried to access the files, said that we had to find our own funding and said that he would not help in any way. I had watched him earlier over another controversial story and he was such an ineffectual dull person who just looked like one of the civil servant drones. The stories about the government all seemed to be about trying to keep records on everyone in the country. I reflected on why we had become a society where we accepted being on record somewhere for so many aspects of life with even families being risk assessed as a matter of course. It was becoming frightening. Another one of the survivor organisations called to say that there were to be events for survivors of abuse to let them know about the new support fund but they had to register to attend, yet another attempt to have a record of them. She said that the party were primed to ask questions about what investigation would be taking place into everything. That night I went to my drama group with Arianne and Dan while Chris looked after my grandson and while I was there a client called hysterical and frightened as she was impacted by the memories of her abuse. I thought that I was continually receiving signs of why fighting for the project was so important.

On the Friday I received a text from the journalist asking to come at 10.30 to film for the show that evening. I was really nervous and my stomach felt uneasy and nauseous as I waited. One of the clients was asked to come through too. It felt surreal as I watched the journalist and his cameraman walk up the path. The journalist was warm and supportive, and the cameraman showed a lot of empathy about the plight. I felt more relaxed and trusting. I said "I think because we exposed what the civil servant said about clients dying the government minister hates us now as she was a friend of his. We had to do it, but we really didn't want her named. Unfortunately, if she hadn't been named nothing would have been done so in a way it was necessary. We just didn't want to destroy her as her directive is probably from further up."

"I don't know how he may have reacted if you didn't do that. Maybe you should have waited?"

"We couldn't she was destroying services for survivors and hurting survivors so many times. Something had to be done."

He looked at me quizzically as if he wasn't sure, but he then organised everything for the interview.

He asked me if the service would survive after the end of September and I said we just didn't know as we couldn't hand over the files and nobody had contacted us to say how to access the new fund. The journalist explained that the government minister had said 40 other organisations had given over information, but I knew that wasn't true. He acknowledged that was probably the case but without evidence he couldn't say that.

At the end of the interview the client arrived and we hugged. I could tell he was nervous and the affinity between us in our role of campaigning had given us a close friendship over the years. I wanted to protect him but he was determined to go ahead and save the service. He went outside with the journalist to be filmed in the park across the road. When they arrived back I spoke again about the abuse rings in the area and the journalist agreed to come back at a later date to speak to the Board.

I arrived home and sat for the two hours until the news was to be on with nerves and stomach pain. I ate my meal and instantly felt sick. When it came on, I felt reassured that the government minister had reiterated that they did not want confidential information so we could use that as future confirmation and he also publicly said we could access the new fund.

Arianne wanted to go and pick up her partner as it was a very wet and windy night so we headed off and went shopping to buy new clothes for my grandson while we waited. I relaxed a bit watching him smile and laugh. When I arrived home, I had a lot of thought about what was behind it all as I often did. On the morning before the journalist arrived I had a call from a solicitor who knew the person who had resigned from the inquiry. I was told that the reason she had felt the government was interfering in the inquiry was that it was solicitors who were conducting the interviews and that each statement was to be reviewed by seven civil servants. I had felt that this meant if anything came out of the inquiry that could impact negatively on the government then it could be buried and therefore it was not ethical. It also meant that costs of further litigation could be assessed. I was aware that I had been given information to be leaked and I felt very honoured to be trusted. I found other information online about potential costs of civil litigation and a Bill to consider them. There was discussion in the Bill about capping future damages. I reflected again how all of this was making people so anxious that a charity of the size of ours would hold most of the information in Scotland hence why it would be better for Government and the Local Authority if we didn't exist, and everyone could be part of a registration process. It was all so incredibly at best protectionist and at worst corrupt. I was glad to be moving away from it all but always resolved to fight for the clients from the background.

Closure

The weekend after the past crazy weeks started in the usual way with me feeling unwell as my body processed the stress. We went to play golf anyway as a way of unwinding on the small nine-hole par three golf course locally. Golf was our release and as we took in the fresh air, we felt more relaxed. As usual I ranted my way round the golf course saying that I just couldn't cope anymore with all that had happened. When we arrived home Ingrid called me, and we spoke for an hour.

Sundays had always been the worst as the anticipation of the week to come would often cause a complete meltdown. We went to golf again, this time at Stirling University. We looked over the beauty of the University landscape admiring the lake with swans and ducks relaxing in the sunshine. Afterwards we decided to go to the local garden centre as Chris was part of an art association who exhibited paintings there. As we walked in I noticed Aggie sitting with her husband. I felt shaky and angry and they looked nervous when they noticed me. We went to sit at a table walking past them to go to it. I sat facing them and kept my eyes on them continuously. They sat eating and appeared not to notice we were there, but they did not even speak to one another. After we had eaten Chris and I went out into the plant area and we almost bumped into Aggie and her husband. The situation felt empowering as we could have confronted them but being there and not reacting felt better.

Later we drove to Cumbernauld, and we went for a walk into the glen where I threw a coin into the wishing well to ask for good health, no nasty illnesses and for my new job to be happy and successful. I asked for a sign that my new job was my future and whether it was right to move on and we saw a sticker on a noticeboard at the start of the fields that said enough is enough and NOW. We laughed at how clear that would be as a message. We said thank you for all that had been resolved.

Afterwards we went to the street where I had grown up as a young child, somewhere I was rarely able to go to. In the dim light of dusk, it looked even more run down and depressing with the decaying flats and streets that were damaged. A wall of the flats had been painted with three doves but in some ways it just made the surrounding area look even more in need of regeneration. As I sat in the car I remembered my childhood where it felt like nothing would ever be safe. Playing in the neighbourhood would have the potential of being threatened by other children one of whom often carried a knife. I remembered that a neighbour had choked to death after a massive drinking session. I had looked after the child of another while her partner beat her even though we were only children too. I looked at the flats where I had lived with the second one having sheets on the window instead of curtains. I said out loud "you can't harm me anymore. I won't let you define me. I'm moving on". As we drove home, and it turned to night I felt at peace.

Chaos continues

In the early hours of the morning, I was contacted by one of the survivor organisations. Sue one of the civil servants who we had complained about added me and the survivor organisation on Twitter. The other one Jackie had liked a status about the STV news story. Clearly, they were not trying to be friendly so it felt threatening to the survivor organisation and I agreed. On Jackie's page was a photograph of her with the government minister standing close and smiling that she had retweeted. I reflected on the fact that he was investigating someone who was clearly a friend. It was worse by each passing day. I wrote to the MSP with a screen shot of the page asking him to investigate it and Chris sent him and the government minister a private message on Twitter to ask for them to stop harassing his wife. We didn't go to bed until after 2 a.m. so we were exhausted in the morning. I went home from work in the morning to rest and within five minutes Ingrid called. Ingrid was at her best when investigating and trying to find answers for why all the issues were happening. We discussed the fact that all the issues had started when Ingrid had reported the serious international abuse case to intel in the prison. We were talking about how one of our contacts had been alleged to be part of organised abuse by a client in the prison. His connections to the church had linked him with a priest in the jail that the prisoners spoke openly of him as a paedophile. It was known that the priest then had connections to an MSP. After that report and Ingrid making the prisons, aware everything had started going wrong. We had thought it was the original client's case but now we thought this had started it. As we spoke an email from the contact came in which was a huge shock as he never emailed anyone, and he had disappeared for months not attending any meetings and saying he may resign his job. We laughed and discussed again how obvious it was that the phones were being bugged. We decided to contact the public protection unit to set up a meeting and see if they could find out any clues and the person to contact that was senior enough in the police.

After Ingrid went away to call the PPU I received a call from a well-known radio programme who wanted to cover the story about the removal of time bar on civil cases. She had to find a survivor as a case study, and I texted all the staff and called my client. He said he couldn't as it may compromise his case. As I spoke to him the mobile rang constantly. It was Arianne in a panic as her tooth had broken off. While she was pregnant, she had been sick constantly and had been unable to brush her teeth through nausea and her tooth had been ruined. It was her front tooth, so Arianne was in a terrible state. We rushed off to the dentist and we were there for over an hour. When we arrived back home there was another call this time from a solicitor's office. It was their press officer and he offered to act as a press officer for the charity too. It seemed to be free of charge which felt very strange. I felt suspicious as I always did about any new contact. He had previously worked with the radio journalist in the BBC, and he said he was a good person.

The next day the radio reporter arrived for the meeting. He was very friendly, and he seemed very empathetic but I had a strange sense from him. Whenever there was a strong connection to abuse I would always have the same deep uncomfortable nausea and pain. I felt shame and distress from him, and he described previous bullying in the BBC. It was as if he needed to talk about it but then I felt nervous as I opened up to him about the difficulties we had with the government and worries about abuse at very high levels and I knew that nothing was off the record with journalists. Trudi said to me afterwards "well what we know about is true if he uses it then maybe it isn't a bad thing."

The strange sense continued when I arrived home as texts and then a call came in from the press officer to ask how the meeting had been with the radio journalist. I texted to say it was good and he seemed pleased. The local newspaper contacted us too to ask for a story about the files. I asked the press officer what to do and he said to speak to them. I called Ingrid and we discussed how strange it all felt. I said I had a sense that perhaps the radio journalist had been in the BBC when the abuse ring at

Westminster was uncovered and the bullying he suffered may have been to do with what he knew about it. The press officer had worked with him and perhaps they were trying to carry out investigative journalism as a way of pursuing further what they had been blocked with.

The next day a meeting was held with survivors who were due to meet the council to ask for funding to be restored to the charity. They were very angry about the funding being removed and it was clear the subsequent meeting would be challenging as the council did not respond well to strong feelings and opinions. I started to feel very ill and nauseous, so I returned home coming back later after a sleep to talk to Katy and Trudi.

Later an email came in from the government from a civil servant who had been recruited to carry out an investigation into Jackie and her inappropriate comments. It was sent to all complaining parties and one of the other survivor groups called to see if I had received a letter too.

"I replied to them to say the Board would have to decide the way forward. I emailed it to them for comment."

"You should make sure you have legal support to give evidence. We are going to do it."

The next day I realised that Talia had not been contacted to make a statement. Much of it all seemed like a cover up. I later discovered Gavin had not been contacted either. I called a solicitor recommended by one of the other survivor organisations and decided this situation needed protection.

On the Friday morning Trudi and three of the survivors Rena, Simon and Gavin all met me outside the council buildings for the meeting. I didn't have enough money for the parking meter so I ran over to them as they stood waiting and asked for a loan of thirty pence thinking this is so inappropriate, but I was in my usual unprepared chaos. We stood talking outside as we waited for Simon to arrive. Rena was in a great deal of pain due to suffering from an auto immune serious condition but she had been determined to be there. Gavin was nervous but determined too. Simon arrived and it was obvious he was really angry but he promised to try to stay calm. We went inside and we were made to wait for ten minutes past the time, an old psychological trick to increase the nerves and the power dynamic. The room was miles along a corridor and I knew Irene would be suffering but she was determined to keep going. In the room were Lindsay the policy officer, Tom the leader of the council, Laura the local councillor and Brian the new head of social work. They all sat around a large luxury committee table with plush chairs and overblown decorative mouldings all around the room. It smelled musty and the atmosphere was claustrophobic.

They all introduced themselves and Rena said "there goes the first question on the list. We were going to ask your credentials".

Trudi and I said we were not there to speak but to support the survivors, but I realised this was not an easy task for me.

Tom was a large blustery man but strangely he was the one who listened the most. Lindsay had pursed lips like there was a bad smell under her nose at all times. There was no animation and she sat bolt upright like her spine could not move and she was fixed in place. Laura looked like she didn't know what expression to have until Rena spoke and said "you don't remember me do you Laura? We grew up in the same area and there were plenty of paedophiles round about where we grew up." Laura looked shocked for a second but as an experienced politician she soon recovered. Rena went on to explain what the charity had meant to her. She described the abuse she experienced and asked what would have happened if the charity had not been there. She asked what was happening to the money it should have had. Gavin then spoke. He had an article about the abuse he had suffered as a child. He described how his parents had been jailed but he was then put back to them by the state where he was abused again. He was eloquent and passionate saying that without the charity he would have been dead. He said he did not want to trust more than one worker and that the charity was what he wanted and needed. He said that the choice should not be taken away from him.

"But there are other charities" Lindsay said.

"If you mean Women's Aid, I am not a battered woman" said Rena "my husband would be horrified if I went to Women's Aid. What would his friends think?"

"The mental health charity is no good to me" Simon said, "I tried there but I had to wait for weeks and then it didn't help me."

"The mental health charity told me to go to this charity" Gavin said.

"Tell me do you think that the staff are manipulating me" Gavin said.

They all shook their heads but looked embarrassed as if that had been discussed.

"Well, I know the government said that and it disgusts me" he said. "I have my own choices and decisions and that is something the charity have given me. Come to one of my counselling sessions Tom and see for yourself how much the counselling can help."

"I would welcome that" he said while looking like that was the last thing he would welcome.

Simon asked why the charity were being asked to give over records, but Tom denied that was the case and Brian confirmed they did not need records, and both denied seeing any of the press saying that was about the government not them. Simon asked, "why are you even carrying out this process to retender when there is a wonderful charity that has been there for 22 years".

"Award winning," said Gavin

"We were given a commissioning process by the government to follow about a partnership approach" Lindsay said.

"So, are you saying the government told the Council to do this?" I said.

Brian blustered and mumbled something that sounded like no.

"The problem with your so-called partnership approach is that it took me years to speak to one charity" said Gavin "I get what I need from one charity I don't want to go all over the place to have my needs met. You never spoke to us to ask what we wanted you just decided for us, and the government decided for us. The approaches you are all using of taking away what supports and helps us will cause deaths. People will die."

Simon asked Lindsay is she had children and when she nodded asked had they been abused. She put her head down and said, "I wouldn't answer that question."

"Well, I was at the charity and a young boy came in. I knew that boy who was tiny had been abused. Come to the charity and meet the children. You won't be sitting so coldly then."

None of them seemed able to make eye contact but not as they felt shame at the prospect. It was in a way that if they did not show compassion, they would look wrong but if they did it would look false.

Simon went on to explain his situation where he had been trying to highlight the risks of the person who abused him still being a janitor for years and now that he was living on school grounds. He explained a horrible meeting he had attended with one of the senior staff in education "when we arrived, I introduced herself and he said we fund you, stopped in his tracks turned round looked at her and said or do we."

Lindsay shuffled in her seat looking very uncomfortable and she said, "we can't comment on other council officials".

"Well comment on why you are taking away my service!" he shouted banging on the table "I was abused by you people employing paedophiles then there wasn't enough to convict him because it was my word against his and then he went back to work in schools. When I tried to tell others by warning them online, I was arrested, and I spoke to my worker at 10 pm the night before court and she came to court to support me and my family. How many of your so-called charities would do that for me. None of them!"

Brian then went on to say well we were unable to restore referrals to the charity because they would not let us see their client information.

Simon became incredibly irate "you just said you didn't want records, you said that didn't he say that?" looking at everyone "this is a disgrace you say you don't want our records then you just said you took the funding away because you wanted records. They did the right thing and didn't give you them, but you then penalised the charity."

"It was more than that there were internal issues" said Brian smugly thinking he was imparting something they didn't know "all we wanted was evaluation data not the files."

"If you mean the grievance it was proven to be malicious" I said "and with reference to the information you wanted we gave over masses of evaluation information and our funding officer was always happy with it. I have emails, a reference from her, masses of evidence that what you are saying is lies. They wanted into our case notes which could identify clients. We said no and our funding was removed because we said no!"

"I think we need to speak about this afterwards" he said

"Yes, I apologise for going into details at this meeting. But we do need to meet as I need to show this evidence to someone."

Trudi spoke emotionally and almost in tears "we need to know what is happening to our funding this year. The funding was agreed in the budget, but we are having to see people out of our own funds as we can't turn anyone away and we won't. You need to let us know soon what is happening."

Tom agreed that would be investigated urgently.

Lindsay tried to imply the mental health organisation could pick up referrals.

Simon was apoplectic with rage "they wanted to charge me £35 a session or I would have to wait over a year. They didn't offer what I needed."

"Yes, they only offer CBT" said Gavin "CBT is not what I need it only puts a plaster on my issues it makes me feel okay for a while but then I will feel worse again as it doesn't deal with the underlying issues."

"Yes CBT was recognised by the review process not to be effective" I said, "the commissioning process came up with our model as the best way forward."

"It wasn't your service" Lindsay said.

"No, I said it was our model and it was."

"Well people objected which is why it was changed to a tender process."

"We will be watching to ensure it keeps the principles of the consultation" I said.

"We want to be part of the consultation" Gavin said, "talk to us to see what we need".

Lindsay looked furious and she tried to deflect the request.

"I think that could be a good way forward Lindsay" Tom said.

She tried to deflect it again, but it was agreed that she should meet them as a way forward.

When the meeting was ending Rena invited Laura to come down to the charity and she said she would make cake for her. Laura was friendly and agreed to do so. Tom discovered from Simon that one of the local opposition counsellors had suggested he should not make waves as he was becoming too high profile. He was keen to follow it up especially as the local MSP had agreed that he should drop it. I shook his hand and thanked him for the opportunity to meet. He apologised it had taken so long and he held back to talk further to Simon.

We all spoke outside about how strange it had been that the elected members seemed to be approachable but the officials very combative and defensive. It appeared that they had misled elected members and they had in some ways been found out, but it may have been a very clever deflection and smokescreen.

When back in the office I was looking at my email screen and two of the folders 'In care' and 'law' moved out of the alphabetic order which should not have been possible. I took a print of the screen feeling very concerned that the hacking was still continuing with the awareness that the folders that had been affected meant there was a strong possibility it was the government doing it.

That night I spoke to Eva from the Board. Eva had been the Board member who really wanted matters publicised in the press and she said it would be important to keep the momentum going. We agreed to meet for a meal the following Tuesday to plan a way forward and we decided to appoint a new lawyer as our lawyer worked for the government and so it was a conflict of interest. We agreed there needed to be an integrated approach with all the survivor organisations or we would never be able to change things.

Return to the Justice Tree

Late on a Sunday evening Chris and I returned to the Justice tree. We sat staring at the light still coming through the gaps in the massive pine trees as it was changing to dusk and the light gradually was fading. It felt like the pines were whispering as the wind whistled through them. In the evening quiet the steam could be heard as could the birds settling down for the night. We felt peaceful and content at the end and beginning of the story and the strange way the wishes were fulfilled or starting. I said "It was predestined Chris. This was my life plan. All of It. What happened to me as a child gave me the drive to make a difference to others. If I had not been ill, I may have pursued a more traditional career or may even have purely been an accountant. If I had not been through the terrible relationships, I may not have gained the strength I needed to fight. Without the grievance I would not have needed personal justice and I would have still been a person who was afraid of what other people thought. My pride was shattered so I could fight with nothing to lose. Without you being by my side giving me the confidence and keeping me standing every time I wanted to give up, I would have run away long ago. Every time we wanted to stop the signs and symbols in our lives would bring us back to where we needed to be. The morning before the week where it all came right, I had cried and thought all was lost. I went to tidy the bedroom as I needed to occupy myself to escape from my fears. I found three things that made a difference. Last Christmas you gave me a tiny bottle full of glitter that had an angel below the cork with a small card tied on it that said Guardian Angel. Next to it was a card that Trudi had given me that contained a necklace that represented strength. On the card it said, "you are the strongest person I know". The final thing was a 50th birthday card with a loving message. That day was the day we went to two art exhibitions where we saw magical paintings and the representation of the beauty of nature. I had asked for a sign and I was given many. So now that I realise what it was all for I can feel free and the survivors who felt like my children as they came into my mind down here in the glen can now grow as I can too. It all had a path and a purpose like the paths in this forest and all paths led us to justice. However, I know this is just the first stage and we have a long way to go. I am going to stay in my job and continue to fight"

Chris stroked my hair and smiled.

The space In between

I had been thrown into the world of campaigning and life was becoming more surreal by the day. Chris found driftwood on the beach, and he sneaked away to paint on it not giving away his plan. He had a painting which showed a chaotic background with a path through the forest apparent through the chaos. The name of the painting had been the space in between. I left for work the next day and there was the driftwood covered in sparkles and glitter with 'the space in between' written on it. Chris explained later that our new home was the space in between of the crazy chaos that life had become. The path of the justice tree still had many twists and turns to travel through before it would reach its end and to remain calm within it all we needed the time to be still.

My story was the story of a world where the horrors of child abuse and exploitation were hidden behind the noise of false prophets and reality television. Each day was full of more and more noise and clamour and image after image of distress with the next social media post of dancing kittens popping up to confuse the brain. The noise would intensify and build to a deafening scream until those listening would cover their ears and hide away. Everyone became an open book, but the pages were hidden from view.

The enemies started to look like supporters and enablers and those who had journeyed along with us on the previous paths were suddenly appearing to lace the path with barbed wire. It was confusing and cloying leading to the feeling of being on a rollercoaster that never stopped.

On the surface it looked like all the options I campaigned for in the past were coming to fruition. That was on the surface and part of the smokescreen. The exploitation was deeper and more insidious than it had ever been. In the past the lack of care had been obvious and explicit. Through the days of exposure of what had been wrong structures were being created to give an appearance of putting things right.

I was starting to put together all the pieces of the jigsaw and I was not happy with the image that was emerging. Abstract confusion was overtaking the learning from the first phase of the battle.

In the space in between, reality was emerging from the abstract. In the forest of the justice tree the wishing well had been turned upside down but the streams continued to flow around it. Life was moving forward despite the lack of hope, and I was sure that finally justice would find a way.

It was a start of a new chapter for me. I now knew why I was drawn to my field of work and had a sense of where it was leading me. It was time to continue the battle and to investigate the information I had gathered over the previous four years. The answers were partly visible but mostly hidden and I realised that I would have to start another long journey to bring them into the light.

Stalling

After Christmas was over and on the return to work everything felt very flat. It was as if all the activity had risen to a crescendo and then splattered to the ground and dispersed leaving a feeling of emptiness. In one respect I was happy to not be in the thick of campaigning with all the stress that brought but on the other it felt like the fight for justice that had been building was stopped never to be continued. The charity was setting up a new service so I was active in my role in a way it would have been without all the chaos. While it felt very good from the perspective of release of stress and ability to sleep, I had an overwhelming feeling that it was all still being covered up.

I had been having regular contact by a new law firm. The government were discussing abolishing the time bar which was the three-year restriction for civil cases to be brought. The law firm were a personal injury firm. They offered the organisation the press officer who had originally contacted us and said we could have free legal services. I kept wondering what the catch was. I had a meeting with the lawyer where I felt the clawing sickness I would always feel when wary of someone. Afterwards I confronted the lawyer saying that I felt I could not trust him. He said he would put me in touch with some valuable contacts to put my concerns to rest.

The lawyers had arranged a meeting with the head of the Professional Footballers Association. I felt uneasy that a meeting to look for a contract to help footballers who had been abused felt a bit uncomfortable and exploitative but on the other hand it would give them the help they needed not using a clinical psychology model that would mean the fact that they were a survivor would be on their medical records. The meeting was very positive and the head was very approachable. I had a strong sense that he and his colleague really did care. However, I reflected that he really wasn't sure what support would look like or how many people would come forward.

The following week there was to be a prevention meeting but on the same day as the Cross-Party Group. I had seen a tender where the inquiry team were looking for support to be put in place, but it had to be delivered by Clinical Psychologists. I wanted to challenge it, but I was unable to be two places at once. Ingrid agreed to stay on at the prevention meeting to allow me to go to the Cross-Party Group. The prevention meeting was becoming very tedious with the obvious division between those who were there to impress the government and say what they wanted and those who wanted a process that would work for survivors. I was happy to leave, and I drove down to the parliament for the Cross Party. That day it felt like the usual routine had changed into something more surreal. As I passed through security, I chatted to the staff there with a feeling of contentment that this was important. Inside I met my colleagues who had attended the previous campaigning meeting with government, and we all took the lift to the large committee room giving a further feeling that it was all not real as the room was one that would have been seen on television for committees being publicised. In the room there were three MSPs. from Labour, Conservative and SNP. There was an additional newer MSP who had been out to see the service and who was very pleasant. She was Conservative but seemed to be far too empathetic to be. Others there were long term colleagues, two survivors and a long-term member who worked in the NHS to take forward a training framework. Another was someone Ingrid suspected to be the "man in the shiny suit" she had reported to Intel and to the police. Whenever he was there, I felt very nauseated looking at him. The chair chaired the meeting in her usual professional way with little movement from the main agenda. I raised the issue of the Clinical Psychology support to the inquiry which led to a wider discussion about clinical approaches not being helpful to survivors. Sharon from the NHS training framework team was very defensive, and it was clear that was the model they would be promoting. The chair had to leave at that point and the vice chair took over. That was when the meeting changed. The vice chair was supportive about the concerns largely my friend and fellow campaigner April and I were raising, and the discussion progressed past the time the meeting would usually end. It was agreed to challenge the clinical model with the recognition it would mean clients would have disclosure as a survivor on their medical records whether they wanted it or not. The survivors raised that training in psychology now promoted that survivors were untreatable. So, there would be a record of them but no support. Fergus agreed to raise it with the SNP as I pointed out that I was not exactly popular with the government. Jan from Labour agreed to raise it too. Very late following the meeting I rushed away to pick up Ingrid who had charmed the security guards at the government to look after her. She said the meeting was a complete joke with most of those remaining either promoting their own services or trying to impress the government. Nothing innovative was discussed. Ingrid would have a cigarette in the car so that I could inhale it as a past smoker and all the way back we inhaled smoke to relax and discussed "the man in the shiny suit".

Escalation

I began to wish I had not reflected that everything had calmed down after the Christmas break. Starting the new pilot service was chaotic and some of my colleagues in the management team seemed to be unhappy that I was not available to rescue them from stressful situations. Trudi was becoming resistant to picking up any additional work from me. Everyone in the service showed signs of stress as the battles continued with the government and we had to fill the gap from the council funding. The service for people abused in care was now having to invoice every second of the work which was causing a great deal of anxiety for the workers. The new service Forward Paths were now trying to have access to the client files, so it was all starting again just with different people. The new manager of the service seemed even more arrogant and dismissive than the previous manager. Gavin had still not received his apology from Jackie and as they do the government had decided to move her to a new department. I was feeling very anxious about holding it all together making sure everyone was okay. Another meeting had been arranged with the public protection unit which had the potential of adding to the anxiety. Ingrid and I set off again for a meeting.

When we arrived, we were taken to a different room from the last time we were at the police station. A different person was in the room and he introduced himself as the head of the unit. We all had a friendly chat but it was as if he had been brought in to show us we were considered to be important or to intimidate us. Gray then spoke to ensure that Ingrid and I were to be convinced that the police had nothing at all to do with the appointment of the head of the inquiry.

I said "but what are you going to do. Either he is the unluckiest man in the world to be a close associate with the head of the most prolific paedophile ring and then a close advisor to a Cardinal sex offender or he is involved in something sinister"

"I can only assure you we will fully investigate his associations" Gray said.

"Well, we are very glad to hear that" Ingrid said, "I reported this years ago and I was dismissed but I know I am right by the horror that befell our organisation ever since I reported it".

"I do not understand why there seems to be more energy put into covering all these things up than there is to investigation them" I said, "I know you will hate me for being a thorn in your side raising all these matters but you will sit there smiling at me and pretending you like me and want to help."

Gray sat and smiled.

At the end of the meeting, we were shown the file that related to the local paedophile ring and we were shocked that we were shown the names. There were seven as the client had reported and the main ringleader was the person Ingrid had suspected. He had died a month previously. Two others were in prison for other offences against children. Ingrid and I left feeling vindicated that we had all been right and that the client was at least listened to at last. We went to the local garden centre for lunch where we reflected that other children may not have been abused if the ring had been investigated sooner. We were glad that we had been right all along about the paedophile ring as now it meant the police would have to stop it operating in the future, but we were extremely frustrated that it had taken fighting as hard as we did to have it uncovered.

I had to put aside my frustrations as later that week I was to attend the inquiry with my client. It was potentially going to be awkward as I had raised concerns in the press that the inquiry was going to name people who made allegations to the person or organisation they had accused. That had the potential of making survivors very scared and upset and that was the case with my client. I was aware that the inquiry team had been sent an email to say not to engage with people from our organisation if they were attending with clients. The rejection of our organisation as a core participant was still in my mind as I arrived to meet my client but I resolved to put it aside and concentrate on his needs. He sat tense but defiant as his bravery always shone through. He had been determined through life to fight back while dealing with terrible flashbacks and memories that made rest and sleep impossible. We went over to the hotel where we were to meet. We commented on the dingy nature of the hotel and the fact that the decoration looked like it was from the forties. We were led to the room by the inquiry support worker, and we were offered dry looking cakes and insipid looking tea in

China cups. The statement taker came in. She looked tight lipped so that when she attempted to smile to look empathetic it looked as if it was a sneer instead. I was fascinated by the nose stud that she had as it looked out of place with the over coiffured appearance and overly prim accent. They handed over the statement and then offered to leave the room to enable the client to go through his statement with me as support. The client said that he would probably not sign it because the organisation he accused could be told, potentially affecting his civil case. The statement taker was visibly furious, and she glared at me seeing me as responsible for the decision. I stared back and the woman looked away.

"I have made my own decision on this" the client said, "you have no right to breach the trust I had when I first came here and gave my statement".

After we left he read through each page scoring out large sections where there was the potential to identify him. It felt upsetting for him as such a lot of his past was being disregarded but the trust was gone. When the inquiry team came back in he was insistent that the statement be changed to be sent to him so that he could go over it with his wife and so that he could seek legal advice. The statement taker sat with a printer beside her saying "I will change it now for you and you can sign it".

"I told you I will not be signing it!"

The support worker said that he would call the client the next day to make sure he was okay, and we left. I made sure he was not feeling anxious or upset and he headed back home.

I called the next day to make sure he was feeling okay.

"Well just as well I have you" he said, "no calls from the Inquiry team and I have been feeling suicidal from constant flashbacks like a movie playing over and over in my head."

I was furious at the lack of care but I resolved not to bring my own feelings into my work with the client. It didn't mean I wouldn't take them to task at the next opportunity I thought to myself.

The big campaign

Following the Cross Party Group, it was agreed that those of us with long term experience in the field would meet the government to raise our concerns about the medical model and ongoing core funding for abuse services. Involved were four of the longest campaigners in the field. My friend April had been a campaigner in the field for around 20 years. She had previously been a manager of an abuse organisation. She raised a petition in parliament that led to the Cross Party group and a national strategy. She spent some time as a professional advisor to the government and she had been involved in the original tender process for the in-care service. Pamela was a specialist researcher who had written many books. She was highly respected, often speaking at conferences. She was a specialist in physical health and she had carried out research into physical health issues with us. Edward was a writer, publisher, and abuse specialist. He had written a book with a survivor. Sylvia had around 20 years' experience in the field as a therapist and specialist trainer. We arranged a meeting with the new head of service Jason, his assistant and Sue. We were encouraged by him. He seemed approachable and he stopped Sue from being offensive each time she was.

Our team attending evidenced our significant experience. We challenged the medical model and he seemed to listen. We said that with 90% of survivors abused not in care there had to be core funding for the specialist organisations with many years' experience. He was open to ongoing discussions with us.

Informing the informant

Following the publicity about the head of the inquiry I received an email from someone who had previously emailed looking for work to say that she could possibly have information. She had previously indicated she may have information about the inquiry. After a series of cryptic emails where an element of trust was developed, we arranged a meeting. Before Dana arrived, I felt very nervous. She was tall and glamorous looking much younger than her years and instantly she made me feel relaxed and comfortable. With her bright blonde hair and biker jacket she was so different from the usual bland professionals. We chatted abstractly about the work of the charity and the work that Dana had done for fifteen years for the procurator fiscal service. From there she had realised the impact on families of murder victims, and she had established a project to support them. Dana described that for years child abuse cases were part of her statement taking and she had developed a concern that so many cases did not progress to a conviction. Therefore, she had started work for the inquiry. The whole inquiry was a shambles from the start. A team were recruited but they sat around on massive salaries for weeks before anything was started. Some could earn £600 a day. The team were the same team as many other large-scale inquiries, and most had worked together many times. The chair and the panel were far removed from the lower levels of the team and Dana had not met them. She developed a good relationship with Josh, one of the senior advocates but the rest of the team tended to exclude her. They were not unfriendly, but they were reserved. She was aware that one was the daughter of a senior member of the legal establishment who had overseen a controversial major inquiry involving child abuse involving establishments who may be investigated by the inquiry. Dana was very concerned about it as she felt this should have been a conflict of interest.

Dana was sent on home visits, particularly to one survivor who should have been assessed as a potential risk. She was aware that there had been alleged government interference in the inquiry which eventually led to the resignation of the chair. After her resignation another of the panel members also resigned. It was all a mess. Each statement had to be checked by seven civil servants. Dana took a statement by an abuse survivor where he outlined what sounded clearly that a murder had taken place. Dana was told to remove that section from his statement. She was very concerned and raised a whistleblowing concern. Soon afterwards her employment was terminated. Dana had seen that our charity had been refused to be a core participant to the inquiry with the right to cross examine witnesses. It was strange and of great concern as the charity had supported over 1500 people abused in care and the inquiry was to expose abuse in care. Dana felt the refusal had to be sinister. The new chair of the inquiry was part of the establishment, and she would have no concerns about government interference making it even more sinister that the charity had been rejected, especially as the reasons were spurious and nonsensical. Dana resolved to help in any way she could. She knew a great deal of information about the head of the other inquiry, including the fact that there were rumours he was in a relationship with the Cardinal. I gave Dana our new lawyer contact details to see if she could help him in gathering statements. I was pleased as I felt it would give an opportunity to have someone else review if the lawyer was trustworthy. I was concerned that his submissions to the inquiry seemed to be unfocussed and easy to challenge. As he was a highly regarded lawyer it felt strange, and I was not sure if he was trustworthy. Dana resolved to go by her gut feelings about him.

Government games

April, Edward, and I had a further meeting with the government as Ingrid and the others were unable to attend. We met to discuss how to take forward the meeting. It was a very awkward meeting as they were all friends with the head of the inquiry that we were concerned about. Nobody mentioned him making it all more awkward. I was pleased they were still campaigning despite the tension that was between us. The government meeting involved Jason, Vera his assistant, and Clara the replacement for Jackie. Clara appeared to be much more approachable, but she terrified me by coughing uncontrollably throughout the meeting.

Jason was dressed casually in a checked shirt and jeans which made us all laugh as we suggested he was trying to appear non-threatening. Vera sat with her usual attempt to appear obliging while showing venomous stares when she thought she was not being watched. April insisted that the group wanted an independent reference group to take forward all the concerns that had been raised. We all felt that would be a way of insisting the government review their processes. I said to Jason "all your previous responses to us have been dismissive, condescending and factually incorrect. You funded a worker to start a process locally to remove our core funding and then wrote to flatly deny it."

"We didn't remove your core funding"

"We have minutes of a meeting that evidence that you funded the council to start a process to remove our funding" I said.

Jason looked shocked "well I wasn't aware of that".

"Well, it appears your team don't share things with you. Perhaps it is not a bad thing that Jackie has gone."

Jason turned red and looked down. "Well, we are willing to take forward a reference group and perhaps that will resolve all communication difficulties"

We were all shocked by the apparent climb down. "But will it be independent of government? Although being held in government premises would be good to ensure that it has credibility."

"It should be chaired by April or Pamela to ensure its independence" I said. "We are all so upset by the horrible way communication has been up to now. For example, Clara a recent email from you where you almost implied, we were fraudulently making claims. I had to walk away from the computer to calm down before replying."

"I feel the same with your emails" Clara said, "perhaps we will all benefit from trying to work positively together."

The meeting seemed to end on friendly terms and we left shocked that there seemed to be a resolution. It had been agreed that April would meet Vera and Clara to take forward planning of the group.

When I told Ingrid she was concerned about April going on her own for her protection so she called Jason to ask if she could be included in the next meeting. She left the message on his answerphone. About a week later there was an angry email from April asking why Ingrid had contacted the government without telling her. Despite the fact that neither Jason nor Vera had contacted Ingrid directly Vera had contacted April to imply that Ingrid had forced her way into the meeting implying that meant she didn't feel April could go ahead on her own. She said that as it was to be a government reference group involving organisations and excluding others wouldn't be right. April realised she had been played and they all wrote to query why it had now become a government meeting. Vera wrote to the Cross-Party Group to request giving an update to exclude them from the process and go over their heads. April objected and they submitted a paper. It was clear the suggestion of a reference group was to exclude rather than involve the child abuse experts.

At the next Cross Party Group, it was clear that there was a tension in the room. There was no sign of the head of the inquiry and most of the group members were acting strangely. Alan, a survivor who attended the group, asked why I had spoken out about him. I explained that I couldn't say but that I had a moral and legal obligation to do so. The Chair of the meeting then gave a speech that he had resigned due to other commitments but she spoke at length about the loss to the group and her own regret as he was a friend. One of the other group members then asked was it due to the press attention. The Chair said no and the meeting moved on but I was very upset that nobody had asked me about it but they made me feel very awkward. I felt humiliated and shamed. Later we all attended a film screening with questions and answers afterwards and I spoke up to ask why we were not pushing an open door for funding. I mentioned my own background as a survivor and parent of a survivor. Later I reflected that I had spoken out through anger and shame and I felt that it had been a mistake for me. I felt the same feelings of shame I had felt when I first told my mother. The group were all due to meet again and Pamela emailed me to ask if I could explain what my reason had been for taking the issue public. I agreed and we all met in the Gyle. On first sitting down Ingrid tried to explain as the issue had originally been highlighted by her but Pamela asked her to stop speaking so that she could ask her questions. Ingrid angrily left the table. I explained as much as I was able to without compromising client confidentiality. I became very upset as I felt my colleagues should have understood I would not have acted without very good reason. We were all very shocked and all upset but we resolved to continue our campaigning despite the personal issues. Ingrid and I were not entirely sure we wanted to as we felt our colleagues should have understood and put friendship aside. It was also clear that the head of the inquiry had lied about aspects of his previous associations saying they were not friends and they hardly knew each other where in reality it was easy to find online that his version of events was not true. April and I had to meet again to take forward a Cross Party subgroup and I told her the full story. It made things feel a bit better but there seemed to be no easy resolution. The subgroup decided to take forward the possibility of a Scotland wide abuse organisation similar to the ones for domestic abuse and rape to enable them to influence policy. They planned to investigate it further. I promised to speak to other abuse organisations about the possibility.

Election infiltration

While all the other craziness was going on I decided to do something even crazier to complicate matters further. I decided to stand in the local elections as an independent candidate and Talia decided to stand alongside me. The local councillor who had always supported the organisation said that he would support us as part of a group of independents with three others too. The world was changing rapidly, and politics was becoming unpredictable. The prime minister decided to call a general election during the local election campaigning in the hope that it would oust the leader of the labour party. Brexit was the main topic of the day even though barely anyone had any idea what it all meant. I felt very strongly that I had been subjected to a hate crime through the grievance and after having the courage to report it to the police I decided to campaign on equality issues and abuse issues. Of course, it was an added benefit for me and Talia to make the council very nervous. I wanted to campaign for a local railway station as a main campaign issue. The Board and all my colleagues thought it was hilarious. While it was initially to protest the local structures and the corruption behind them, I started to secretly feel I could somehow make a difference. Going through with it would take a great deal of courage as there would be contact with the elected members who had tried to destroy us and the head of the council.

I decided to engage with the local community council to find out what issues local people had. I was very nervous at my first meeting knowing that Laura would be there. The meeting involved one of the senior council officials who had been invited to discuss the local community development plans. I found that challenging him eased my nerves. I asked why there was austerity in the council and not growth as growth was the way to build a positive future where austerity would just mean cuts year after year. People were losing hope. Bin collections were now monthly, and people were experiencing rats in their gardens. The area had been fighting for the railway station to meet the growing community and I had been pushing for it as all my children had struggled to work in the big cities due to lack of transport. I asked why, at a time of austerity the council were paying massive local government pension contributions or they were paying them to fund managers at a cost of around thirty million. As I challenged people noticed me and Laura looked furious. At the end of the meeting, I was asked to join the committee and I agreed feeling excitement about being part of something new and grassroots. I told Chris that regardless of what happened at the election I wanted to stay part of the community.

Chris agreed to become my election agent and I became the election agent for Talia. We went to an event to give information on being a candidate. I noticed the council workers looking into the crowd and they looked momentarily horrified when they saw me, before covering it. Other elected members fidgeted in their seats uncomfortably. When we left Chris kept laughing at the cheek of his wife to face her enemies. I was determined to be at as many hustings as I could to be seen and to put forward the issues I cared about. I went forward with excitement and asked the local equality council to allow me to be a candidate. I was shocked when the answer was no as only political parties would be allowed. I sent an email back to challenge the decision, but they would not budge. I was very disappointed as the equality council had stopped me speaking when I attempted to discuss in the equality group they organised that I had been subject to a hate crime. I felt that I should have been included as a disabled person with a background as a disability activist. I wrote a complaint and a meeting was organised with a manager. Even more irritating was that my own hustings for my own charity was being organised by one of the staff who was trying to promote his own party. He kept trying to stop me being involved. I insisted and Talia decided to be there too. After much campaigning Talia and I were able to be involved in three hustings. We arrived at the one for our own organisation to be met by three other candidates with a very awkward introduction. The questions were all relevant to childhood abuse and it was clear there were people planted in the crowd to discredit the organisation and bring up the previous battles with the council. I decided to inform the crowd about everything that had happened and the others on the panel were shocked and distressed as they had been misled and lied to about it. It was becoming clearer that whoever had the agenda to close down the organisation had been implying that we had not completed reports or evaluation information. I gave an open invitation for anyone to come to the office to see everything that had been provided. At the next hustings Talia and I were the main contributors making it obvious the party candidates did not really know what the issues on equality were. At the local community council hustings, I found myself up against Laura. I was shocked to see that she was shaking uncontrollably. I spoke up for the local community issues while it was obvious Laura was only interested in promoting her party. The sense was always there that the other parties understood I was a risk as there were matters to be covered up that I could expose.

On the day of the count, it was obvious that Talia and I were not going to achieve many votes but the 120 votes I achieved made me proud of some success. It felt like in some small way justice was starting to happen. To stand up and not be afraid was something that had been very important for my ongoing recovery.

A few weeks after the result there had been a complaint that I was on the community council as while my postcode was for the area I was on the periphery. The complaint was anonymous but it was clear that I would not be tolerated anywhere in the area by the council. I was upset. I loved the people I had worked with and enjoyed being involved in my community. Every block was beginning to affect my wellbeing more.

Lawyer, ethics, and the campaigner

Our new law firm had offered a great deal of support, but I had always kept an open mind as I had been contacted by a number of lawyers all of whom wanted the survivors to be told about them. The term used was ambulance chasers in such circumstances, but this lawyer did seem more ethical. Pat the main contact was warm and friendly but with a very significant edge. However, he introduced me to Lynn who was extremely pleasant and approachable. It was clear she really wanted to make a difference and she was approachable to survivors. I really liked her. I attended the parliament with two survivors to give evidence on time bar and some weeks later the Bill progressed through parliament to remove the time bar. The lawyers wanted me to send a leaflet to all the clients so that they could seek legal compensation. I held back as I felt wary still. The press officer seemed to never achieve very significant coverage despite his significant contacts. One of the survivors had started a major campaign to find survivors to come forward to the inquiry to achieve justice He developed a campaign team involving survivors, the organisation, and the lawyers. He organised a few vigils and I was encouraged that the lawyers came out to stand in the streets with them, particularly Lynn. However, I was concerned that the lawyers did not use him to find people for them to make more money. Every vigil we held more and more survivors would come forward, often from the homeless people in the area. He was frustrated at the time it took to have interest and in the number of people who would help so he grew trusting of the lawyers. He arranged a meeting for me with the police as they had released a leaflet that failed to tell survivors about the range of organisations that could support them. The press was paying attention to his campaigns. He brought together people from across the UK and Ireland to join him.

Forward Paths

The government new service to replace the previous one for people abused in care had rebranded itself to be called Forward Paths. It offered people holidays, household appliances, cars and even a horse as a way of giving people who had been abused support in something called a support fund. I was still very concerned about it as I knew when people started talking about the abuse it could make them dissociate or become re-traumatised but I knew that any small amount of help could make a huge difference. Due to all the campaigning by the survivors Forward Paths were to fund our previous service to allow it to continue. Finally, the survivors had been allowed to meet the government minister. It was obvious at the meeting with him that his civil servants were taking note of the survivors who were shouting the loudest against the new service. Many had been treated like they should have a begging bowl out and they had felt humiliated. I had been right that it would make them feel suicidal. The government minister promised the service would continue then shot off at speed. Following the meeting the survivors who had been shouting loudest were suddenly being offered far and beyond what other survivors were given from Forward Paths with the service directly approaching them. One was asked to be on a government advisory group. Another was allowed to be on a government committee. They all knew they were being targeted but decided to take what was offered to see how far it would go. I was very concerned they would be made to feel important and then let down when no longer needed.

I was approached by Florence the new manager of the service to meet up and discuss working together. Florence was a tiny Canadian woman who appeared to be extremely pleasant and unassuming. She presented as very empathetic about everything I had been through with the government and attempted to play to my ego by saying the government feared me. I was very wary of the over-the-top attempt at friendship as she had understood nothing was ever straightforward. On the day that I was campaigning for the election I sat outside the polling station for an hour while Florence attempted to convince me she was trustworthy and gradually and insidiously try and convince me to hand over the client records. She told me that Jackie was hated in the government and that people were glad I had battled with her. She told me that the government were scared of me due to all my press contacts and coverage. She seemed to be playing to my ego. It all felt so false, and I was aware that just like the clients I was being manipulated. I felt sick and resolved to be very wary. A day after the call Florence wrote me an email to confirm the conversation which did not reflect the conversation and I knew I had been tricked. I refused to sign the contract with the new service as it had permission to access the client records and insisted on a meeting with the lawyers in attendance.

Florence glowed with charm and sweetness in the meeting. The lawyer Pat came in a full three-piece suit. I felt anxious so I included Sharon and Michael two of the managers and Trudi sat in too. Florence showed no sign of nerves despite all the others in the meeting. She led the meeting to make it clear what was expected. All clients would have to be signed up to the new service to be paid for.

"But many don't want anyone to know who they are, they don't want the new service." Michael said, "Do we have to tell them they can't have our support then?"

"Pretty much" said Florence "the government want everyone signed up to the service. No details, no money."

"But that is so unethical" Michael responded "to have support they have to compromise their right to privacy. What makes it worse is that we have to ask them to do so. That makes me very unhappy."

"Well, we could compromise and let them have a few months to register. After that no registration, no money." Florence sat back in her seat looking triumphant. "If you want to work with people that's fine but we won't pay you. Then you will have to prove that all the hours of work your counsellors are paid for are seeing people we have registered."

"But how can we do that?" I interjected "You are one of our main competitors and to give you details of our salary records would make you able to undercut us in any tender."

"We won't be competing with you in any tender I can promise that. Our work will be more prevention not service delivery."

"How are we supposed to trust you? I said, "You have proven to be untrustworthy in the past."

"Well, you will just have to." Florence scoffed "I don't see that you have any choice."

"The wording of the contract will have to be changed." Pat said, "There can be no breakdown of salaries and our auditor will carry out any audit."

"No, it has to be our auditor." Florence insisted. "Nothing else will be accepted."

"We have been all through this before." I said exasperated. "It will be our auditor and our financial information will be confidential."

"I want an agreement clients will not be forced to register against their wishes." Michael said. "I will not frighten people that way."

"Well, we will just have to see." Florence smirked.

Some weeks later the contract was amended as the lawyer had requested and it was signed. However, Florence came back to insist that details of any new clients were passed over. I wrote one of my long emails to object. I had also become aware that the organisation running Forward Paths had tendered against us for our service put out to tender by the council. Our organisation had not progressed but the other one had. I confronted Florence as she had kept insisting our auditor gave more and more detail of the financial information. Florence responded to deny that she had said the other organisation would not tender against us then denied she had any influence. I was furious at the ongoing lies. It was becoming obvious the agenda to close us down was stepping up and that any dirty tricks possible would be used.

New beginnings

I was engaging with a campaigning organisation, and it had started to be clear that they were being monitored by the government. I travelled to Perth to speak at a conference they arranged. I was unsure if they could be trusted but had a sense that this would be a positive way forward. As always when speaking publicly I was extremely nervous, so Chris travelled up with me. I noticed Sue sitting at the back of the room with three others who were taking notes and who looked like civil servants. The speeches by the survivors were extremely moving and I felt inspired to protect them by joining the campaign, but I was nervous as trusting others was a huge challenge. At the break I went to the toilet and Sue followed me.

"When are you speaking" she said.

"After the break." I said.

"Well good because I only came here to see you speak."

It was said in a threatening sinister way which made me more nervous and more determined. My very measured, planned speech was suddenly no longer relevant. I returned to the room where I started my speech by referring to the paedophile rings, I was aware of and the reasons why the council and the government wanted rid of those who could expose it. I was aware everything I said could be used against me but didn't care. I spoke about the cover up and the threats to campaigners. I spoke of my emails being hacked and my phone being listened into. People cheered throughout and I felt perhaps this crowd were on the same journey as I was. Sue left straight after my speech but not before speaking to two of the main organisers of the event.

A month or so later it became clear that the two who had organised the event were being offered a huge amount of rewards by the new service and they stood up at an event to speak about how the new service had changed their lives. One of the main survivor campaigners for the past ten years was on video promoting the new service. It was becoming clear if anyone was a threat to government the new service would offer them money while others were being rejected. I did not feel any bad feeling towards the survivors as after a life of nothing to be offered so much was something they could just not reject but I knew when the help stopped they would be left bereft and feeling used. Florence herself was in direct contact with the survivors who had previously shouted the loudest.

I spoke to one of the other organisers of New Beginnings the campaigning organisation about my concerns. They spoke to the others who had promoted the new service and a dinner was organised to discuss it. In the end he didn't appear as he had been unable to find the restaurant but Chris and I spent all evening with the others and we developed a close to trusting relationship. We agreed to work together in future.

The main people running the organisation were Douglas, Nick, Penny, and Kim, although Kim was more of a researcher. A few weeks after the issue with the government the members who were involved with Forward Paths resigned and decided to go in their own direction to focus on their own campaigns. I started to be become more and more involved taking part in Skype meetings. I spoke at an event they held to launch a people's inquiry into child abuse due to the failings of the existing inquiry. I gave another speech that was recorded. I was aware that the inquiry could tell the perpetrator if they had been named by the survivor. Survivors were frightened by the possibility. One had asked to meet the chair of the inquiry, but she refused. Another survivor had given a statement to the inquiry and they had let the police know. The survivor then had death threats as there had clearly been a leak, particularly as the police would then put people on a vulnerable person's database and tell social work. I had complained on behalf of the survivor, but the inquiry chair had condescendingly dismissed the complaint and lied about what the survivor said. I mentioned the issues in my speech, and I also raised that many survivors were concerned that other high profile abuse cases would not be covered. They felt there was a conflict of interest by one of the inquiry team. Another speaker at the meeting was Robert. I admired Robert greatly as he had contacted me regarding the abuse of a young girl with learning difficulties who had been abused by a paedophile ring. He had been arrested for raising the issues and he had still refused to back down. Another speaker was a tireless campaigner into ritual abuse cases. The meeting felt inspiring. I joined in with another of the Skype meetings and then joined the Board of the organisation. It felt that this would be so important. I felt strangely nauseated at every contact with them which I found hard to analyse but I was determined to keep an open mind and not be scared. The researcher Kim was wonderful with masses of valuable information and the ability to form links.

The council

The council had finally put out to tender the service for abuse survivors and had a two-stage process. Trudi and I applied through the tender process, but we did not even progress to the next stage despite over twenty years' experience working with survivors. The organisations who progressed were ones with no real experience or track record. The Board asked for the lawyers to take forward a judicial review and they reported it to the counter corruption unit of the police. The lawyer met with me with a senior advocate. The advocate said there was nothing we could do as it could cost hundreds of thousands and we wouldn't win. I felt close to tears as I realised I had been right not to trust the lawyer as I knew I was being managed to not take matters forward. The next week I met the police anti-corruption unit with Eva. It was explained to us it was no longer the counter corruption unit which could investigate all public bodies. It was an anti-corruption unit against the police. Strangely the other unit had been disbanded around the time I had spoken to the Justice Minister about it. There was now no avenue to investigate public bodies. The police informed us it was unethical practice by the Council but not a crime so they could not intervene. I reflected that while the Council had won, at least aspects such as the lawyer were clearer. I felt they had not won as they could not be comfortable covering up the abuse of children when in private moments. One of my contacts spoke to me about the early days of the organisation when it was run by the council. There had been a ritual abuse group where three women reported ritual abuse locally. The previous manager had not taken forward child protection concerns and people were still being abused as the children of the survivors were being used by the ring. It made the later destruction of the files more of a concern as evidence of the abuse rings was lost. The new service would mean any future information that came to light would be back under the control of the Council.

Survivors and informants unite

Over the space of a few weeks the problems with the emails had escalated and it was clear there was sabotage happening. I reported it to the cybercrime unit as a potential hacking issue. We discovered that a hacker had signed into my email and used it to steal funds. A private email I sent to the lawyer was forwarded to the government. The cyber-crime unit warned us that we would be an ongoing target and they advised us to keep records secure and not online. We had previously had to report many of our files being deleted by a hacker. They were the files of the abuse in care service but fortunately we had no client information online.

I had just been through a long call with the IT Company about the email problem when a message from Dana came up on my Facebook. She asked how everything was going and then dangled a tempting suggestion that she had interesting news about the local community. I agreed to a call as I felt that I would be unable to wait to see what it was. Dana had a strange almost hypnotic way of talking when she called. She gave me information that she was working with a senior solicitor to take statements for him, but he was a lawyer who had worked for the previous First Minister and the senior advocate who had been accused of covering up the abuse of the young disabled person. He had links to many journalists, and he had been part of some major Inquiries. Dana gave me information on the case. It involved a police officer in the local area who had been accused of sexual abuse of a 15-year-old boy and a guest at a wedding. Another young man had accused him of online grooming and stalking but the boy had been arrested for wasting police time. His father was also a police officer. While the main case was online and obviously true much of what I was being told felt strange. There would be no purpose for me to hear the information either as useful in the campaigning or to be able to evidence the case. I felt that I was continuing to be given information either to see if I would hold the secrecy or to see if all the onslaught of horror would eventually frighten me enough to withdraw. The links that Dana had were beginning to not feel coincidental. I could not help liking Dana but I was aware that many of the other protagonists in this drama were very clever negotiators or manipulators. I laughed as it all as I was obviously moving closer and closer to the truth.

Over the time of being more public others had contacted me to speak about their concerns about sinister cover ups. A young girl had appeared at the office with a huge dossier of information she had uncovered. It mentioned the case Robert had been investigating, the Dunblane case and other cases in Edinburgh referred to as the Magic Circle and Fettesgate. I pulled all the information I had with other information given by Dana and others from New Beginnings and I could see that there was a pattern. The case of the chair of the inquiry case was linked to it all too. I received an anonymous dossier about him, posted to the office so clearly people knew things but they were scared to come forward. One of the volunteers met a homeless man in Glasgow who referred to the Magic Circle and the fact that it involved rent boys who had been procured from the organisation the chair of the review was involved with. Another contact spoke to me about possible trafficking and corruption in her area and links to a politician. It was clear that the common theme with many of the informants was that they had been discredited or made out to be mentally ill. It was also clear that some people who were shouting out about abuse were planted to look erratic and discredit those who were real campaigners. I kept an open mind about all of it and sat and observed. I reviewed details from all the client files to bring more and more pieces of the jigsaw together.

Threats on a sinister path

The lawyer contacted me to say that he had a letter from the inquiry giving a transcript of my speech at the launch of the people's inquiry where I raised concerns about the inquiry. The letter warned me against speaking out and it threatened me with being accused of a criminal act if I spoke out in a way that would stop people coming forward. I was furious and I contacted Dana and New Beginnings. Dana and her colleague who was a senior advocate came out to see me. Both had previously had important roles within the inquiry and they informed me that they had been warned not to interact with me. They said that the threat was very sinister as in fact they were calling on the law very loosely but trying to scare me. The advocate had been offering me advice as my organisation had been refused to become core participants to the inquiry. His view was that this was very strange as was the warning as we were the largest organisation with knowledge of in care abuse. He and Dana had been investigating a case linked to Fettesgate and they had a long discussion about a possible way forward for that. They knew of a very senior judge who had been accused of child abuse and they had information about two of his victims. The information backed up much of what I had known from our files and from New Beginnings.

I had seen one of his victims commenting on a newspaper article to say that the judge had abused him in a caravan. Dana had information that one of the other victims had been paid off and he was now living in a luxury flat in Edinburgh. They were aware that the victim had used the judge's cheque book and that this was at one point evidence and a Freedom of Information request could perhaps uncover this information. The victim had apparently stolen the judge's car. Dana and the advocate were going to visit a potential witness but they were concerned as he now had dementia. They wanted me to dig further and see what else I could discover. All of us thought that due to Fettesgate there could be links to the chair of the review. I decided I had to speak in detail to New Beginnings about the chair of the review as someone had to know what I knew. New Beginnings organised a further meeting in Perth and Chris took me up to meet them.

From the moment I arrived I felt very uncomfortable and ill. The conversation was very intense. I was careful about what I shared as I felt there were potential risks and I suddenly felt a sense of how overwhelming it all was. Part of me wanted to give so much away to see what would happen with the information and give clues as to whether they could be trusted.

Douglas was part of a maverick radio show and he said he would make sure the issue was publicised. Kim undertook to carry out research into some of the reported cases. The Sunday Times offered to publicise that I had been threatened and that the survivor who had come forward had received death threats. The story was pulled when they received the same threats from the inquiry. It was beginning to feel more and more sinister, and it felt very much like a cover up. I had always tried to keep an open mind but my mind feeling confused and bewildered. Straight after the meeting in Perth I took very ill and spent the next three weeks feeling unwell physically and emotionally. It felt there was nowhere else to turn.

Who do you really know?

The New Beginnings issues progressed throughout the year becoming stranger and, in some ways, worrying. I really liked them all but never felt that I fully knew them or why they wanted me to be involved. They organised a series of workshops over the year from March to October and I agreed to be involved.

Douglas was the un-appointed but obvious leader of the group. He was tall and imposing with a heavy beard and thick greying hair. He always wore a full three-piece tweed suit giving the impression of a country gentleman. He compered all the meetings and brought in his friends to many of the events. He was involved in an alternative online media channel. Nick was a very kind and friendly man of around 50 although he looked much younger. He was very affected by ME and he often walked with a stick. He was very uninterested in his appearance often wearing band t shirts and jeans instead of dressing up for the events. Kim was painfully shy and would not make eye contact with anyone. She would mumble when spoken to and look down at the ground. She affected an appearance of not caring what anyone thought. Her clothes were often combats or trousers with chains and zips. Penny was the sensible and level-headed one of the groups. She was also affected by ME, and she was careful not to push herself too far. I found her to be kind and thoughtful. She was the natural leader.

I attended another event in Perth where one of the men attending became very upset and dissociative. I was asked as a counsellor to speak to him and support him. We went into another room where he was pacing and crying. I managed to calm him down by working on his breathing. He told me he was having flashbacks and memories of his childhood. He had memories of a curly-haired blonde child, only around three years old. He remembered her being murdered and her body buried. He said the case related to the case of those who were senior in the legal establishment. We returned back to the room where a speaker spoke about the number of children and young people who disappeared from being in a care environment. They often entered the exploitation market where they were used in the dark web. I was extremely shocked, and I reported it to the public protection unit. They told me it must be a fantasy as no bodies had been uncovered. They said no children had been reported missing, leading to the alarm being raised. What I had heard stayed with me and I was unable to let it go.

Petition process

One of the clients had taken forward a petition to save the service. He petitioned that the clients had not chosen the broker model. They wanted the service where they felt safe. As we were the service he was referring to we were asked to give evidence. I wrote a paper where I raised serious concerns about the broker model. We were already aware of client suicides and we were still sure the new service was high risk. It opened the door for people to speak with no services for them to go to. The service was also extremely costly at up to £5 million a year with only £1m going directly to survivors. Staff costs for personal outcome co-ordinators were close to my salary and management costs were significant. Most of the costs were on staff salaries with a limited amount of money to survivors. Survivors were given funding for all sorts of random things. Counselling was provided by high cost, private counsellors. It transpired that the private counsellors were part of a service established by the organisation who held the tender. So, they were paying themselves. They refused to broker our service, despite the longstanding experience. The committee were very supportive and they asked the survivor back on more occasions. The government gave evidence too but it was not very effective. We questioned the medical model further as part of the petition process. The petition ran for a few years in total. We were asked to attend the committee to give further evidence. I attended with Douglas as he was now on the Board. It was a nerve-racking process but I felt we gave a very good account. Soon afterwards it was confirmed at the committee that the government had written to them to say our funding would continue.

Media moans

I woke to morning television which was increasingly becoming more bizarre. A debate about whether people should publicly display affection involved one who was for and one against. The whole debate had been created by a photographer capturing one of the royal family in an intimate moment with her husband. This then created the spin of further debate. I reflected on how often this happened. A minor issue would be escalated with debates and comment and it then became a large issue. This was followed by a debate on the burka following negative comments by an MP on social media. The irony that nobody would have paid attention to what the MP had said without all the press coverage seemed to have been lost. This effectively increased the discrimination. Our morning television when we had just woken up was creating our reality for the day about what should be important.

The last week had been flooded by Love Island with various beautiful young people brought onto morning television to discuss their appearance on the show. The constant coverage was creating a media frenzy and the young people were battling to be the most interesting to create celebrity for their future.

The couple from Love Island were saying that being in the public eye made them experience Twitter trolls. Comments online included 'she is breathing in so much it hurts to look at'. 'Why wear a bikini'. 'She should get a boob job to go with all the other plastic'. The girl from Love Island was bullied at school for being shy and insecure so she highlighted to the online trolls that they could have impacted on her mental health with this further bullying. Her message to trolls was to remember what you are putting out there if you are trying to find a job. You are leaving a footprint of who you are. The guy tried to show he was not bothered while trying to be empathetic. Both were trying hard to be popular in the public eye, raising popular issues. The guy was talking about his own bullying for being overweight. The issues were important but they felt like they were being discussed for headlines and profile. The media was now all about distress and what people suffered under the mask of raising awareness.

Criticism of social media had become a common thread before tweeting about it later.

Next the show considered, Victoria Beckham's secret to a happier life. It seemed loosely connected to her fashion range.

There was a piece on crystal healing with the presenter saying that people were bound to be sceptical. The interviewee was punting a book on the power of crystals. "Do crystals really have powers" was flashing across the screen.

A celebrity was talking about her new book, an eating disorder and her battle with mental health. Denise Welch: my anxiety struggle was flashed across the screen.

Dr Alex was talking about skin difficulties.

Is Tom Hardy planning to leave acting behind?

There is no harder job than parenting!

A health scare for Matthew Perry. He asked for privacy as he heals.

Lady Gaga is making a comeback with a residency in Vegas.

I put my head in my hands and reflected on how insignificant matters are the news, but the real news was remaining hidden. Some of the ridiculous items were items about body dysmorphia due to weight gain followed by a cooking segment of high calorie meals and desserts.

The end of family

It was the birthday of my mother and Arianne contacted me in a rage.

"I was just looking at gran's Facebook. She had a message from Jan, Chris's ex-wife wishing her a happy birthday. What is going on?"

"After I feel out with your gran after your auntie assaulted me your gran and your aunt made friends with her to hurt us. She was invited to your gran's wedding too so I couldn't go".

"That is so messed up! Arianne shouted. I am going to say something to her!"

Arianne put really.... on the status and my mum contacted her immediately to try and justify the contact. She then sent an email to me to try and smooth over why she was still in contact with Jan. I found her email to be cold, unfeeling, and unconcerned. I responded with a long email expressing all the years of hurt and distress that my mother would support someone who had tried to kill me. I acknowledged that I had ensured that Morag's children should stay with their father but made it explained that it was a child protection issue as Morag was so dangerous and that her ongoing drug use since childhood made her an inappropriate parent. I had witnessed her being abusive with her children.

My mum was colder in the next response, and we decided to meet at the garden centre locally. My mum insisted that nothing was to be discussed.

On the day I took Arianne, Dan, and Thomas with me. We took the baby too in the hope that it would diffuse the situation. When we arrived, my mum refused to leave the car saying she would not come in unless nothing was to be discussed. I felt my distress rising and tears started pouring from my eyes.

"You refuse to speak to me and yet you let my sister try and kill me and then you went on to support her and block me from your life for years. You broke my heart and to make it worse you befriended Jan. Now you won't speak to me. Fine we will go in and have lunch a pretend nothing has happened."

My mum smirked and opened the car door. We went into the restaurant and as always, I paid for lunch for everyone. I felt numb and a sense of unreality and I carried the tray to the table. As I sat and they all made small talk I felt a roaring sensation in my ears. My body started to twitch and I was aware I was possibly approaching adrenal shock. I ran out of the restaurant and sat trembling outside trying to stabilise my pulse.

Arianne and Thomas came out to check I was okay and Arianne asked if it was a panic attack. I explained about adrenal shock due to the long-term steroid use for the lupus and the subsequent adrenal insufficiency. Thomas went back in to speak to his gran but she sat and ate lunch calmly and refused to react. Thomas was shocked at her coldness. I managed to calm my system despite crying uncontrollably and feeling embarrassed at the scene to others around. My mum eventually came out with Dan, Thomas, and my grandson.

At first, I tried to speak to my mother calmly but she continued to ignore me. I said "I should call the police again. They always told me that Morag could be charged even at this late stage if I decided to press charges."

My mum reacted to that "Morag has moved forward with her life. I won't allow you to do that".

"She tried to kill me. What kind of mother are you?"

"She has moved on why don't you?"

"I lost my mother for 14 years. I can't visit you unexpectedly or call you. I can't see you at Christmas or wish you a happy new year. I can't call you when my life is bad or good. I lost my mum."

"No wonder I couldn't turn to you when my dad abused me. How could I turn to you when I didn't trust you? When you told me you couldn't bond with me as a child as you didn't remember me being born."

My mum just stared coldly and went into her car.

I begged her to listen but she closed the door.

I was shaking uncontrollably and the children all hugged me in shock.

"I didn't know she could be like that" Arianne said. "Forget about her. Honestly, she isn't worth it."

"Are you okay to drive?" Dan said.

"I will be better driving to try and settle myself".

We drove home speaking about it incessantly and in complete shock. I knew that even the minimal contact I had with her mother would be ended and I felt lost and alone.

When I told Chris I could feel his fear of the impact it would have on me going forward.

"My mum could die or be seriously ill and I will not be told. I will never know. I could lose her and we could have not spoken again. How do I cope with this? "

"I don't know" he said "all I do know is that she is evil. She knows what this will do to your health and she doesn't care. Somehow you will have to move on without her."

I lay all night in the foetal position with tears soaking the pillow. I could never understand why my mother had never loved me. Perhaps I was unlovable. Perhaps that is why I had experienced so much abuse in my life. I knew that was wrong but on some level I just wanted to die to make the pain stop. There had to be some reason but there was no explanation and no sense. If not loved by your mother how can you be a person, how can you exist?

As I always did in life when Monday came again I put off my alarm, found fresh clothes and drove to work. My feelings were buried in the way they always were and I laughed and joked with my colleagues as if nothing untoward had happened. When Chris called to see how I was I just said fine and went back to obsessively organising my emails. Work was always the way to cope and work would be my solace and a channel for the pain. The survivors knew my reality as it was theirs too. To be able to make even a small difference gave it all some meaning.

Another one!

I was contacted by a new government civil servant brought in to liaise with the abuse organisations. She asked to come and visit the service with Clara to meet me. I had built a positive relationship with Clara and I felt hopeful that perhaps she would give a positive impression of us to this new person. I prepared presentations about the service for the visit. Norma was friendly and enthusiastic. She worked hard to convince me that she was new and not affected by anything that had gone before. She seemed very impressed with the service presentation.

While she was speaking to one of my colleagues Clara and I were able to have a chat. She told me Jackie had also said clients should die to make change in government and the team were glad she had been moved due to the bad press. She said Jason was aware of how badly things had been managed.

Norma promised to work with us to improve the relationship with Forward Paths. I was sceptical but I felt it was important to give her a chance.

Audit and the future

To ensure that we could not be discredited in the future we asked the government to carry out an audit of our service. Florence had said she couldn't be sure clients were "real people", Clara from the government signed a confidentiality agreement. She checked our client lists against claims and found them to be accurate. She also evidenced that our client numbers were correct. She checked random files to ensure that clients did exist. She carried out another audit after six months. The external financial auditor carried out a through finance audit on the service. Florence had no further way of criticising us. Jason agreed that Forward Paths would continue to fund us.

The government announced that they were allowing abuse organisations to apply for core funding. We were triumphant that our campaigning with the Cross-Party Group had been successful. We realised that would not necessarily mean that we would be successful but we had ensured survivors who need help would be able to access it. That had been my goal and dream from childhood that survivors could access the help they needed. It was something that had not been available to me and my son. We did manage to achieve the funding with conditions that other organisations didn't have but at least we could support our clients. We started to notice that many were challenging the medical model. Personality disorders were being challenged and complex trauma was coming to the fore. We hoped that we had been responsible at least in a small part for some of the change.

The fly in the ointment

While it was great that our funding was secure we were aware that we were not receiving any counselling referrals from Forward Paths. We raised our concerns regularly but nothing changed. We were aware that referrals were being sent instead to the lead organisation in the Forward Paths consortium. They were running a private trading arm with a high unit cost, much higher than the cost of our service. We were also aware that many of the counsellors were newly trained and not trauma specialists. We were suspicious this was another attempt to eventually close us down due to low client numbers. However, most of our long-term clients remained with the service and the lawyers sent many new referrals to us. Florence said they would not allow us to record new referrals that did not come from them unless we agreed to them being registered with Forward Paths. I called Norma to raise my concerns. She was clearly caught off guard and she promised me she would speak to Florence and come back to me.

The new government

I drove to Arianne's house to collect her for a day out shopping for my younger grandson's birthday. The phone rang and it came up on the hands free as Norma. I realised this could be a long call and pulled over into a lay-by. Norma was clearly rattled from the conversation the day before and she had spoken to Florence. While it was clear this new government official had been chosen for her diplomatic skills, she was obviously struggling with being torn in many directions with different perspectives being sold to her. She tentatively attempted to explore the issue of referrals.

"You see Florence wanted to arrange a meeting with the two teams as there have been some practice issues reported."

"What with her staff from our workers or do you mean with our staff" I mumbled over the words as I could feel the tension rising.

"No, your staff there have been some practice issues and Forward Paths would be reluctant to make referrals in those circumstances."

"I'm sorry but that is a very serious allegation" I said. "There is absolutely no evidence of malpractice and all our team have supervision regularly by qualified supervisors. If there were any issues they, would he highlighted to us. You are questioning the professionalism of our staff and that is very serious. If this gossip and hearsay does not stop, we will be forced into making a complaint. When Florence was in the meeting with Jason, she turned to the side away from us and mumbled that there were complaints, although not quite complaints about our team. When questioned on it she had nothing to say."

"I'm sorry I may have misheard what was said" Norma ever the diplomat interjected "I'm sure there was no suggestion it was anything serious".

"Well, it must have been serious to block referrals. We have had many very serious concerns raised about Forward Paths but we have left it to the clients to personally raise concerns. We don't discuss gossip and hearsay as if it is fact" I was in disbelief that I was hearing this.

"Well, I will speak to Florence about it again but it will depend on the support workers making referrals and Florence was clear they are not being told to refer to anyone, including the umbrella organisation."

I was furious "I have already told you the support workers are promoting the umbrella organisation. In any case there are many people on the waiting list, some of whom will have been waiting for over a year who could be seen by our workers to keep them safe and stop them having to wait. It can be traumatic to speak on the helpline and then wait so long."

Norma spoke tentatively as if she knew her next comments would be controversial "but your workers are not trained to identify what people need. They are counsellors and not all clients need or want counselling."

"Our workers have always assessed need and they have always referred on where we could not meet that need. Forward Paths can deal with practical support, but we know that most people need counselling too. The reason for the development of our service was identified by the government following the report in 2008 into abuse in care. It was recognised that clients needed a service that would offer therapeutic support along with advocacy and informal support. Our workers provide much more than counselling. They can offer informal support and advocacy to access other services appropriate to their needs. They can do all of that while keeping people safe. Over the years we have referred to the NHS and the NHS have referred to us. We always worked together with others."

Norma seemed to murmur agreement "but why would we choose your service rather than any other that would not be fair on the others. It could cause issues."

"If you look back at the landscape of abuse organisations prior to Forward Paths you will see that there are only a few specialists. Nobody was interested in working specifically with those abused in care. We set up a partnership approach, but we were the organisation everyone referred to. We gained ten years' experience, and we have the greatest capacity with workers all over Scotland. You are leaving clients at risk of suicide rather than referring them to us for help." Norma again seemed to murmur agreement.

"So, you are saying only you would have the capacity I can see that."

"Would it not be fairer for the large piece of work for the £100,000 to put that out as a competitive process to all organisations to allow the Forward Paths umbrella organisation to bid too?"

I was shocked "the Board will be furious about this. We were promised the £100,000. It was an agreement to reduce what we were due on a commercial basis which was about £100,000 more. The Board agreed to reduce the income to have a more secure, non-zero hour, arrangement for staff. They were fair and reasonable and now you are going to change from that promise to keep the umbrella organisation happy with some promise that seems to have been made to them behind the scenes."

"Well, I will have to have a think about it. Obviously, I need to rethink. That may take some time."

"We have been waiting for months since we spoke to Jason for all of this to be organised. The staff and the clients have been still concerned and worried not knowing if the service was secure. This is extremely unfair. For the client to being referred to agencies who look for records but can't offer counselling support. For the chaotic way of working. We already know about at least four suicides. How many more will have to die. Forward Paths are paying people to say what they want and promote them. They are splashing clients over social media and the press because they are so grateful about that money. Where will they be when Forward Paths and the money are gone, and they are left thinking they were used. It is disgusting! People who have been abused are being exploited to show a glossy service."

Norma asked, "when you met Jackie was there a good relationship to begin with?"

"No, she was hostile from the first time we met her. She and Sue came in and criticised our report saying we clearly didn't understand psychological research. Why should I because I was not a psychologist, and it was a report not a research paper. They were very condescending, and they then presented the broker model saying it would be going to tender but no point in us thinking about it as there would be no service delivery involved just brokerage."

"She actually said that" Norma said in disbelief.

"Yes, ask Talia if you don't believe me she is on our Board now and she was with me in the meeting. She went on to say she saw services being delivered by the NHS. I said but our service was started because the NHS wouldn't work with our clients. They saw them as untreatable. I said clients would die. She said maybe it was necessary for clients to die for change to happen. I was horrified and in shock."

"You won't go to the papers about me, would you?" Norma sounded worried "Of course I wouldn't. You haven't done anything wrong. You and Clara have always been very nice to us. I didn't feel good at all about going to the papers. It was hurtful. I don't like being in the press. I prefer to work behind the scenes."

"Why do you think you were treated like this?"

"It all started with a so-called grievance in our team. I had been very ill for a while. My adrenal gland wasn't working, and I could barely stand up without being dizzy. It was potentially life threatening. The Board gave me the chance to work from home as my reasonable adjustments for my disability. Two of the managers decided if they could get rid of me, they could take over as I was surplus to requirements in their eyes. They spoke about it on a night out. They then invented spurious allegations and asked people to sign up. They did not know it was not true. Three of them are still with us and they really regret it." I burst into tears and could barely speak. The whole horrible episode flooded back. "I feel so responsible for all that we have been through as a charity. Without that grievance and without my health issues nobody could have attacked us" I was sobbing as the pain kept coming back.

"I want to give you a hug now" Norma said, "I now understand why you feel the way you do."

"We did nothing wrong and yet we have been treated so horribly. There is no explanation for it. Jackie treated us like enemies right from the start. She would divide and conquer. Other organisations were our friends, but Jackie suddenly started involving them in everything and giving them funding to have an organisation to rubber stamp everything she wanted. It created division and made us even more isolated. Our referrals were given to the umbrella organisation. We were purposely isolated."

"All I can say, and I shouldn't be that I met Jackie. I was already 85% convinced that what I was hearing was true before I met her. Afterwards, and I only had one question to ask her, I was 100% convinced. I realise what you must have been through. I have no reason or desire to meet Sue."

"I am meeting another organisation next week. I hope that you won't feel I am dividing and conquering" she said.

"I don't like this division" I said, "I want us all to work together for the good of survivors. That is why I am trying to bring everyone together to form an umbrella organisation."

"I think that is a great idea, Norma said, "It will be constructive for all the organisations to work together."

The conversation was starting to falter. I felt exhausted and humiliated for becoming so upset. "What happens now".

"Well redress will be announced on 23rd October and you, me, Sharon, and Florence can meet afterwards perhaps for a coffee at the parliament. We will speak on the phone on 19th and on Monday I will speak to Florence again to see what we can do next."

I drove on to Arianne's house calling her and Chris on the hands free to explain while shaking and feeling ill. I couldn't believe we seemed to be back to square one again. I felt like we had been successfully played. Chris reassured me that we could go back to the fight if necessary and that I did have the strength to keep moving forward. Arianne reassured me that crying was okay as it showed me to be a human being and not just the CEO.

Return to campaigning

On 21st August 2020 the plans for Redress for people abused in care were announced. I took time to read through them becoming more and more shocked and frustrated as the information started to sink in. It was clear that if survivors were to pursue Redress, they would have to give up their right to raise civil cases in court. The amounts they would be able to pursue were a flat fee of £10,000 followed by a scale up to £80,000 dependant on the severity of the abuse. They would have to evidence that severity. Organisations involved in abusing children would have an incentive to pay into the scheme as the level of Redress would be restricted to lower amounts than a civil case. I contacted Pat, from the lawyers but he didn't answer his phone, so I then called the press officer and Lorna, one of the partner solicitors. Lorna was at the hairdressers, but the press officer called back. As he did Lorna texted how angry she was. The press officer was furious and he promised to try and achieve press attention.

"Typical they would sneak this out on a Friday" he said.

Lorna called after the hairdressers furious and distressed. The lawyers had put a substantial amount of time and effort into cases and some were settling for hundreds of thousands. Both Lorna and I recognised that for some survivors £10,000 would feel life changing and it was guaranteed so they may be reluctant to wait and see if they could be successful in a civil claim. Many had significant health issues so pursuing a civil claim may be time that they didn't feel they had. They agreed that it was time to start campaigning.

Pat called next and he was equally furious. He suggested involving politicians to insist on changes to the Bill. I agreed to be involved and it was decided to have a campaign meeting the following week.

I was asked to give evidence to a parliamentary committee about the waiver attached to the redress scheme. I wrote a submission in advance and met with another campaigner to discuss it. We agreed we were on the same page with it. We attended the committee and presented our concerns about the waiver and other aspects of the Bill. We were shocked as another of the long-term campaigners supported the waiver. The survivors were furious with her. Despite numerous meetings with MSPs the Bill was passed with the waiver. COSLA had entered into the situation at the last minute by agreeing to pay into the scheme if the waiver was in place. This agreement ensured that some of the unsure MSPs voted to agree to it. We realised how much of the issues we faced had been connected to this. The files that we had protected for the clients would assist them in achieving the highest payments possible.

The life changer

"Hyper haggis" the child abuse campaigner I mentioned at the start of this story had contacted the organisation many years before. His original contact was to ask for support to seek compensation. He had reported to the police, but they were concerned that he had limited memory of the abuse. They felt that by working with the service memories could be recovered. I was very confused as he had sent a detailed testimony of abuse, but this had not been reported to the police.

I was very unsure about him, but my colleague Sharon persuaded me to join him in his campaigning. She was concerned that he was campaigning alone with no support. I agreed that we would join a campaign outside a church building in Glasgow. I was conflicted as he stood and gave a testimony of his abuse. It didn't tie up with him having no memory as his account was very detailed and it had no effect on him to speak out. We stood with him for hours. He repeatedly called journalists to ask them to come to interview him. Eventually a journalist did attend, and he became excited and exhilarated.

From then he decided we had to support his campaigns. He called me regularly with new ideas to attract press attention. If I didn't respond immediately, he would threaten me that he could discredit me and the organisation if I did not do exactly what he said. I was frightened of him as he had told me one night when drunk that two of his partners when younger had died in his arms in unexplained circumstances. He told me one had died from choking on a chicken bone on a night where there were a crowd using drugs. He said that she was in his arms when she died. He told me about his pregnant wife who died of natural causes in his arms. I found information from one of my colleagues where he had told her his wife had died of a drugs overdose. He said after her death his was admitted to a psychiatric hospital because he became psychotic. On the call where he told me about their deaths, he also gave me a long explanation of his pattern of destroying people who care for him or who he was too close to. His original testimony was full of stories of times when he would black out but be covered with blood. He explained that he had put someone's feet on a windowsill and then jumped on his legs to break them. In later testimonies he took these aspects out and never again mentioned the first woman who had died. I was convinced from that night that they had come to harm at his hands. However, drug related deaths were often not investigated too deeply. In many calls he would give me different versions of the events as if he had to speak about them.

I found emails where he complained about his early worker and tried to have her discredited. I was concerned that the reason for his attack on her was because he had told her he did not remember any abuse and she had referred to that in communications with the police. He knew abuse had taken place in that care home due to press articles. Much of his testimony didn't tie up. I later discovered he had a conviction in England for dishonesty. Other survivors and his counsellor told me that he had taken some of their stories and made them his.

He linked me up with a journalist friend and persuaded me to hold an event in Glasgow inviting survivors and interested parties to highlight the intention to close the service. At the end of the event, I had to break up a fight between him and another survivor by stepping between them. The other survivor called him a liar and a con man. He said he had lied about the abuse. I supported him in a complaint to the police about the attack.

A few weeks later another survivor emailed me copying Jim in to say that he had conned her out of money. I was very worried. He seemed unconcerned when I confronted him. I was worried about connecting further with him in isolation. I connected him up with our lawyers for additional support for his campaigns. I felt it would help us maintain boundaries and safety.

Jim was very jealous of my campaigning with New Beginnings as he felt they were competing with him. He was obsessed with press coverage and notoriety and he did not want to share it. New Beginnings tried to support him by assisting in one of his campaigns, but he then wrote to them with a very worrying long letter. It was paranoid and threatening. It accused them of being dangerous.

Around that time, he told me that the police had asked to meet him alone and that Forward Paths had asked to meet him. He wrote me an email to say he thought they were grooming him. He said the police warned him against us and they offered him a job. In the letter to New Beginnings, he told them that the police did not trust them. I found these very inappropriate things for the police to say. Forward Paths offered him money for his campaigns. He said Florence was scathing about us.

The lawyers started paying for his campaigns. They provided lawyers to come along and support him. He would send demands for more money and he demanded the lawyers pay for a brochure for him. At a campaign my colleague Sharon raised concerns with me that he was giving out his personal number to people. She asked me to speak to him as she was too afraid of him. She said he had previously been sectioned for threatening to kill a priest and she had reported him. I spoke to him about the risk to him and others because he was not a trained therapist and from that day he started to turn on me. He started to behave in a very bullying manner towards me. He told me my disability was affecting his campaigning. One night when he was holding a meeting for some survivors over from Ireland he ordered me to buy take-out meals from everyone and bring them from my house to Glasgow, a 45-minute journey, immediately. My family were furious. When I arrived, he was angry that the food was cold. On one campaign he called me when I was in Glencoe on holiday and ordered me to buy black tablecloths. He threatened me that if I did not do so he would discredit me. He told the team I had offered him a paid job. When I spoke to him about it to say it would not be possible for me to do so as he was not trained he turned on me saying I was arrogant and I thought I was better than him. I was becoming very worried so I raised it with my Board and they agreed the next campaign would be the last.

The final campaign was a three-day campaign in Dundee. On the weeks prior to the event, he sent bullying emails to the lawyer insisting his accommodation, posters, banners and train fairs were all paid for well in advance. He was aggressive to her, accusing her of not doing it. About a week before the event, he sent me a text to say he had been offered no support and he was floundering. I texted back to ask what support he needed. He didn't respond. I was aware he had support from Sharon. We had tried to stop the campaigning many times but he kept threatening us and the lawyers that if we didn't continue he would discredit us.

When we arrived at the hotel he was obviously using a substance such as speed due to his behaviour and presentation. He was dismissive and rude to me. Later that evening Douglas, one of the New Beginnings team brought a young woman to see me for help as her daughter had been abused. While Douglas waited Jim became angrier as time passed and some of the clients had to hold him back to stop him attacking Douglas. When I returned to the table he turned on me, shouting into my face. He said my association with them would affect his campaigns as people thought they were paedophiles. He told me that he had been told my husband and I were paedophiles. To try and calm him down I spoke to him about the times others had tried to say negative things about him, referring to the client who had attacked him. Instead of calming him he became more irate accusing me of saying people disliked him. He kept shouting in my face I could discredit you, would I! He shouted that the press officer from the lawyers was an alcoholic and that I should not be working with them. He said they were stealing his campaign. The other survivors were becoming very upset, so he left the room. When he returned, he was calm, and he insisted I come with him to do a radio interview in the morning at 7. I said my husband would bring me to it but he insisted I attend with him in a taxi. When we arrived it was clear the radio journalist had not expected me to be there. I said I would go but Jim insisted I stay. He showed me a rambling script he had written. It was very critical of the government and Forward Paths. I told him my organisation couldn't be associated with it. He then went on radio and did a totally different script. I was aware he had been trying to upset and worry me.

We then went into the square where the event was taking place. It was extremely cold. With lupus my body can't cope with extremes of hot and cold so I was starting to become very unwell. He insisted that I carry heavy boxes from a church to the square while he spoke to the minister. He put up a banner with his personal details on it. I asked my husband to take the banner down. He called me over to him and he started complaining about the press officer from the lawyers, who was walking around the square, saying he hadn't organised the press. He said again that he was an alcoholic. He said that he would call him often obviously drunk. He then said he was going to show me what he did previously with a drunk person who irritated him. He grabbed me on my chest and pushed me, then pulled me back and pushed me again. I stumbled and ran back to my husband as I could see that he was angry and ready to react. I said, "leave it, it will just make things worse". Jim moved away and started speaking to passers-by and one of the survivors came to the square. I was very ill due to the cold and shock so we went into the shopping centre to warm up. I bought tights to put on under my clothes and went to the toilet to put them on. I started to feel my stomach becoming unwell and the next thing I remembered was coming to on the toilet floor, as I had passed out. I asked Chris to take me home. I returned to the square and by now the lawyers had arrived. I burst into tears and said I had to go. They looked very shocked.

The journey home was an hour and we blasted the heater. I lay down for a while then said to Chris "I need to go back I'm supposed to be speaking at an event tonight. I can't let down those who are attending, particularly as the police are coming." We travelled back to Dundee. When I arrived Jim said angrily "what are you doing here?" The others looked shocked. I gave my talk feeling anxious and with my head pounding. Jim said to my husband I need Valium to bring me down. He was clearly still on speed as he was speaking so fast and sweating profusely. My colleague Sharon told me he had behaved in an aggressive way to one of the other survivors, accusing her of inappropriately using the budget. I told her we would have to end our involvement in the event. Jim was furious as he said he could not continue without us as he needed counsellors to be there. I emailed the Board to explain that he had pushed me and been aggressive. I returned home. The journey home was extremely difficult as my heart was racing. My head was intensely painful with all the pressure.

After the event Jim kept demanding to speak to members of the Board. They decided not to speak to him as he was seen as a risk. He wrote a long letter to them. Within it he described a fantasy where the female police officer who had been in Dundee had raped him. He related this to saying that I had said the police were grooming him, despite that being what he had accused them of. He then started involving other survivors to attempt to turn them against me, New Beginnings, and the charity. He started writing to the government, press, politicians, and survivor organisations repeatedly every day. When newspapers didn't cover his story, he started threatening them. This went on for months until he submitted a complaint. We were aware that the complaint was supported by Forward Paths. We later became aware that Forward Paths had encouraged him to complain to the Scottish Charity Regulator OSCR. The complaint was untrue so the Chair of the Board responded to say it would not be upheld. Jim wrote to the lawyer on the Board of the organisation threatening a Christchurch attack. He also wrote to press, government, and Forward Paths to threaten an attack in Alloa. We were all terrified and put extra security in place. The police took the threats seriously and they started an investigation. I kept saying to them how dangerous I felt he was especially when the cases of the death of his ex-partners had never been properly explained. He wrote to a politician who was the chair of the cross-party group and numerous other politicians. She called me about it while I was in Newcastle with Chris. He was there for the Channel 4 Artist of the Year competition as a wildcard. On the morning of the event, I became very ill with terrible stomach upset. I panicked and drove home on my own leaving Chris to take the train back. I felt so humiliated and frightened.

OSCR were copied into an email where he was abusive and threatening copying in many journalists. He said in the email OSCR were investigating us. He said in the email I was a narcissist and many other insults. One of the OSCR staff called me to say OSCR were not involved in the email sent. She then went on to question me about why this had happened. I told her it was a very difficult and upsetting situation where I had been assaulted and harassed. She asked me what I had done to bring this on. She questioned me about the council investigation many years previously. I told her that was resolved at the time but the report was put to council in private so we couldn't release it. I told her that at the time I had explained this to her colleague, and it was closed off as the government had seen the report and continued to fund us as had the council for another two years. Her questions seemed so inappropriate I was worried about whether it was actually OSCR so I later googled her. She followed up by an email and I responded to say I had been very upset and concerned that she had called me.

The police decided to arrest Jim. When he was arrested, I was at the office. The police called me to say to stay at home and not go out. They told me he had resisted arrest and then had been causing a severe disturbance in the cells until the early hours of the morning. They let me know when they had put him on a train home and reassured me that there was an injunction where he could not go near me or enter Alloa. I wrote to OSCR to inform them he had been arrested.

Jim went on to speaking about me daily on Twitter, speaking now about false allegations and saying OSCR were investigating. One of his friends tagged me on Twitter challenging me to come and see him and answer questions to him and "ex members of staff". He said I had stolen fundraising money. This was mixed up with the accusations against Trudi but I realised he must have been linked up with those involved in the grievance. I was very confused. I realised there must be a leak who knew me and them.

The world changed

In March 2020 the pandemic hit and life changed beyond all recognition. We recruited a new business development manager and on the week he started he came in with what seemed like a heavy cold. Although the pandemic had been discussed we did not realise how dangerous it was. I was worried but tried to dismiss my concerns. On the Thursday I started to feel a scratch in my throat. On the Saturday we had a craft fair to run a stall at. All day I felt very unwell and I kept coughing. By the next day I couldn't breathe properly and I had a fever. My stomach was badly affected. For the next nine weeks I spoke to the doctor every day. My steroids were increased and it took weeks afterwards with relapses to bring them back down. Chris became ill a week after me. I was terrified as he was up all night unable to breathe. As Covid did not have a test at that time the doctor had presumed it was Covid. For weeks afterwards I was severely fatigued. From then on I had food and other allergies meaning I could only eat a very limited diet. I was diagnosed with kidney failure and high cholesterol. The doctor felt my ongoing health issues could be long Covid.

In a strange way I felt more relaxed than I had ever been before when lockdown was introduced. My health was always at risk from germs and viruses but now everyone was in the same situation as me having to take care. We ordered food through online shopping and we had regular zoom calls with the family. I became very familiar with zoom and realised I enjoyed online meetings. I had so much more time to work. I developed new services in schools bringing the budget up to almost £2m with 60 more staff. I developed over 30 training packages and delivered them online internationally. This extra work gave the organisation security as we did not rely on the government funding. Just before the pandemic the government informed us that they had decided to carry out a review of us again. They referred to a clause in our funding contract where it stated they could carry out an external evaluation at any point. We were not aware of any other organisations in the funding portfolio facing it.

Two consultants were appointed. We met them but insisted meetings were recorded due to our previous treatment. It became apparent they wanted to review the whole organisation not just the government funded part. We told them we would not agree to that. They then wanted to review our staff qualifications. We were aware they wanted to promote that those who offered trauma therapy should only be clinical psychologists. Our team were counsellors and psychologists, not clinical, so we refused this level of scrutiny. We were aware some organisations were led by survivors with no qualifications. We knew we were again being singled out.

A meeting was arranged with the new head of the government department and one of his team. Jason had been moved on. In the meeting I challenged our previous treatment including the previous review in 2014 carried out by someone who had behaved inappropriately with me in the past. I mentioned the terrible treatment over the years and the different way we were treated. When the minutes of the meeting were sent everything I had said was ignored. I insisted the minutes were changed to reflect what I had said. The government official contacted the Chair, not including me, asking for a meeting. At the meeting she was pressurised to leave the minutes without my part. She asked me what I wanted to do so I agreed just to let it go so that we could complete the review.

The reviewers organised meetings with the team. The team asked if the meetings could be recorded. The reviewers produced slides to reflect the meetings. They misrepresented what was said to fit their own agenda. They wanted to say that all services should offer CBT and EMDR but indicated that our team were not trained in those fields. The team had given excellent evidence of the approaches they did use and gave a good account of their experience. This was all excluded. I transcribed the recordings and challenged them that their report was biased. I wrote a complaint to the government. The review was never referred to again and the government never followed up. The person who had asked to meet the Chair without my knowledge was moved.

We returned to the growth of the service. Through time the service became very respected. Excellent relationships were developed with local authorities and partner organisations. I attended around six online meetings each day. I delivered training to other organisations offering wellbeing support. We were commissioned by a bank to support their staff. I delivered the international training every few weeks. The trauma training was attended by over 400 people. Some were from Australia, Canada, Singapore, Indonesia, Greece. It was so exciting and feedback was fantastic. I realised we were being recognised as trauma experts. Each time I delivered the training I realised more about how trauma had impacted my own life. It felt liberating. Through time I was asked to speak as an expert at many events. I felt that at last I was moving away from the destruction of my reputation. Funders were coming to us to offer funding for new and exciting projects.

Despite all the positive aspects and just as we started to relax a major issue faced us.

Do investigations ever stop!

We received a letter in November 2020 from OSCR saying they were carrying out a formal review. They asked for our policies and procedures. They asked what had happened with the council review in 2014. They referred to the situation with the client and they asked about our relationship with our solicitors. Initially we were unconcerned as we knew we had professional policies and procedures. We sent our policies and other documents requested within three days. We responded regarding the council review to reiterate what I had already told the OSCR employee who had called me. Our lawyers asked another solicitor to respond on our behalf to many of the points including the relationship with them. Within two weeks a newspaper contacted us to say they knew we were being investigated. We knew the fact we were being investigated meant funders would presume guilt so our press officer said that he had managed to ensure the story did not go forward. However, it was very clear now that there was a leak within the organisation.

I spoke to our partner organisation that I had met after the grievance as I knew that she had some concerns about internal sabotage that we may be facing. She told us that Jim had contacted her for support. He had criticised us to her but she refused to engage with him. She told me she had felt that he was vulnerable and mentally unwell but now felt there may be something more sinister. She decided to put in writing to me her concerns about Sharon. In the letter she said that another of our partner organisations had been sabotaged in the same way as our grievance. It was one of Sharon's colleagues and friends who had instigated it and they felt he had been motivated to do it by Sharon. I had known her for a long time and she had been one of the first to apologise so I did not want to believe it. I reported it to the Chair and we decided to watch and monitor the situation. It was worrying as only a small number of people knew we were being investigated. As a member of the management team, she knew. Over the years since the grievance, she had been promoted to a senior management post. Sharon and I were friendly colleagues and we delivered the training together.

Months passed and there was no response from OSCR. Eventually they wrote to say the person investigating was on holiday so there would be a delay. They followed up by saying the same things three more times. Chris wrote a complaint to them due the affect the delay was having on me. I was struggling to cope. He also complained that they had investigated us based on the complaint by the client as they must have seen how abusive he was to me. I also complained to say the OSCR staff member should not have contacted me at the beginning as it had been so upsetting. The timescale complaint was upheld as was the concern that I should have not been contacted directly under the circumstances. They confirmed they would change their policies. However, they insisted they were right to investigate the client complaint.

Eventually a time was set to meet the Board. Our lawyers told me this was an unusual approach, especially as we had sent all the information and there was no evidence of any concerns. The lawyer insisted that the meeting should be recorded. OSCR contacted the lawyer off the record to suggest to him that I had founded the organisation and that I was in control of the Board. The Chair was furious as it indicated that she could be controlled by me. It was also untrue that I had founded the organisation. However, we were aware the government had presumed that in the past so we had suspicions about their involvement.

Prior to the meeting a document was sent with points that were to be raised in the meeting. It was full of inaccuracies and misrepresentations. The meeting was due to go ahead a week later. The Board members who would be in attendance and three of the managers were contacted to arrange the time. The same newspaper and journalist then contacted me to ask if the Board were due to meet OSCR. This time the story went forward. A small part of it was the OSCR investigation with the rest being an attempt to destroy my character. It included many of my previous campaigns with a spin on them to make me look like a constant troublemaker. I was devastated. The press officer told me that he had contacted the journalist and he was adamant it was a reliable internal source who had given him the information. There was a further article the following week that reported the grievance and council review. It also alleged that I had failed to report the local paedophile ring to the police. I was so angry and upset that for weeks afterwards I felt suicidal. All of my work to help others had been used against me. I reviewed some of the journalists' previous articles and I realised he had worked with Sharon on stories. He was also a contact of the press officer. I became more suspicious but still did not want to believe it could have been either of them. It had to be one of only a few people who knew about the meeting with OSCR.

The meeting with OSCR asked the questions in the paper they had sent us previously. The Board were able to prove the faults and inaccuracies. OSCR had to apologise repeatedly for their errors. They confirmed that they did not usually respond to individual client complaints. At the end of the meeting, they asked about the qualifications of our staff and whether we would let funders know what they were. This had never been part of the original inquiry so we knew for sure the government were involved. OSCR wrote to us after the meeting with very bland recommendations. We realised this was so that they could report there were recommendations but they had to admit there was nothing of a regulatory nature or concern. In all the responses they submitted to the press they used wording that was negative in tone about us.

OSCR provided minutes of the meeting. I had recorded the meeting due to my disability. I would regularly record meetings as I could not write notes with my sore hands. We were able to write to show that the minutes had been seriously misrepresented. When the final response was received to inform us that the investigation was complete with no concerns we were informed that the staff member who started the process was no longer working with them. We reflected on how many staff had been moved or left from those attacking us over the years. It felt like an indication of how corrupt it had all been where people had to move on to hide the mistakes.

We hired a new press officer. He was able to ensure the papers reported that the paedophile ring had been reported to the police. I complained to the police for misrepresenting the situation. They decided to take forward an investigation both into the police reporting the situation inaccurately and the failure to fully investigate the paedophile ring. I had a long interview with the police to cover everything that had happened.

I submitted a subject access request to OSCR and a Freedom of Information request. I also submitted a complaint to the Ombudsman about them. The Freedom of Information had nothing in it as OSCR said by providing more they could compromise their relationships with other organisations. It was clear to us that would be their relationship with the government. In my subject access request was pages of awful letters written by Jim. I was appalled again that they would have taken this seriously, rather than see it as abusive. There was one paper with the name of who reported it not available. The information presented was awful in that it referred to me and one of my children as abusers. The other information in the paper made it clear it was not from Jim. It could only have all been known by one person and that person was Sharon. I was so shocked I couldn't sleep all weekend. I called the Chair and Pat. We decided not to do anything about the information due to the relationship Sharon had with the clients. They would have been devastated to lose her. However, I realised that was the beginning of the end for me in my job as I couldn't continue to live day by day with the corruption and vindictiveness. I could only presume either Sharon had been very jealous of me or she had been used by an external body. I also realised how much she had been involved in stirring up Jim throughout the situation with him. She must have been actively involved in the grievance.

While this was all happening, Jim continued to harass and stalk me. On Twitter he kept writing threats. He shared the newspaper articles. I had to call the police over and over to gather the evidence of ongoing stalking. He sat outside the police station in a neighbouring village with placards protesting the justice system. The paper that covered the OSCR situation covered it as a story. They had a long-term relationship with him as they had previously covered many stories for him. He had previously been due in court and they ran a story about him having his first Christmas tree a few days before. The case was postponed as his lawyer had Covid. Throughout the time I was very fortunate to have a support worker from Victim Support as the court delays were so upsetting.

Finally, the court day arrived. I was so ill a few days before I didn't know if I would make it to court. The previous evening, I was told not to attend. I was so worried the case may have been dropped. I knew the court had agreed to drop the assault charges to persuade him to plead guilty to the stalking and death threats. I was happy to do so as the assault had been a small part of everything that happened. Later that day I called the procurator fiscal and they said he had pleaded guilty. He was to come back for sentencing a month later. At sentencing he created a disturbance in the court. He refused a tag and the judge jailed him for 60 days. He was given a five-year restriction order not to contact me or Pat. The press picked the story up, especially the death threats about a Christchurch attack. He was released from jail after 30 days. He started a campaign on Twitter to say that he had been a victim of a miscarriage of justice. He seemed to have forgotten that he had pleaded guilty. He involved others and it seemed to be people who had been involved in the grievance. The contact could only have happened through Sharon. The police said there was nothing I could do as he had not contacted me directly. I was becoming so exhausted with it my life was eaten up with it. I decided it was time to move on.

Return to the dark places

I had made the decision to tell the Chair I would be looking for another role. She persuaded me to wait until things had settled because I had not experienced a time at work without stress and attacks. I reluctantly agreed. There had been a call into the office that the client at the start of this situation wanted to speak to me. We knew he had been hiding in his siter's attic and I was so pleased that he seemed to be coming back to life. I tried calling a few times but the number was wrong. Eventually, he called again and I was able to speak to him.

Over the years Ingrid and I had continued to investigate all we could about the case. Ingrid knew a lot of people in the area. We had discovered the cellar he had referred to did exist but it had been filled in. We had found links to other paedophiles in the area. The meetings with Gray, the public protection officer had confirmed that there had been an abuse ring with the main perpetrator now dead. We had found links between local politicians and the leader of the ring.

He came to the office to see me with a suitcase of evidence. We spoke about the parts of evidence I had found that corroborated what he had reported. He told me that his stepfather had sold him and other children in the family to his contacts for money. He said the family had been supported to resettle from Poland by a local Lord and his family. He said he first experienced abuse by him and his son. He had often felt that this abuse at a high level had made him a serious threat to those in power. I agreed to support him in pursuing his case again. Three days later his brother contacted me to say he had been sectioned and he was now in hospital. I was very concerned as he had not seemed mentally unwell. His advocate confirmed to me that he felt the same. He had been shouting outside the local MSP office about the abuse and cover up and he was arrested. The charges were later dropped. I had worked with abuse clients for almost twenty years and I had seen no signs of him being mentally ill. He was angry about the abuse cover up and he was experiencing trauma symptoms but he was not a risk to himself or anyone else.

He was kept in for months. I spoke to him when I could but his phone was removed from him regularly. At his request I looked through his evidence. It was clear there was no record of him having a mental illness. It was clear from the records it had been recognised that he was being abused from around three or four but no action was taken and he remained with his abusers. They were allowed to foster other children. The jigsaw pieces were falling into place as the council could have faced litigation and accusations of cover up of abuse rings.

His brother and sister-in-law called me and they confirmed everything he told me and much more.

The stepfather was selling the children and blackmailing someone in the archdiocese of the church. He was involved with a local well-known crime family. The family had potentially broken into our previous office. On another occasion the alarm stopped working and files were stolen. We were told squirrels had probably cut through the alarm wire. Around 500 files were missing. When the office was originally broken into with files trashed after the DVD was released it was discovered it had been a local crime family who were involved.

The brother said the boys had also been abused at scrapyards owned by the crime family.

The mother and stepfather had three children between them, and they fostered the client from age 2 or 3. They made it clear to the family that they hated him. They also fostered the other children who may also have been abused.

At a family get together our client started having memories about the first instances of his abuse around the time of a family wedding. He could remember the clothes worn and photographs confirmed his memories. His sister's family started to be very nervous. He was very young when the abuse started.

His stepfather sold him and at least one of the other children to the main abuse ringleader. The other child was the client's witness against his stepfather. He was given a £22,000 pay out for the abuse by the ringleader. The stepfather ran off to live abroad.

The main ringleader's sister was involved with another of the abusers. His son was also involved. A nephew may also have been involved.

Local politicians were also mentioned as possible abusers. Children were taken out in a car to be abused by one of the abusers and his wife.

A cellar was built at the house. It was dug out under a wooden garage. Children who were being abused were locked in the cellar and babies may have been brought. There was discussion about a dead baby.

Another possible witness had come forward who had been raped and abused as well. Other victims were named by the client's brother.

The family were able to own flats due to being paid by abusers.

Another victim/ witness was put in prison for killing his sister's abuser.

The police and the organised crime ring may also have been involved with selling drugs.

He said a local senior politician was involved with the catholic church and they were involved in the abuse.

I was shocked that the brother's account put in place so many pieces of the client's account and it also filled many in many missing pieces of our investigation over the years. It all made sense.

All the evidence led to the archdiocese and this then led to possible links to the "man with the shiny suit". It reminded me that a local politician was told three years ago that two powerful people had it in for us.

I was so shocked and horrified after hearing the evidence from the client's brother and sister-in-law that it took me weeks to settle. I was horrified that this had never been properly investigated.

"The man in the shiny suit" revisited

The advocate who had been to see me with Dana was finally achieving awareness of what had happened to him and some of the matters he had raised were being publicised by supportive newspapers. We had kept in contact over the years and I was delighted to see online he was finding justice. He had tried to fight the inquiry for dismissing him from his job. They had accused him of investigating beyond his remit. It seemed to be that his findings were very worrying to the establishment. The daughter of one of the abusers, a senior lawyer, was finally achieving recognition with one of her abusers being extradited to Scotland. It was recognised that her father had abused her. The case was linked to the testimony given to me by the survivor at the New Beginnings conference as a senior politician, now dead was also accused. He had mentioned him in relation to the case he had highlighted to me. He was highlighting the death of a former lawyer and active political party Vice-Chairman that had originally been recorded as suicide. It was now recognised that it could have been murder. The lawyer had files on a high-profile paedophile ring named the "Untouchables". The information was described as a conspiracy theory as many of the cases were.

The information he had uncovered about so called "rent-boys" being taken from a care setting to be used by members of the legal establishment and their contacts was highlighted. He questioned why the inquiry had not pursued his findings. He posted on Twitter that the scale of abuse for young girls who were in care could be as significant as Rotherham. Abuse of young care experienced young people was linked to an organisation that the "man in the shiny suit" had been convenor of at the time of leader of the largest paedophile ring in Scotland. There were accounts that it had all been linked. Two survivors had come forward to say they were abused due to the same organisation. They highlighted their own concerns about "the man in the shiny suit".

Another campaigning organisation entered the debate. They had contacted me on several occasions about the football abuse cases. One of the paedophiles in the abuse ring had been connected to one of the football teams with many abuse cases emerging. Spotlight posted online the evidence that "the man in the shiny suit" had joined the organisation as convenor on the same day as the paedophile ringleader became CEO. It was clear that wider recognition was happening. It was now not only online as the organisation at the centre of it all had referred themselves to the police. Despite the concerns it was clear they had continued to receive large levels of government funding. I was shocked as the agenda for many years had been to remove our funding when we were the organisation who supported survivors. The mainstream press were starting to cover some of the historical cases. Some of the most significant rings were finally coming to court, including a ritual abuse ring in Glasgow. I felt it was finally time for justice.

Endings and new beginnings

After all the pressure of the past fifteen years I decided it was time to make changes in my life. I was offered another job and I called the Chair to tell her I was leaving. I explained to her that after the stalking of the last four years and the possible internal betrayal it was healthier for me to try something new. She was upset but understood my reasons. I spoke to Eva and we agreed I would stay connected for anything that may arise with the abuse cases. I planned to continue to support a few survivors. The final weeks were difficult as I managed endings with people across the organisation and externally who had come to mean so much to me. I realised how valued I had been by those who counted. At the final AGM Pamela came to speak about how much I had meant to the cause. I was so delighted as Pamela had been an inspiration to me throughout my time in the abuse field. I had spent years highlighting cases, despite many attacks on my character. It felt like the right way to end.

Some months later I discovered that many things were going wrong with the organisation. It appeared that they were being rescued by a large amount of funding from the government. I wondered what the conditions would be and I thought so it continues....

The final battle – full circle

My local political party asked me to put my name forward to be selected as an MP. I was surprised but felt it may be a way to make a real difference so I agreed. I passed initial selection and was given details of a hustings where I would give a presentation and there would be a vote from the local political groups. I was given lists of names and contact details of local people in the party who could vote. I felt sick. Included in the list were many of the local politicians who had treated us so badly in the fight with the local council. They were involved in the cover up of the paedophile rings and the attempts to discredit me. I felt a mix of unsafe and inspired by the fight for justice.

I sent out a publication giving details of me and my background, asking for a vote. I received an email back from one of the groups in the area where the abuse had happened. She challenged me about being a lifelong member of the party and asked was a member of the party when I stood as an independent candidate against Laura. I realised this was a start of an attack on me. Even though I expected it I felt the past horrors flood back to me. I wrote to the party to complain as she was the head of the local party and could influence others. I looked at their Facebooks and all the party members who had caused us to lose our funding were connected together and with her. They were also linked to Morag, my sister.

I was very nervous but I went forward to the hustings and Chris was part of the audience. We had previously been close to the local party in our area but they all ignored Chris and tried not to make eye contact with him. The other area had all turned out and the room was mobbed. I was taken into a room with the other candidates. One had been unable to attend due to a family illness. There was another female candidate who was very pleasant and professional. There was a male candidate who had no professional background. When I mentioned researching current political issues he laughed and said he wouldn't bother with that. He seemed confident.

The first candidate came out shaken and confused. The candidates were to go in one by one and all were to be asked the same questions. She said there was a question about bad press and was there anything in her background the party should be concerned about. I felt shaky as I realised the question was meant for me. The male candidate seemed unconcerned.

I was ushered into the room. It was full of people, mostly men and there was an aggressive feel in the room. Chris was looking very concerned. I recognised the women who had sent me the email from her Facebook profile. The second question was the one about bad press. I was passionate in my response. I said any bad press I would have was due to miscarriages of justice that I was trying to expose. I said I was proud of it and I would do it again. The other questions seemed targeted with none about national politics but not as blatant. My initial speech gave a great deal of detail about my professional background and achievements.

At the end we were taken into a room for the count. I realised the woman who had questioned me was on the selection panel. She had allowed me through the selection process to then attack me. The count was all in favour of the male candidate with all the female candidates having 10 votes between them. It was a landslide.

I felt humiliated as even my local party didn't vote for me. I had complained about a year before about disability discrimination and sexism by one of the local party. I felt I was being punished for doing so. He was well connected in the area and had a great deal of influence. Chris told me afterwards the male candidate was awful just saying he would do his best to everything and that any bad press would just be about his golf swing. He said the group were marking their paper for him before I spoke. He spoke as if he knew them all.

I was going to leave it but I felt it was a sign that the party was still full of people who would cover up abuse and attack me for trying to expose it, even years later. I wrote a complaint to the national party outlining everything from the past. They didn't respond but it felt like closure as they had to hear what had happened.

The justice tree in the end

Chris and I felt we had to go for a walk to the justice tree. It was a winter's day in February. The air was frosty and the trees were sparkling. The ground was white with frost and ice. The snowdrops were starting. We walked carefully through the glen. It had so many echoes of the streams, the wildlife, and voices in the distance. We stopped at the concrete wishing well, still sitting upside down. I stood on it and wished for a positive and healthy future. I realised how much my health was affected by the knowledge of what human beings could do to one another and what had been done to me. The work of Pamela highlighted the links between childhood sexual abuse and physical illness. So many of us had serious illnesses in adult life. The abuse destroyed us in so many ways and led to facing multiple discrimination. However, standing there I realised the strength I had developed and the fight to change things for others. I said to Chris "I wanted to make things different for the children today and in the future. I wanted to stop them suffering the way I did. My life as a survivor led to me experiencing so much more abuse as an adult. My son was abused. I saw this experience with so many other survivors. I didn't ever have justice. I wanted others to have justice. I wanted to educate the world on what trauma is and what it does. I wanted to save the files for the survivors. I would have been devastated if anyone else had control over my history and my story. It was so important it was under my control and I wanted to make sure that was the case for other survivors. I wanted survivors to understand their strength. I wanted to challenge the conspiracy theory narrative and make sure people understood these things were real. I wanted those who abused children to be exposed. I wanted those who facilitated that abuse to be exposed too. In all that people had no right to harm me."

Chris said "you achieved all that. How many people has your organisation supported over the years, how many lives were saved?"

"In the beginning when I started we supported around 300 people a year. Last year we supported over 5,000. Over and over survivors gave testimonies that they had not killed themselves due to the support. It makes me so emotional."

Chris took my hand "realise that you did what you set out to do. You took that job because it meant something. You achieved it. You fought back. The government and councils were not able to take the files. The survivors now have their files for redress. You know that will make a difference to how much they receive. You linked with the lawyers for people to win civil cases. We have seen cases where survivors have achieved significant compensation. You fought for that. You will always be the invisible person or the one attacked but does it really matter."

We walked on through the forest to the justice tree. Chris pointed out that there was so much growing around it, even in winter, that made it still look like a living tree despite it lying on its side. I sat on the tree trunk and smiled.

"I do feel I had justice. Many of those who tried to destroy me didn't succeed, they are gone. They used so many people to do what they did. They must live with their own conscience for the rest of their lives. I always feel that I did everything for the right reasons. I can feel those we lost around me; I can hear their voices. This will not be the end as I will continue to fight for them, just in a different way. I feel my life meant something and my past failed to define me and set my course. However, it did make me follow this path. Justice is finally in my heart and my soul is free."

www.ingramcontent.com/pod-product-compliance
Ingram Content Group UK Ltd.
Pitfield, Milton Keynes, MK11 3LW, UK
UKHW022203110125
453409UK00011B/370